Published by:

Classic Pet Books
7890 Jasmine Loop NW
Sauk Rapids, Minnesota
56379

Printed and bound in the United States of America

Translated from:

Ein Leben mit Boxern
Third German edition, 1987
Verlag: Gollwitzer, Weiden

First published in 1960
Second edition, 1980
Third edition, 1987

My Life With Boxers

by

Friederun von Miram-Stockmann

A new translation from the Third German Edition of *Ein Leben mit Boxern* (1987)

Containing over seventy additional pages of the great Boxer breeder's writings that have never before been published in English

With over 600 sketches by
Friederun von Miram-Stockmann
to illustrate her story

Translated from the German by Calvin D. Gruver

Friederun von Miram-Stockmann in the popular photograph of her "Boxer wagon"

This is the story of a young talented art student who became the most famous Boxer breeder of her time—and perhaps of all time. It is the history of a breed, the German Boxer, and the role played by her Vom Dom kennel in shaping that history. It is also a story of tremendous sacrifice and hardship for her dream.

In the expanded Third German Edition, published in 1987, numerous essays by the author—some published and some not—were sought out by the publisher, Ingeborg Gollwitzer, and prepared as an appendix to Frau Stockmann's great story. These essays are included in this edition, as well as some additional material found by the translator. None of it has appeared in English before.

This limited edition has been prepared primarily as a gift for donors to the American Boxer Charitable Foundation, Inc., an organization totally dedicated to funding health research on Boxer-related illnesses.

For additional information, contact any American Boxer club or visit the World Wide Web site of the American Boxer Club at

http://www.akc.org/clubs/abc/abc-home.htm

Contents

List of Photographs

Translator's Notes

Translating is not a matter of replacing a foreign word with the English equivalent. No translation could ever be literal, word for word, or it would make no sense. Instead, the translator must convey the meaning of the original. I have used words, phrases, sentences and paragraphs as we use them in current American English. Any errors along these lines are therefore mine and not Mrs. Stockmann's.

When it seemed a citation of the original German word might be useful, I have included it in brackets [ ]. That is also the way I have handled all clarifications that were not in the original.

Those readers who are familiar with Boxer history will surely notice that I refer to the Stockmanns' kennel as "vom Dom," rather than "von Dom." Vom Dom means "from the cathedral," whereas von Dom means "from cathedral." "Vom" is a contraction of "von dem," and is the correct usage in this case. How the error of "von Dom" crept into English writing is unknown and unimportant, but it was an error nevertheless. When the kennel name is of feminine gender, then it must be "von der. . .," which is often listed simply as "v. d. . . ."

Mrs. Stockmann frequently used the words "Champion" and "Sieger." A Sieger (feminine is Siegerin) must have a working title to win, thus not all Boxers in a conformation show are eligible for the Sieger and Siegerin titles. In a Sieger show, there will be a fawn and a brindle Sieger, as well as a fawn and a brindle Siegerin. All classes have been divided by color in Germany since the beginning of Boxer breed shows.

Sometimes she almost appears to use the words interchangeably, but not quite. It seems as though a champion must be the winner of several shows, but if that was the case then—it has changed now. She definitely seems to place a higher value on the title "Champion." To escape the possibility of a misinterpretation, I have used the words as she used them.

The same procedure has been followed for all of the dogs' names. They are in the original spelling.

In some cases, Mrs. Stockmann misspelled places and names from her America trip. I have corrected those, when I recognized them as errors. If I have missed any, it was certainly unintentional.

Several people deserve special thanks for their assistance. From the German Boxer Club, Rosemarie Westphal and Detlef Mell were reliable resources for help whenever I was not clear on a passage. Mr. Mell was a great help in locating articles and getting permission for me to insert them in this book. Otto Donner graciously allowed me to reprint the obituaries of Mrs. Stockmann, which he wrote for *Boxer Blätter.* Barbara Pieper of Tree Towns Boxer Club allowed me to include a letter from Frau Stockmann and several photographs, all from her collection of Mazelaine memorabila. Vera Albers (Bavaria's Boxers) saved me a great deal of hard work by taking over the task of indexing the book.

Finally, I would like to thank my wife, Meredith Medler, for reading the manuscript and offering valuable suggestions for improvement. Her encouragement, editorial skills and broad knowledge of German and German history have been a great help to me. Any errors in translation are, of course, mine and mine alone.

Calvin D. Gruver
Sauk Rapids, Minnesota
Fall 1998

Germany During The Lifetime
Of Friederun Stockmann

Friederun von Miram-Stockmann was born in Riga, the present capital of Latvia. At the time of her birth, Riga had been a part of Russia since 1710. When she writes of her "homeland" it is Latvia and not Germany that she means. She was, however, a cultural German. There were many such Germans living in the eastern lands of Latvia, Lithuania, Estonia and Poland—reminders of the long-distant past when the Teutonic Knights conquered and ruled much of that area. The Von Miram family itself was of minor nobility.

She had a happy childhood in a loving family. Her attentive parents quickly recognized an artistic talent in their daughter, and sending her off to far-distant Munich for art studies was just another indication of their devotion. It was also a sign of the Von Miram family's general prosperity.

One of the prominent themes in Mrs. Stockmann's book is her conviction that childhood experiences shaped her whole life. Since she wrote the book as she approached her seventieth birthday, it could hardly have been just a passing thought. Yet we can be permitted a friendly smile at the suggestion that her unfulfilled childhood wish to own a dog produced a later desire to have thirty or forty of them. The reader can easily recognize a born animal lover in her, something that was as much a part of her personality as her artistic abilities.

When she was born on New Year's Day, 1891, Germany had been a country for twenty years. The unification of the German states came with a quick victory over France in the war of 1870/71. A confident, prosperous new nation—leader of the world in education and science—Germany's future seemed bright and promising. But one of the last stages of the 1870 war had been a total blockade of Paris by the German troops. Unwilling to surrender, the people of Paris eventually were reduced to eating rats. It was not forgotten.

A little over forty years later, Germany and France met again on the battlefield, but now many more nations were also involved. No easy victory this time. World War I was an ugly war, and it had a great impact on the Stockmann family. Indeed, from that time on the family's fate is deeply intertwined with the history of Germany. Her story, to a large extent, becomes a tale of her private battles against the consequences of Germany's history.

With her husband at the Front, Mrs. Stockman was alone at home with a small child and a pack of Boxers. In 1916, the Allies imposed a blockade on Germany. It was a total blockade, both from the sea and the land. Areas east of Germany were closed because Russia was on the Allied side, and the British navy successfully stopped all maritime shipments to Germany. Before the war, over half of Germany's food supply had been imported. The blockade brought the war to Germany's civilian population, including the Stockmann home.

By the winter of 1916/17, there was some starvation in Germany, and that winter became known as the "turnip winter." Turnips, a vegetable fed almost exclusively to pigs, became a staple in the German diet. Complaints that the blockade was only hurting civilians fell on the deaf ears of the Allies.

In November 1918, the armistice ended all hostilities. But the following peace conference turned out to be a conference of only the Allied countries. Germany was not permitted to participate. Here began a great discontent and sense of betrayal in Germany, a feeling that the Allies had tricked them into laying down their arms and now were imposing distasteful conditions on them by force. The Treaty of Versailles, which officially ended World War I, became known in Germany as "the Decree" [Diktat].

Resisting the treaty's terms was difficult. All through the peace conference—well over a year—the Allies maintained their total blockade, thus forcing the Germans to endure warlike conditions even in a time of peace. Fear of another blockade was enough by itself to motivate compliance. But the high reparation payments demanded by the treaty angered the whole country.

Finally, in a move of utter contempt for both the Allies and the German people, the leaders of Germany allowed the economy to slip into an unbelievable inflation. Economic historians still view the German inflation of 1923/24 as the most extreme in modern world history. At the peak of the inflation, the government had a dozen presses printing money twenty-four hours a day. To mail a letter at the end of 1923, cost 100 billion marks for postage. When a new government came in and ended the inflation in 1924, the exchange rate for the new currency was one trillion of the old marks for one of the new. Long after World War II, there were still some bars in Germany with this currency serving as wallpaper.

Of course, it meant severe hardships and heart-breaking economic setbacks for many Germans. Luckily, the Stockmanns avoided bankruptcy. Out of the experience came the wonderful but sad story of her new hat.

Scrounging the countryside for food, which the Germans called "hamstering" (from the activities of that animal), became a daily ritual during the years of the blockade and later inflation. Mrs. Stockmann's difficulty, however, was not how to feed her family but her dogs. She remarks several times she could easily take care of the family; the dogs were the problem.

The new currency, plus a new government, brought back political and economic stability. It lasted about four years, then history intervened again. This time it began with the depression in the United States, which hit Germany immediately and much worse in 1929/30.

By 1933, unhappiness with the incompetent government was so severe that a massive political shift occurred, bringing the National Socialists (Nazis) to power. A fringe party for ten years, suddenly the Nazis, with their program for a total overhaul of the political system, seemed an attractive alternative.

In numerous places in her book, Mrs. Stockmann makes clear her dislike of the Nazis. At the time, this surely must have been a strain in the family, for her husband, Philipp, was in the National Socialist party. That had disastrous results for him. Although a civilian, he was arrested by the Allies as a war criminal in 1945.

With another war came even greater hardships and personal danger than in the earlier one. She allows us to get a glimpse of the callous ways of the Hitler government in conscripting dogs for military duty. Toward the end of the war life became extremely difficult and dangerous. Strafing Allied fighter planes roamed over Germany almost unrestrained. People transporting goods on the roads, as she often did, were frequently made targets by overzealous pilots. Both day and night, the waves of bombers dropped their loads. Every city over 100,000 was bombed severely (with the exception of Heidelberg), as were also many smaller cities. What a great relief it must have been when that war finally ended.

A few final words have to be said about the postwar arrests by the Allies. The exact motivation is not clear. Probably the shock and extensive publicity about the extermination camps—which came just before the end of the war—brought forth an Allied determination to punish the German people. Strict control of the food supply by the occupation forces kept the Germans' diet near a starvation level for another two years. And then there were the arrests of German civilians. By the beginning of 1946, the commander of the American occupation force, General Clay, could report that "over 150,000 dangerous Nazi criminals" had been imprisoned. They filled the old concentration camps with them.

Of those 150,000 arrested, about 10,000 eventually came to trial. The rest languished—some died— under very severe hardships in the internment camps for some two years and were then released.

Fewer than ten Nazi criminals of any significance were found in the 150,000—and not a one of those was a major figure. To make it even worse, we now know that the American military and intelligence people were actually helping some known major Nazi war criminals escape to foreign lands, while in Germany they were busy arresting teachers, government workers and civil defense directors as "dangerous Nazi criminals."

Philipp Stockmann's crimes seem to have been that he directed civil defense in the small town near their farm, and he had also been in charge of housing allocations. Fourteen years older than his wife, he was sixty-eight years old when arrested. As his wife tells us, Philipp Stockmann was an ardent patriot and a blind follower of the German government. The readers can judge for themselves as to whether he deserved his fate.

Once the Cold War developed in 1947, American policy changed sharply. The Germans were now slated to be future allies. Marshall Plan aid came, dietary restrictions were lifted, a new currency was introduced, and finally a new Germany was born in 1949. That same year Mrs. Stockmann made her America-Great Britain trip, a highlight of her life.

For all intents and purposes, her story ends with the eight-week trip to America and Great Britain. After a half-century of turmoil, stability now returned to Germany and to her life. She lived until 1972, over a decade after she finished this book in 1960. She continued her breeding of Boxers during the twenty-three years after her trip. In 1961, she celebrated her seventieth birthday and her fiftieth year in the German Boxer Club, plus saw her book appear in print.

Ironically, she bred what she considered her finest Boxer just after she had written this book. For the second German edition in 1980, a short note written by Mrs. Stockmann and later found in her literary remains was published as an Epilog. It contained a description and picture of the great Godewind vom Dom, along with what might be described as her literary farewell.

It is a marvelous story she tells. We might be left wishing she had revealed more of her family's personal life, but that was apparently not her way. Her story is about the creation of a dog breed and within it, the role of her "vom Dom" kennel. As such, it is one of the most valuable sources for the history of the Boxer breed.

Calvin D. Gruver
Emeritus Professor, Modern German History

A Child's Unfulfilled Wish

*"If a dog starves when young,
it will never be full again."*

This old breeders' saying explains my own existence.

My father was a doctor. He passed on his warm love of animals to his children. My mother proved to be a very creative artist. For this love of animals, and also an instinct for art, I thank my parents.

Father never tired of trying to bring the animal world nearer to us. Once he brought home a breeding pair of white rats. Another time it was a parrot. Unfortunately, mother never liked it because it always pecked her. These animals all disappeared quickly from our house.

I will never forget my first encounter with a dog of my own. One day father seemed to take a long time removing his overcoat, and then we discovered a little Pug in his pocket. It was about as little purebred as possible, despite its black muzzle. At that time, though, the black muzzle was believed to be a true sign of a Pug's blue-blooded ancestry. For just one mark cash, father had purchased the joyous enthusiasm of his children. But it was a short-lived happiness. To mother's horror, the unmistakable signs of a dog's healthy digestive system began popping up in the little corners of the house. The very next day, the little Pug had a new master. But that short visit was enough to win our hearts.

Despite mother's advice we still longed for a dog as a playmate. Of course, we lived on the second floor of an apartment house. Who would take the dog outside? Neither father nor mother had time for that, and our servants didn't seem reliable enough. Thus the unfulfilled wish became a dream. Later, as life made the dream possible, it became my hobby. It's possible that my whole life would have been different if that childhood wish had

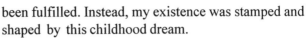

been fulfilled. Instead, my existence was stamped and shaped by this childhood dream.

Perhaps it was just fate. My playmates once claimed I was born under the dog star. And when I asked my father about it, he said there really was a dog star. It was Sirius, the brightest star of Canis Major, the big dog. I was very proud of that, and nobody could take away my faith in the dog star.

There's another childhood memory that strikes me as evidence for this fatalistic view. Once at a Christmas market, in a little shop with brightly-colored ceramic wonders, I saw two plump, fawn Pugs with black masks. I wanted them both, but the price almost exceeded my cash. The kindly shop lady sensed the emotion of my wish and made it possible.

When I went to sleep that night, the two Pugs sat on my night table, and as often happens with imaginative children, play and reality melded together. I imagined that I had forgotten to feed the dogs. Restlessly I tossed around in bed, until I thought of Illa, the private fairy of our children's room. She ought to help in this situation, I thought. Again and again I said softly, "Illa, please feed my dogs, feed my dogs, Illa!" After repeating this many times I fell asleep and dreamed of my Pugs, both now well fed and no reason for further worry.

The next morning I was astonished that father wanted to take my temperature. Our governess had told him that I had repeatedly cried out in my dreams, "Illa, feed my dogs!" As a good physician, father wanted to learn if I had been delirious.

Today I know these little ceramic Pugs brought the Boxer into my life.

Dogs—The Idols Of My Childhood

In the winter we lived in the city. But in summer, with its glorious vacations, we usually moved to my uncle's large estate. There were dogs there! Flocki, a white watchdog, looked like a little short-haired polar bear. He was a wonder of his kind. My uncle needed only to draw a line across the meadow with his cane while Flocki watched, and Flocki would never let one of his herd cross that line. Under such circumstances, it's understandable that the dog's fame greatly exceeded his farm. With children, he was also very friendly, but since he was usually "on duty," he seldom had much time for us children. Even at night he slept with the cows.

Also loved by us was a Setter, Don. He was a talented boy! My uncle bought him from a poacher. Don's glittering achievement was a trick. When uncle pointed at somebody and said, "Take off that hat!" Don would immediately leap up and remove that person's hat. It was a country-type joke. Thank goodness, Don had more sense than we children had. He simply refused to obey us when we told him to take off someone's hat.

The king of dogs at my uncle's place was actually a little Dachshund named Bill. Even my mother couldn't deny Bill his respect. When uncle travelled abroad, Bill could live with us in the city.

Bill was a hunting dog in the grand style. I'll mention only two of his many heroic tales. Once after a hunting drive Bill turned up missing. All searches were in vain. Two days later, some forest workers heard a dog baying. Normally they wouldn't have paid much attention to that, but uncle had promised a big reward for Bill's return. So the workers followed the call. They came to a swampy area, as is common in the Baltic forest regions, and there in the marsh they saw a moose standing, guarded by a little Dachshund. This giant of the wilderness seemed almost glued to the spot. His tiny enemy wouldn't let him budge, even leaping at the moose's hooves whenever it tried to move. Of course, the dog was much too small for such an animal, and the workers could not get Bill to come with them. He absolutely refused to leave his prey. Finally they contacted my uncle, but it was hours before he

arrived. He then shot the moose. Only after that could he call his little hero to his side.

The other story involved a Baltic baron who was one of uncle's best friends at that time. He was a Dachshund fan also, and owned a whole pack of long and short-haired Dachshunds of all colors. So it was a big event when he accepted an invitation from uncle to go on a large hunt. The baron was proud of his pack and often pointed out that they were all purebreds. How well you could prove that in those days I don't know. I assume that all of them were really purebred, as was little Bill. But the others were much stronger and more colorful than Bill.

When they left on the hunt uncle didn't say much. He just took Bill in his arms and climbed onto the hunting wagon. When the group returned that evening, however, uncle beamed from ear to ear, while his friend sat with a sour look on his face. Soon the story of the hunt became the topic of the evening's entertainment. They had taken a fine buck. The whole pack had been turned loose on the track. As long as possible, the buck had defended himself while surrounded by the entire pack, but not a one was willing to attack. Only Bill dared to attack, and in the wink of an eye fastened onto the buck's windpipe, holding on until the animal collapsed.

When the hunters arrived, they were greeted with an incredible picture. There, on top of the dead buck, stood Bill, and in a circle around him stood the proud pack. Not a one had dared to go near Bill and his prey. Of course, Bill was the hero of the day, and the most significant dog of our childhood paradise.

During the winters I began to collect candle wax and form figures from it. Perhaps every art—beginning with the primitive cave paintings—began in that manner, human beings trying to represent the unreachable. My idol was always the dog. No wonder that little Bill embodied this idol. Thus my first piece of art became a Dachshund, and this Dachshund, in turn, became the reason my mother discovered a sculptress' talent in me.

Still, I never wished to own a Dachshund. My dog would be strong and demand respect. The giants intrigued me, the Great Danes, St. Bernards, Newfoundlands and so on. But I learned that they no more fit me than the smaller breeds. And the German Shepherd? Oh, I liked them, but they weren't original enough. I still find them beautiful today, but I wanted my dog to be something special.

My brother once received a boy's almanac for Christmas. Inside was a large, colored chart with pictures of all the different dog breeds. In vain I tried to buy it from him, and my desire only made it more valuable. At night, when he was sleeping, I would sneak it out of his room and study it by candlelight. Yes, literally study!

The book wasn't very modern, and the author was hardly an expert. About the English Bulldog he wrote the following: "A very strong, medium-sized dog, hard to train, likes to fight, but true and courageous. It is easy to recognize whether it is purebred, because it will have a split nose [hare lip]. It has short, crooked legs and was used to fight bulls and bears. This English dog has a German cousin. They are called Bullenbeisser or Bärenbeisser and are larger and more manageable than their English cousins. There are fanciers who see a great future for these German cousins."

When I read that I knew which breed I had to have. But it took a long time before I got one. The Boxer breed in those days was still fighting for its existence. Indeed, there was already a young club for breeders, but there was no clarity about breeding guidelines. Only the name was unique. Bullenbeissers had become Boxers. That was to be an expression of its fighting nature. Munich was then almost the sole residence of the Boxer, and very seldom did a buyer succeed in bringing a Boxer to the world outside of Munich.

I begged Father for literature about my future breed. But there just wasn't any to be had. Only years later did I get something from the German Boxer Club in Munich. For those who are interested, I have included exact dates and the early history of the Boxer in Appendix I.

My First Dog

My mother was just as determined to make a sculptress out of me as I was to get a dog. In order to achieve that goal, she allowed me to make some short detours. Thus I was able to get a little billy goat for a model. That never worked out because he was too restless and I lacked experience. He was also mischievous, and when he charged a glass mirror his departure was certain. I gave him to a little boy, who had cried and cried in my father's office over a hurt finger. He was the son of a rich farmer, so I knew that my problem child would have a good home.

My next model was a black tomcat. He did encourage me to create a nice cat group. But he remained shy and wild, and one day decided to make a try for freedom by going through a closed window.

After that, mother advised me to use human models. But since I believed that humans only approached the beauty of animals when they have their clothes off, that didn't work out either. Anyway, I doubted very much that human beings could ever compete with such wonderful creations as horses.

Eventually I became a student at the School of Art in Riga. Their pedagogical methods were old fashioned. As I began overcoming the first difficulties, I learned that real satisfaction came only when I worked for myself. In this way I reached that moment when the object created by me escaped its material limits and came to life. I worked with body and soul. Years later I learned that one can also create and shape new forms out of living entities.

The best of my works were photographed and sent to a professor at the Academy of Art in Munich for evaluation. His judgement was positive, thus helping me achieve the most important requirement for studying in Munich. When I left I made my only childhood boyfriend angry, because I assured him the first thing I was going to do when I reached Munich was buy a dog.

Sirius, the dog star, was really a good star to watch over me. I was eighteen years old when my mother brought me through Berlin and on to Munich. The journey lasted for days, and in many ways was exciting. Well supplied with numerous good rules and directions, I began my young adulthood on my own. An elderly spinster became my landlady. I shared the boarding house with a Swiss girl of my age named Lilli, and our studies were held in a beautiful studio the professor arranged for his students to use. At first I was most interested in the evening life-study classes. There were some fifteen or twenty students in this group, including many interesting—and also many untalented—people.

I had promised my mother I would visit two old friends of hers every week. They had two grown sons, but I never tried to get beyond conversations with them. One of the friends at least had a Fox Terrier, which actually belonged to her son, a lieutenant. This lieutenant seemed to make a great deal out of his rank. He repeatedly stated his principles for a love affair. That interested me quite a bit, but only in a platonic way, since I wasn't willing to accept a Fox Terrier in place of a Boxer. In the meantime, much to the horror of my landlady, I picked up a tree frog instead of a dog. Of course, that wasn't any type of substitute for a dog wish.

The loneliness of a large city far from home began to affect me. Only one of my fellow students actually interested me. He had assumed a sort of supervisory position in our study group, and it seemed to me that he was the most intelligent and talented among us. I would have liked to know his name, but in those days it was out of the question for a young lady to ask such a thing. Eventually, a dog-related incident led to our acquaintance.

For a whole week, the young man never attended studio classes. When he returned, he had a slight limp. Because of his dog he had a small accident. Usually, when he was away he left his dog with a friend's family, and whenever he returned there was always a boisterous reunion. But this time the dog leaped up on his master, and both went falling down the stairs. That caused the slight injury to his leg.

His report on the accident had my undivided attention. I asked him what kind of dog it was that could show such joy. He explained to me in general terms that it had a big head, a black face, and a coat like a tiger. I asked if that might be a Boxer, but he wasn't really sure. So I asked him to bring the dog along sometime to the studio. No, he didn't think that was a good idea, because there might be problems in the studio. But I did receive an invitation to visit my new acquaintance and get introduced to his dog. Of course, because of my mother's rules I had to decline the offer.

From that day on, however, we had an endless supply of conversational material. I never even noticed that my distant manner changed gradually, and I began to be attracted to both the dog and his master.

Pluto, The Dog From Hell

Gradually I learned about Pluto's history. His owner had wanted to get a dog for the same reasons as I. One of the daily newspapers contained an ad for Boxer puppies, but he assumed—as did most people then—that they were actually Bulldogs. The breeder, however, soon convinced him that the Boxer was a unique purebred breed.

My friend fell in love with the dog, just as I had with that Pug of my childhood. Pluto was a light-fawn brindle, with a black face and not a single white hair on his body. Proudly the breeder pointed out that the father of Pluto was the ancestor of all the Boxers and Bulldogs in the region around the city of Bielefeld.

My friend introduced his new dog to his landlords without any trouble. On the next day, he took the puppy to work with him. It was a lithographic firm, and there was a large courtyard which could hold many dogs. But this area was dominated by a big, aggressive, biting Great Dane. No one dared to go near that dog during the day. Even his owners were very cautious with him.

On this day, the Great Dane was occupying himself with a huge bone in front of his house. Then though the doorway of the courtyard trotted a little round fellow with a big head and a black face. His legs, with their big paws, made him look almost clownish. Innocently it trotted over to the giant animal. The amazed Dane just stared, but soon the little one moved toward the bone, and suddenly the giant came to life. With one jump, he was on his feet and on top of the small Boxer. Screams echoed down from the upper windows of the building, where Pluto's master and other employees watched the proceedings below. It seemed as though Pluto was done for.

The Dane stood up, and clenched in his mouth hung the small dog with the brindle coat. Perhaps he was considering whether to swallow the little guy whole or first tear him to pieces. Then the lifeless small body began to move. Little Pluto raised his head and began squirming around in his loose hide.

With the front paws paddling in the air, he raised up and moved his head backward until it lay on the forehead of the Dane. Lightning fast, he latched on with his small, needle-sharp teeth and clamped his jaws shut in the manner known to his breed since ancient times. The Dane became upset. He loosened his jaws, but Pluto, now hanging free, continued to clamp down on the Dane's right eyebrow. No longer was the giant the champ of the courtyard. He shook his head back and forth, swung his front paws wildly above his forehead and muzzle trying to get rid of that burden-some insect. But it was all in vain! Pluto hung on! The Dane began to howl. Again, in vain!

Wildly jumping around, the Dane ran across the courtyard and back. After a while, the young Boxer grew tired of the fun, loosened its grip and slid to the ground.

Panting heavily, the Dane just stood there. Pluto, however, calmly trotted over to take his first booty, the big bone.

Slowly, with his tail between his legs, the Great Dane moved over to the other side of the courtyard and laid himself down. After that incident there was an armistice between the two, with each giving proper respect to the other.

A year passed, and Pluto's master gave up his job in Bielefeld to go on his own as an artist. He left his Boxer with his mother in Mainz. She liked the dog, but wasn't capable of controlling such a lively fellow. In a short time, Pluto was chasing after any wildlife they saw on walks, wouldn't come when called, and tried to mix it up with every dog that was bigger than he was. In other words, Pluto went to the dogs without his master.

Finally, my friend allied himself with another artist and they established themselves in Starnberg. Pluto moved there too. His wild years seemed to be soon forgotten. Most important was that he now displayed a wonderfully kind attitude toward the landlords' children.

So it was a shock when one day the three-year-old began shouting, "Pluto knocked me down, Pluto knocked me down!"

That was impossible! Immediately they found the criminal. There he stood, ears down, with his muzzle and head all wrapped in twine. In front of him lay a hammer. When he was freed from the twine he spit out a mouthful of stones. Then they started questioning the children. They confessed they had filled Pluto's mouth with stones, then bound up his muzzle and head. They planned to hit him on the head with the hammer "to see how it would rattle." No wonder Pluto decided the matter had gotten out of hand. He simply knocked his torturers down.

I knew all of that and more about Pluto, but I had still never actually seen him. Finally I received such an impassioned invitation to go tobogganing at Lake Starnberg, that I just could not turn it down. Everything was arranged with the help of my friend Lilli. How complicated it all seems today, when one thinks of the appearances that the young generation of that time had to maintain!

On an ice-cold, but glorious day, a new part of my life began. The little train chugged me along to Felddaffing. Glorious winter landscape, a brilliant sun! It was a day out of a dream!

We spent the morning tobogganing in Felddaffing. At noon we drove to Starnberg and the family that my friend lived with. The reception was wonderful. But I really was not much interested in the family because my attention was riveted on a dog: medium-sized, very sturdy, striped coat, big head, and a black, powerful muzzle. Plus dark eyes which constantly fascinated me. There was a bound- less primitive power in his eyes, but also much tenderness and an enduring desire for love. As I reached out with both hands toward him, he slowly came closer. Perhaps both of us felt that we had met before in an earlier life. Then up he sprang and began licking my cheeks. Oh, for so many years in my childhood I had dreamed of this dog!

Everyone present wondered at Pluto's behavior. Usually he was reserved, almost shy, when meeting strangers. But I wasn't surprised, because I knew: This was my dog!

In the evening, the three of us strolled to the train station: my friend, I, and Pluto. At our farewell, my friend said, "I will have to give you Pluto now; one day you may take him with you. But until then, visit him often in Starnberg, because he needs a lot of friendship and love."

It was the first time my friend used the intimate Du when talking to me, and I thought he was being very fresh with me. But it did not upset me. Still, it took me three more months before I could bring myself to address him as Du. And with that, this romantic episode of my life came to an end.

Pluto And The Boxer Club

Thus Pluto became my first Boxer. And much, very

much later, his former master—Philipp Stockmann— became my husband.

Summer arrived, and with it a four-month break back home on the Baltic. During this time I flattered my way into getting permission to give up my former apartment in Munich. When I returned, I found a nice boarding house with many other young students. Soon I was the favorite of my landlords. Eventually, Pluto moved in, and he rapidly conquered the hearts of the other tenants.

I was industrious and I worked hard. Best of all I was no longer alone. Often on foot, sometimes by bicycle, I made excursions with my constant companion Pluto. He even went with me to my classes in the studio in Schwabing. My tuition was so high that the well-known professor was quite willing to overlook the dog's presence.

So I ought to have been satisfied since all of my wishes had been met. Why wasn't I then?

Well, some questions still required answers. Pluto was already five years old. Two characters seemed to be combined in his personality, and I was never able to overcome that. He was the model of obedience at home. No dog since him has ever been more obedient to me. When I said "phooey" to him, he would refuse to take any kind of food, even spitting out what might be in his mouth at the time. You could tempt him with the most delicious treat, and he would refuse it until released from the command.

But if I took him to the woods, he was a different animal. He trembled with anticipation of the hunt. The hair on his back stood up, and when he took off no call or command could get him to return.

It was the same on the street when we met another dog that was bigger than he was. Smaller dogs could actually hurt him without response. At most, he would just toss them aside. But woe unto any that were bigger! How much grief and trouble I had with that dog!

A spoiled dog and an inexperienced girl! How could they ever get along together?

Then I heard of a club for breeders of purebred Boxers. They were even supposed to have an accurate stud book for the breed. And all the available breed literature would be there too. Could that place help me train this dog? But I couldn't muster up the courage to go to the club's main headquarters alone. That might sound ridiculous today, but at that time I was full of inhibitions and tripped over my own feet. So I prevailed upon my friend until he finally agreed to follow the path that became our destiny. He visited the main office of the club and brought me back copies of their publication, *Boxer Blätter*. Especially important to me was a brochure on the Boxer and a breeder's record book.

I Want To Be A Breeder

Impressions of a new world stormed into my life. My dream became reality. Out of a girl's obsession developed a real situation, with enthusiastic men and women being involved. Even scholarly questions—which I never even dared to ask then—played a role.

I was in heaven. For the next week, no one could even talk to me. Seldom had I ever dedicated myself more to my studies, but as with many others who have tasted the fruit from the tree of knowledge, I wasn't really happy.

I began to look at Pluto with new eyes. Where did my ideal dog go? There was a great separation between the desired image of a Boxer and mine. Why, I asked myself, is a short back nicer than a long one? Why do the legs have to appear to be straight when viewed from all angles? Were these merely the opinions of others whose dogs happened to look like that?

It was later explained to me that everything which best fulfils a purpose is also beautiful. Long backs, sway backs,

faulty extremities, all hinder the performing ability of the animal. Mostly, such faults are the result of thoughtless breeding and careless attitudes. In nature, the tendency is toward producing the form that serves the animal best, and that is also the most beautiful.

I had to get off my high horse. My dream that I was the owner of the most beautiful Boxer came to an end. But I still loved my Pluto as much as ever. After all, I had made so many sacrifices for him. A change of living quarters, the difficult confession to my parents that I had a dog— those things happened because of him. But how many times must I stand helplessly to the side as he carried on with his fighting?

I tried everything to stop his fighting. He couldn't go out in public without a muzzle on. But what did Pluto care about that? He would jump the first big dog he saw, put the muzzle up near the dog's mouth, the dog would grab onto the leather, then a quick jerk back and the other dog was standing with the muzzle in his mouth and Pluto was free to use his teeth.

The worst thing about dog fights is when bystanders get involved. I was always trying to hold back people who just wanted to wade in and start beating. That did no good at all, in fact made the dogs even more vicious. Sometimes I even received blows intended for the dogs. One time an officer, who just happened to come along, pulled out his long sword and began striking the dogs with the flat side of the blade. In doing so, he also whacked me on the finger. A year later my finger was still swollen where it had been hit.

But that didn't bother me much. The worst came when Pluto started another fight right in front of the same butcher shop where he had one three days earlier. The owner of the store finally lost all patience. He raced out with two apprentices, they grabbed Pluto by the collar, jerked him off the other dog and beat him until he was as limp as a diaper. Somehow I managed to save Pluto. I was totally exhausted. Crying never has come easy for me, but this time my whole world was out of order. I don't know who angered me more, Pluto, the other dog, or the butcher and his apprentices. When I got home I locked up Pluto, threw myself upon my bed and cried all afternoon.

The next day I took Pluto on the leash to my friend's studio. Pluto was completely undisturbed by his beating. He pranced alongside me as though he were overjoyed by the beautiful spring weather. I never even glanced his way. Secretly I tied him to the door knob, rang the doorbell, and quietly disappeared.

For two weeks I never met with my friend, even avoiding any chance encounter. But finally, I just had to get rid of some of my anger. With the help of a young admirer, I played a trick on the butcher. Gradually the anger and disgust eased away. But Pluto had once again overloaded the debt side of his account with me.

Then I received a letter from my friend. He told me that he was worried about Pluto. The dog would not eat, lay around completely apathetic on his mat and seemed to be very heartbroken. Who wouldn't soften after that? The lonely Sunday hours had already become difficult for me. And when I read that Pluto tugged on his leash in the direction of my place whenever on a walk, that every time the doorbell rang he ran eagerly to the entrance and then slinked back to his mat when it wasn't me at the door, well—I couldn't hold out any longer. There just was no other choice, I had to make up with the dog and his master.

Now I faced a breeding problem of general significance: my ideal that I had created in my mind began to break up piece by piece. Should I abandon Pluto because of that? I did not wish to capitulate and give up completely on him. Gradually I hatched a new plan. If Pluto were not exactly what I dreamed of now, could it perhaps happen with a son of his?

As the year once more came to an end and my long-desired vacation at home neared, I promised Pluto, "I will

return and we will then go to the Boxer Club, and I will buy you the most beautiful Boxer bride that I can find. It will be difficult and cost many sacrifices, but you'll see, I will do it!"

My Breeding Program Begins

Vacation time passed, and I moved into my rooms again. Of course, I was not entirely aware of what I had decided to do. Breed dogs in a boarding house in a large city? Almost an impossibility actually. Any city dweller would know that. And then there was the matter of money. My student's allowance was generous, but dog food and license fees cost money. Every trip on the train now cost double. I would have to give up going out at night, the theater, dancing. Would I give up all that for a dog? Of course!

So one day I found myself standing with Pluto in the offices of the Boxer club. I was rather downhearted, because I knew what Pluto's weaknesses were. It was even worse because my affection for him was much too visible.

Naturally, Pluto was examined carefully. Just so I wouldn't seem too ignorant, I pointed out his poorly cropped ears, his dewlap, his long back and steep hindquarters. After some consideration, the verdict was pronounced.

"Your dog is of a somewhat older type, but he's a powerful and charming male. You may register him. And you can even breed him!"

That was like pouring oil on my fire. It was so simple in those days to get an evaluation of "Good" at a show. And that approval from an expert sufficed—along with a two-mark fee—to register my dog in the stud book of the German Boxer Club. So Pluto became officially Pluto vom Dom, No. 1521.

The kennel name of "vom Dom," meaning "from the cathedral," sounded almost religious. In later years, the name was often labeled pretentious, especially abroad. Reality was a bit more prosaic. That had been Pluto's notorious battle name when he was living in Mainz with my friend's mother. His brawling and cat chasing in the area around the cathedral had made him a celebrity of sorts. Anyway, Pluto became the first representative of my kennel in stud book number IV of 1911.

For me, there was an innocent joy about it. Pluto, along with his parents, whom we laboriously identified, would remain forever in that stud book, but at the same time forever forgotten.

Eventually our conversation took a decisive turn. Mr. Schmöger, who at that time was the leader of the Boxer Club, casually mentioned that he knew of a good Boxer bitch for me. She had a pedigree, was five months old, good on the leash, shook hands, jumped over the hurdle, and was even housebroken. Supposedly, they wanted fifty marks for her. In the opinion of the expert, that was a gift. They gave me the address of the breeder, and after that there was no more stopping me.

Way down in Giesing, we found a little house with a small garden in front. When I rang the doorbell and the door opened, the first to greet us was a fawn bitch with two young dogs, one a brindle and the other a fawn. I reached first for the brindle, since Pluto was also one. But I was disappointed to see that he was a male. The other one, however, was a lively red-fawn bullet with a face that was all white on one side. Like many beginners, I had a dislike for those features, but the decision had already been made. Pluto had jumped over the low fence and was already forming a close friendship with his future kennel mate. With tail wagging, he fastened his eyes on me, then licked the little bitch's ears. His look said it all. How could I refuse him?

The four of us made our way back home: my friend and I and the two dogs. Silently I walked along, but finally I could no longer hold back a sob. My friend asked if I were not happy. Oh, yes, I was happy all right, but that

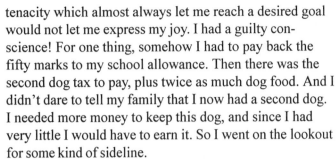

tenacity which almost always let me reach a desired goal would not let me express my joy. I had a guilty conscience! For one thing, somehow I had to pay back the fifty marks to my school allowance. Then there was the second dog tax to pay, plus twice as much dog food. And I didn't dare to tell my family that I now had a second dog. I needed more money to keep this dog, and since I had very little I would have to earn it. So I went on the lookout for some kind of sideline.

After numerous hesitations, I rented a studio together with my friend. We began producing drawings and articles for advertising. That helped a bit, but with the high tuition for my professor and the upkeep for two dogs, I needed a lot of money. The easiest solution would be to stop my lessons for a month and save the tuition. After all, I was learning just as much in our studio as I was with the professor. And I was successful at it! Hardly nineteen years old, I had the joy of seeing my statue of a Boxer—an idealized version of Pluto—exhibited at the Glass Palace in Munich.

Laska

Many dogs have accompanied me through life. Every one was somehow tied to my existence and thus had its own story. All have earned the right to their own monument, but I can only do that for those who became exceptional canine personalities and, with my influence, became a part of the history of Boxer breeding.

Laska was one of those. She received her name from me. It's Russian and means "the loving one" or "the friendly one." That fit her fine, and she was beautiful and became more beautiful every day. But she was solid wood between the ears. She was not a brawler, but she picked up other tricks to torture me.

Laska had been housebroken for a long time. One night though, a stomach disorder caused her to demand to be let out. To do that, I needed to conquer five floors of stairs, but I had young legs. So Laska went outside. She took her sweet time, and only after twenty minutes were we back in the warm bed. You could excuse that once, but Laska's now stomach seemed to reset itself to a new rhythm. The next night she did the same thing, and the next night and the next night. Then I lost my patience! After letting her whine awhile, eventually I took her downstairs.

In slippers and a coat over my nightgown, I went down the stairs, but unfortunately I had waited too long. She relieved herself in the stairwell. Then she made a big fuss to get outside. I opened the door, it was pitch dark outside and a light rain was falling. Laska took her time. She wandered to the corner of the house and then went around it. I called her, but she didn't hear me. Or maybe she didn't want to hear me. All of a sudden it was as though she had disappeared from the earth. I ran farther and farther after her, but all to no avail. The wind tore at my coat and it rained even harder. The city seemed to be dead. I headed for my studio, and I ran for forty-five minutes to get there. My braided hair was wet, my coat stuck to my body, and my slippers dripped water and mud.

Finally I reached the studio. It was as dead as all the other houses, and I did not have a key for the locked door. There was no sign of Laska. Maybe she was hiding around the corner and laughing at me. Or perhaps she had already gone back home?

No choice remained but to return. I moved as quickly as possible. It was freezing, and the city frightened me. Then a policeman stopped me. Where was I going? He asked. I begged him to let me go, I was only looking for my dog. Because of my unusual outfit he asked for my name and address. When I told him the street, he became suspicious. The distance seemed too much. So I decided to tell him the whole story, whereupon he became much friendlier. Finally he let me go, but with the good advice that I should never run after a loose dog, because you will

never catch it. It's better to go in the opposite direction. He was sure the dog was already back home.

I have never forgotten that man. His advice was really not bad, although it didn't work in this case. Laska was not at home.

The next day I found her waiting at the door of the studio. She gave me a joyful greeting.

Laska had another specialty: she was a born tightrope walker. Any balcony or barricade crossbar enticed her into a daring balancing act.

Dizziness was unknown to her. One time when we were strolling along the Isar, Laska jumped up on the bridge railing, hardly more than a hand wide. No one watching dared to do anything. Far below roared the waters from the distant mountains. I didn't try to do anything except speed up my steps a bit, and it seemed as though the bridge had no end. Finally we were across. I called Laska, and she came right to me, as pleased and proud of herself as she could be. She was quite conceited and knew when she was being admired.

Once, sometime later, she almost lost her life playing such a game in my hometown of Riga. Loggers often floated rafts of sawlogs down the Düna, and in the still areas of the river sometimes there were hundreds of logs jammed together. Laska ran out on one of those, way out to the end. But the log was not large and could not hold her up when she was on the end. She slipped and fell in the river. It wouldn't have been so bad, if there had not been logs on all sides. There wasn't enough room for the dog to swim. Whenever she tried to climb on a log, it would spin and she would go back under. We were helpless and confused. Then a dock worker came over and used a long hook to move the logs around so Laska could swim to shore. Oh, yes, she could take your breath away at times!

Laska developed wonderfully. Everywhere she went, she drew attention with her cocky manners and white muzzle. But eventually I knew I would have to face the consequences. Why did I get the bitch? I had told my parents a fictitious tale about Pluto being so beautiful that he was used at stud, and I had received Laska as the payment. But it bothered my conscience, and I wanted to get free from that because in no way was it my nature to lie. Decisive action has always been a principle of my life.

Once again spring arrived, then summer and the vacation at home. It was time for a discussion with my parents. Decisions had to be made. My allotted three years of study had now run out. But where should I go with my two dogs? At home, nothing but a city apartment awaited me. And I did not wish to move to my uncle's in the country. It seemed as though the only thing I could do was try to live from my artistic work. Because that seemed impossible to me, I felt completely lost.

My friend, on the other hand, had it all figured out. In a serious conversation, he pointed out to me that there was only one solution: get married! Then we could get a little house outside the city, and—above all—the vom Dom kennel would blossom and bloom!

What else was there for me? I now had to inform my parents that I not only had two dogs but also a fiance`. That was quite a bit for one conversation, especially since my mother had always viewed me as a spinsterish artist. But, all in all, this picture of my future had its attractions. And it was probably the only real solution. But I asked for time to consider it. I wanted first to return home with my dogs, and then we would see how it worked out.

A Breeder's Choice

There was another important decision made at that time. Before I left for home, I took my dogs to visit the offices of the Boxer Club. Mr. Schmöger was pleased to see the two Boxers again. Above all, he was happy to see

how Laska had developed. When I told him of my plans, he gave me some advice which he had probably thought of long before. Give up the idea of using a dog like Pluto on Laska, he urged, and then gave me the address of a gentleman in Riga who had purchased two purebred Boxers. That was where he advised me to find the breeding partner for Laska.

His words really bothered me. Why did I get Laska in the first place? I felt like the apprentice magician in Goethe's *Faust*: "I am no longer the master of the spirits I created."

Home is still home, especially when dear, familiar faces are waiting. The dogs were overjoyed to get out of the crates after the sea voyage. They charmed my parents immediately. Father beamed when he saw Laska, it was love at first sight. Already the Boxer Club had informed Professor Jos, the owner of the two Boxers in Riga, about my situation. Even these organizational matters met the approval of my parents.

Of course, I didn't like the two other Boxers. They were better than Pluto, but they were also heavy, dumpy animals. If I were going to be unfaithful to Pluto, then it would have to be with the most beautiful dog I had ever seen. And I had already found him. In the *Boxer Blätter*, I had seen a picture of a new star: Rolf von Volgelsberg, a brindle with a small white stripe on the face and a small three-cornered spot on his neck, a mark that many of his descendants still have today. I had read the description of him, along with a report of the sensational success of his first times in the ring. And I already felt that only the best breeding matches should be made if something good were to be achieved. The great successful breeders always have a sixth sense, a wisdom that was also repeated to me later by plant experts.

As so often happens, Laska came into her first heat at the wrong time. Now I began to realize why people turn down bitch puppies. It was not a pleasant situation. Add Pluto's love drive to that. Also I had to walk them separately, which

Friederun Stockmann feeding her pack. At the far right is Rolf von Vogelsberg

Mrs. Stockmann at about twenty-two years of age with Rassel vom Dom

Mealtime at the Vom Dom kennel

Bedtime at Vom Dom kennel

took a lot of time. And there was no way I could get rid of the procession of dogs that parked themselves outside our door, as though they were my father's patients.

Only my younger brother found joy in the situation. He perched on the balcony and shot at the waiting crowd with his slingshot. Whenever he hit one it would leap into the air, never figuring out where the pain had come from. My brother enjoyed that immensely.

But even those twenty-one days passed. Pluto's love pains subsided, and he became his old self again.

True to the agreement with the Boxer Club, I let Laska's first season pass unused. Anyway, a great event was coming up. I wanted to show Laska for the first time at a dog show in Munich. Thus her slender figure should not be spoiled.

The First Time In The Ring

As often happens in life, what seemed to be the most difficult problems solved themselves. Introducing my dogs to my parents was nothing at all. And when I informed them of my marriage plans, and our artistic and sporting plans, they agreed without any ado whatsoever.

Of course, I was nervous! There was a little stir when I introduced my fiance` to our old pastor, and asked to be married as soon as possible. They misunderstood the urgency, so I explained there was a dog show in Munich in September and I wanted to be there. I did not wish to come back to Riga. That's the way it always went for me: my dogs! How many misunderstandings, moral disappointments and other unpleasantness have I had to put up with because of them?

Again and again it came back to me that I was not normal when it came to my dogs. It all just rolled off my back. My parents understood me because they loved me. And my husband? I wouldn't have married him, if he didn't have an understanding for the nature of this hobby.

With our marriage, he came under my star. And it stamped and shaped his life, just as it did mine.

My husband rented a small house in Fürstenfeldbruck near Munich. It had a big garden, attached field and two outbuildings. And beyond that, we had my mother's dream of building us a villa with a studio—and a real kennel, I had added softly.

When we said good-bye to my homeland through the train window, we never suspected it would be forever. It was also a last farewell to my dear father. We began our trip into a future that could not have seemed brighter to me. Yet our first setback already awaited us.

Both dogs were in their travel crates in the baggage car, and the conductor had been tipped handsomely. We picked the route that would be the shortest time for the dogs in their crates. If we had only known what lay ahead of us!

Our departure was in the afternoon. When we arrived the next morning at the border, we went through the train and discovered that our dogs were not on board. Immediately my husband demanded a thorough search. I wanted to break the trip, but in the end we had no choice except to go on. There was nothing more we could do. We left behind enough money, with the instructions to do everything they could to get the dogs to Munich as quickly as possible. It took us two full days and one night to reach Munich. Up to then, they had not found a trace of our dogs.

I was very exasperated when we pulled into our new home—Fürstenfeldbruck. My attitude did not get better, when there still was no word the next day. After four days, we still had not a clue as to our dogs' whereabouts. Our telegraprams around the region were useless. Nor was the railroad's offer to pay damages any consolation. All I could think of was the suffering of our dogs. I couldn't sleep or eat. For seven endless days it went on.

On the eighth day, exactly a week after our departure, we received word from the station that our two dogs had arrived. I hardly dared to ask if they were alive, but they did still live!

I can't even remember how we went to the station. At the doorway to the baggage room I shouted out, "Pluto! Laska!" How wonderful it was to hear their voices answer me.

We jerked open the crates, and out they leaped, healthy and happy. They were certainly very lean and ragged, but their joy to see us was enormous.

All during those days I had not thought about the dog show. Now the thought burned in my mind. Could I show Laska in this condition? My husband assured me that she looked marvelous compared to me! So I made a quick decision. The worst was behind us; I would feed the dogs well and see what they looked like on show day.

During a long trip it's not hunger that tortures the dogs, as long as they have water. Much worse is that the digestive system fails when there is no natural elimination. Both of our dogs had to recover from that. After a bowl of milk and two raw eggs, they began their return to good health. Both animals had good appetites, but never as though they were starved. Our guideline was not to feed too much at one time. The body has to get used to receiving nutrition again.

A warm, soapy bath followed their meal. And after a good drying with a towel and a short trot in the late afternoon sun, we had two rather restless but happy Boxers snoring away under the table. For the first time in our new home, I too slept deeply and without nightmares.

Three days later Laska looked much better. Careful feeding, lots of brushing, careful clipping of the hunger-hair that had grown out on the hind and front quarters, filing down her long nails, all had a noticeable impact. But did I dare to show her that way? My husband advised me to try it, and if it failed, then try it again at a later show. At least she wouldn't need another hunger treatment before that one.

Show Business

Laska's entrance fee had already been paid. If I did not show her I would lose that fee. So I decided to show her, especially since she had recovered very well.

For someone in the sport of purebred dogs, every show has to be attended if possible. It's just as interesting for the participants and spectators as a horse race for horse lovers. The evening before, spirits are high. Everyone knows that the first prize will soon be home on the mantelpiece. Sometimes we forget that there are often thirty or more competitors and only one first prize. Those who get the second, third, and fourth prizes are never happy about it. Therefore nobody should envy the judge.

Yet every dog show is a holiday for the dog fancier. Every true fancier takes defeat calmly and tries to find value in the judge's verdict. Only those who learn that defeat can produce success will move forward as breeders.

It was a cold morning as the exhibitors stood outside shivering and waiting for the doors of the hall to open. When we finally entered, two veterinarians, both in white coats, stood on opposite sides of the doorway, They were examining the dogs. My heart skipped some beats. Would my girl be declared too thin? Not at all— I could pass!

We entered a large hall in which rows of wooden crates had been constructed. Laska had received a number, so I sought out that crate, put my sweetheart inside and attached the chain to her.

Next I checked out the ring, that place where the judging would be held. Boxers were divided by color and sex for the judging. It takes a lot of practice and experience before an exhibitor learns how to present the dog's best qualities to the judge. For that reason, one hears the often-repeated chant that only the best-known breeders and handlers win, and the novice has no chance. That's just hot air, as became clear to me on this very first of my shows.

Gradually the ring began to fill with people and dogs. Everything was new and strange to me. The man in the white smock, sitting at a table and paging through papers, turned out to be the judge. Two other men wore armbands with "Steward" printed on them. The stewards had numerous duties. They had to get the dogs into the ring on time, control the crowd, and take care of the awards. Actually, their full duties were to see that the show proceeded in an orderly manner.

Fawn males always began the ceremonies. This time sixteen animals entered the ring. I knew from the exhibition report that this class would have the most significant representatives of Boxer breeding at that time. From Munich alone, there were three often-decorated fawn Boxer dogs in the ring.

For a layman at ringside, it's very difficult to judge the dogs in the ring. Those sixteen dogs seemed to differ only a little bit in their coat colors. Yet the judge graded them as excellent, very good, good, satisfactory, and lastly unsatisfactory. Only one will get the first prize, and that will be the only person satisfied with the judge's opinion.

It was difficult to judge this fawn class. Many duels were fought out in the ring. In the end, a four-year-old undefeated champion, Knieps Remus von Pfalzgau, took the prize for fawn dogs. This dog had gone from one victory to another, but when he finally suffered one defeat after years of campaigning, his owner brought him home and shot him as punishment for the loss. What a disgrace to the sport! But in Munich, he still stood undefeated. And at that moment in Cologne, in the von Eigelstein kennel, lived a four-month-old son of his who was destined to go far beyond the fame of his father.

Although Remus' competition consisted of well-known and frequently-victorious animals, none could best him. Further proof for this judgment lay in the fact that not a one of those others played a role in future Boxer breeding.

The next high point after the fawn dogs came with the brindles. There was a favorite here too: the multi-winner, Sieger Rolf von Vogelsberg. His most respected opponents were three Munich dogs, among them his younger son, Schelm von Angertor.

Hardly breathing, I followed the judging of this class. I was hopelessly in love with Champ Rolf. It was for him that I broke my pledge to Pluto. It was he who I had already decided would be the sire of my future breeding program, although I had only seen pictures of him in the *Boxer Blätter.*

Champ Rolf won. How could it be otherwise! He was the biggest, the most noble, and had the best head. The second place dog was a glorious animal too, with even better color and more substance. I thought for a long time about buying one of the two.

In no time at all, it was Laska's turn to go into the ring. Just to be safe, I had entered her in four different classes. It was immediately apparent that she could not compete with the older and better groomed bitches. The fawn bitches also had a famous winner among them.

When it was all over, my booty consisted of a Reserve trophy and two Fourth Places. I won something else too. Although only a beginner, I learned that losing was also a part of the sport and could be very useful. Laska eventually had her successes and became all we had hoped for, especially in regard to her beauty.

Becoming A Breeder Is Not Hard

The experience of the show impressed me greatly. Finally the time for Laska's second season approached, when she would be eligible to breed. I sought advice from the Boxer Club again. Albert Schmöger, my old friend, greeted me, and I asked him about finding a stud dog for Laska. Rolf von Vogelsberg? Now the leader of the club rightly informed me that Rolf was indeed a great Sieger, but the best breeders were not always those that ran after the biggest hit of the day. Furthermore, he continued, many breeders who used Rolf complained of unsuccessful breedings or, if successful, then of puppies that were difficult to train. He advised me to think it over first.

But I had already decided. Was it my heart or my instincts that led me to Rolf von Vogelsberg? To this very day, it has been this one great dog that determined the Boxer type produced in my breeding program.

Once again my life began to resemble that of Goethe's apprentice magician, as events began to overwhelm me. First, Laska's breeder checked in. He offered, in his words, a splendid deal. Laska's mother was in heat, and he would give her to me if I would just breed her to Rolf and give him a pick of the litter, a male puppy. I hadn't wanted to expand my breeding program so fast, but could I afford to let this opportunity pass? At that time, I had not heard of this tactic used by some breeders to give away an old, well-used bitch to somebody in exchange for a young male puppy. Traudel, Laska's dam, was one of those exploited creatures. Still, I took her and bred her to Rolf.

But once again I had to buy my future success with a failure. Traudel von Steinhausen had a litter of eight. Four were males that were either stillborn or died shortly after birth. Of the four survivors, I picked out a very plain male without any white markings as my future star. On the eighth day, his mother rolled over and accidentally crushed him. These setbacks were hard on me, and it didn't help when my husband reminded me that he had often said dog breeding wasn't the right job for me.

But he didn't know me very well yet. Even when the little bitch, who looked exactly like her crushed brother and was my next choice, turned out so poorly that I was happy to give her away—I never for a moment thought of giving up on Boxer breeding. Really! And here's how ironic fate can be. The two other surviving male puppies, one a fawn and the other a brindle, both with flashy

markings, I also gave away. One to my brother-in-law and the other to a friend of my spouse. Those two dogs, the first two of my breeding, enjoyed successful show careers and brought home many trophies.

Now things really began to overtake me. Several well-known breeders put their dogs up for sale. Among them was Rolf von Vogelsberg, and even if everything went wrong I had to have that dog. It's a good thing that my husband wasn't a spoilsport. When I told him that I really did not think we needed to use my dowry to get a lot of new furniture, and I would rather spend it for dog breeding and hoped to get Rolf von Vogelsberg for 1,000 marks—he merely told me that all our property was held in common, and I should do what I thought was best.

It was not a hard decision. With the financial question solved, I took all my remaining dowry, which was exactly 1,000 marks, and offered it for Rolf. He became mine.

Good-bye to Pluto

Much more difficult was the problem with my conscience. I could not keep two male dogs at that time. Pluto had certainly done everything necessary to earn my affection, yet I still had to decide against him. It was not out of conceit or for the sake of some future success in the ring, but because of a creative drive to see new forms emerge from living material, much as I had done in my art with lifeless material. It shocked me when I began to understand this, but that didn't matter. I could only do what was within the realm of possibility for me.

Pluto went to that family, where I had first met him. They gave him love and understanding. That it still did not go well for him was his own fault. He was seldom punished, yet he fell into his old habits again. As he had done earlier when he was with my husband's mother in Mainz, he now began to terrorize Starnberg. He had regular brawls down by the lake. One time the police even took a shot at him, but he always returned home victorious. His owners began to dread each new day. Finally, they watched from the villa window as Pluto jumped a six-point buck near a small wooded area and tore it apart. With that, the bell had tolled for Pluto in Starnberg.

An acquaintance of the owner had a young relative, a logger by trade, in his hometown in the mountainous region of Upper Bavaria. This relative had a reputation as a scrapper and wanted a reliable dog to be his companion. Off went Pluto. About a year later, the former owners heard their last news about Pluto. He had saved the life of his new owner. It seems that one night after dark, ten fellows jumped Pluto's master, whom they had long hated. In the mountains, knives are always at hand in such brawls. Knocked down and about ready to be done in, Pluto's master managed to get two fingers in his mouth and whistle. That had always been Pluto's signal. He snapped the chain that held him, and in seconds had the attackers scattering like straw in the wind. Pluto had arrived in the nick of time!

If one can believe the whole story, then Pluto also left behind some descendants. Supposedly, in a remote mountain village a farmer had a Boxer bitch that he was very proud of. A regular devil in a dog's body. Pluto bred this bitch. One could assume then, that Pluto's riotous soul still lives on.

I always had a guilty conscience over being unfaithful to Pluto. And later, when I often had to give up one of my dear Boxers too soon, I had the feeling that it was a type of punishment for not being true to my first Boxer, who always remained mine in my heart.

Life goes on. It doesn't allow you to dwell on such thoughts. Lord only knows how so many people learned that a young woman from the Baltic wanted to breed dogs! People from all over Germany offered me bitches. In no time, I had six of them. Of course, they were not really suitable to advance my breeding. Most of them were older

dogs, used to having their own places. There was no end to the bickering and fighting that went on among them.

Later, it went the same way for me with farming. When I bought a small farm, suddenly everybody seemed to be offering me worn-out cows and horses. That's a sort of tuition you have to pay in life. But it didn't hurt anything. It taught me quickly that not every animal is suitable for breeding. It also taught me that dogs are not like other animals. They have souls, which makes acquiring and dispersing them a very personal matter. It's a lot simpler with cows and pigs. Even the most noble of all animals, the horse, does not arouse the kind of emotions a dog does.

Birth

The most important time for any form of life is when it leaves the protection of its mother's body, crosses the threshold to life, and begins its struggle with the world as well as it can.

This beginning of life was always something special for me. A sort of magic, which still remains with me. And with it comes the knowledge that one is personally responsible for that little life. Freshly arrived, it will grow and develop, like a kernel of grain, and be loved and have a hundred hopes for its future. Whether an animal or a human mother, all see birth as something holy and momentous, and whoever doesn't sense that will never be a true breeder. At most, they might be called a producer of dogs, but not a true fancier.

Because I have always been deeply aware of that responsibility, I tried in every way to keep some control over the lives of those little creatures whose existence was of my doing. In the wild, dogs and the other canine family members usually seek out a small, dark cave, for a place to bear their young. In America, they use a shallow box with newspapers strewn around in it. House dogs have gotten used to a lot of things. But those dogs never struck me as too happy about it. I have even seen loving breeders put feather pillows in the whelping box, along with blankets and upholstery. The more sensible use hay, straw, or wood shavings. When the birth process begins, the dam starts to get restless, to turn around repeatedly and paw the ground. That has a purpose in the wild. It aids in labor and expands the den. But how does it work with a feather tick underneath?

Bitches don't have much understanding for an artificial whelping area. The denning instinct is so strong in them, that I just let mine—once I had the space—go out in the yard and dig their deep holes. I just let them have this pleasure, because when I knew the right time had come, I also knew where to find them in their whelping beds.

Finally Laska's time had come. The coupling with Rolf von Vogelsberg had gone well. I think I counted not only the days but the hours to her whelping time. Usually a bitch carries for nine weeks, or 63 days. Little variations often occur and should not raise concern.

Laska's whelping box had been lined with fresh straw. She didn't seem too interested in it. The earlier whelping with her mother, Traudel, had been quite uneventful. She was an experienced bitch and had handled it all by herself in the middle of the night. But not with Laska. Our princess wanted to be pampered and praised. How many would she likely have? A usual Boxer litter runs from four to eight, but it often goes over or under those numbers. For an average, maybe six or seven.

Laska stretched our patience to the limit. On the sixtieth day of her pregnancy we could easily see the little forms moving within her when she relaxed on the floor. On the sixty-second day, we saw the first signs. Laska turned down her noon meal. She picked up an appetizing piece of meat, but then, with a regretful look, put it back in the bowl.

A second sign: that evening Laska sought out her

whelping box. If we talked to her she wagged her tail, but she would not leave her nest.

A third sign: Laska became restless and began to pant. Her body trembled, she whined and came to us, but then quickly returned to the box.

Those were difficult hours for us. We became worried. Laska became more and more restless, her panting increased. She repeatedly cleaned her genital area. In-between, she often held her breath, her stomach muscles would tense, then her labor contractions began. Out of her vulva came a balloon filled with fluid. We didn't have a clue. Neither my husband nor I knew anything about the whelping process. The only thing I could come up with was the old advice, "Please, look it up in the encyclopedia."

Not bad advice. Soon we found the subject "Birth," and it confirmed what we saw taking place. The water bag served to prepare the birth canal, and it should not be interfered with or opened. In all the dog books that we had read up to then, there had not been a word about that. And it could be so important! How was a beginner supposed to learn that? We read further in the encyclopedia, "When the water bag breaks and the fluid flows out, the birth will follow shortly!"

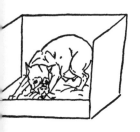

It almost seemed as though Laska had been waiting for those instructions. She gave out a short cry, and a little dark body pushed itself into the light. At first covered with a thin, translucent skin, it looked like a cucumber in a cellophane package. Laska picked it up in her mouth and placed it between her paws. She eagerly licked the little one all over its body, then she began to bite through the umbilical cord, remove the sack and eat the placenta. It was all done as calmly and naturally as though she had done it a hundred times before. Of course, it was all instinctual, as her ancestors had done for thousands of years before her.

Yet there are always people who are sure they know better. They interfere in the natural process and take

Goldi von Pfarrkirchen with her puppies

Petra vom Dom with her puppies and a foster child

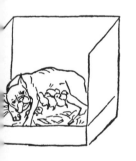

away the afterbirth to prevent the dam from eating it. Thoughtlessly they destroy important hormones and take away what should be the mother's first nourishment. In the wild, the mother is not able to search out food immediately after whelping, thus eating the placenta is of great value.

We were positive that Laska would do the right things. And our trust in her proved right.

After achieving the first birth, and making sure the little pioneer checked out fine, there came a resting pause for the mother. Holding the little one in her front paws, she pressed her warm soft nose against it and comfortably snored away. This rest after the firstborn is quite typical. It often lasts two or three hours, sometimes much longer, but there is no cause for alarm.

We sat full of awe in front of our young mother. Wasn't she wonderful? Not all new mothers go down that first path so instinctively and certain. I've seen some bitches who were so horrified by the first birth they had to be restrained to keep them from running away.

Laska's labor now began again. Four more puppies arrived rather quickly, and then, after another rest, two hours later came the last.

Thus ended the most difficult and wonderful hours of Laska's young life. Both the floor of the whelping box and the puppies were now cleaned and dried. Laska needed the bare floor in order to keep the puppies clean, but all around herself she had built a nest of soft hay.

Gradually it became calm in the whelping box. As a sign of that, Laska now lay stretched out on her side, offering the puppies full access to the lunch table. The puppies nursed, now and now and then we heard a little peep from them. We fed Laska a whipped egg yolk, with a bit of sugar flavoring—it was her favorite treat—as a reward for a job well done. For ourselves, we made a cup of good coffee. We were as tired as though we had too given birth, but then hadn't we?

The Puppy Nest

Who is the breeder that does not revel in the joys of a hundred expectations when looking at the whelping box the day after the birth? If everything is in order, the dam will be lying calmly on her side, and the puppies may nurse whenever they wish. Providing there is enough milk available, you seldom see them nurse. Most of the time they sleep. Sometimes there is a little one nursing alone because it had not been too successful in the struggle to feed with its siblings. If the mother has enough milk, it can catch up on what might have been missed earlier.

No bitch should be allowed more than six puppies. That is certainly enough. True breeders will follow that principle. Yes, there are bitches that seem none the worse for raising eight or nine puppies. But that is exploiting the mother. The extra puppies should be removed, if the mother is to enjoy her healthy offspring.

It's not easy—for beginning breeders especially—to put aside the extra puppies. Just choosing them takes serious consideration. The experienced breeder first culls the weaklings. Then the mismarked next. Puppies with too much white and excessively light coats should not be kept. But if all are healthy and well marked, then one sets aside the extra bitches, for if they are not owned by responsible breeders they are often exploited and pushed from one owner to another. Recently it has become the trend for single women to buy a bitch puppy. The Americans call it a "house pet." These personal bitch puppies are usually much tamer, softer, and obedient than the male Boxers.

One does have to be cautious in culling bitch puppies. Most important is the type of head. Beginning breeders should certainly seek advice. The Boxer Club has prepared

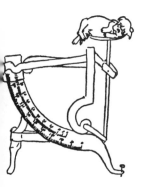

its breed wardens for that, and it has proved to be well worthwhile.

Laska saved us the trouble. Her litter consisted of four males and two bitches. In breeder jargon that would be "4,2." We were happy about that because it spared us the hard decisions—there were no breed wardens at that time.

After a while the young mother became restless. She no longer wished to nurse her young and turned herself over onto her stomach. It was time to let her outside to relieve herself. At first, every new mother resists this. The slightest squeak from a pup pulls her forcefully back to the nest. It takes some patience on the breeder's part, and sometimes a little trickery, to get the job done. Thereafter, the dam is again a peaceful, caring mother. In a few days, the breeder's anxiety begins to ease. If the mother is rich in milk, which Laska was, she will gradually begin to leave her babies, once they are full and lying peacefully in one big pile. If for nothing else, just to make a quick round of the house and grounds to be sure that all is in order.

During the first week, the puppies' little tails are docked. I have always done this by first tieing them off. Still, that's not really necessary. The puppy's pain is quickly gone, and it returns immediately to the mother's nipple for consolation after life's first injustice.

For the beginning breeder, this great event of the first whelping is full of joy. So it was with us too. Every day we weighed the puppies, always recording the exact amount. Puppies weighing about a pound at birth grow slowly in the first week. Then they begin to show a remarkable growth. It isn't unusual to record a gain of over a pound a week for each puppy. A four-week-old litter of six puppies could easily weigh over 25 pounds, almost half of what the mother weighs. And she has to produce the nutrition for all of that growth. Isn't that a marvelous performance?

It's touching to think of all the care that a mother dog gives to her young. Her big soft tongue is constantly at work. Through her licking she controls their bladder and bowel eliminations. Their stomach muscles are much too weak to do that without aid from her. You can sit and watch this maternal care for hours without tiring.

And there is something new every day! After eight to ten days, the little ones begin to blink. In a few more days, they are staring at the new world with big blue children's eyes. There are some little wise guys who—even before their eyes are open—let their siblings know of their existence by actually growling.

Between the third and fourth weeks, little needle-sharp teeth begin to break through. That is the time when the breeder must help the mother get free of the pups. I tried to offer warm milk to Laska's children. But her nipples were still streaming , so I wasn't very successful, even when I beat up an egg in the milk. That made me some-what unhappy. Then I reheated the gruel and suddenly realized that it was too warm and too runny. But after I removed much of the liquid, it seemed as though the puppies had a complete change of heart. They tore into this new preparation and emptied the bowl. How limited is the human mind! Weren't the appearance of those sharp teeth an indication that the time for mother's milk was ending, and solid nutrition was beginning?

Now I began to chop up fresh meat and liver. Along with that I cooked oatmeal. The pups were completely happy with this mixture. Of course they got some cod liver oil too. They ate that, but preferred the better tasting things.

After about four weeks, they started to get curious and tried to leave the whelping box. That allowed them to do their jobs outside, keeping the box clean. Since the mother began losing interest in keeping them cleaned up after they started eating solid food, it was good that they could get out of the box when they needed to.

Up to then, we were able to keep them in the box. The situation changed, however. If the pups couldn't get out now, they scolded and screamed. You must allow that,

since it's the first step to housebreaking them. Anyway, the room's growing barn-smell will hasten that step.

We prepared a special room now for Laska. She had a crate there, which the puppies could visit or leave as they pleased. Sawdust covered the floor. With that, we had set up a nice healthy nursery for her children.

Of course the crew had to be named. How else could I report their latest heroic deeds? Up to then I could only say, "The one with the white feet..." or something like that. You couldn't do that forever! Each one had to have a real name. I was the first breeder to start the practice of using a distinct letter for each litter. The first was the "A" litter; the second the "B" and so on. I did not actually do that with my first litter, but now there would be order! Thus came litter B. Among them was a big brindle boy. Would he be the star of my kennel? I gave him the name "Benvenuto." It means "the welcome one." Later breeding experience taught me not to burden them with such high-sounding names. But sometimes such illusions are all the breeder has until the pup is grown. So it was with our "Ben."

Generally, a growing pup is one of the fancier's greatest joys. Travelling and showing are second place to this quiet joy of the breeder. Perhaps the anticipation of future wins is a part of it. A breeder might raise a hundred puppies, for months go back and forth between anxiety and depression, and maybe after a year still not know if the faults will disappear or increase. It is in these worries that the charm of this sport lies, a certain magic from which no one can escape.

Sometimes I would sneak away from my work. If my husband looked for me, he would find me at Laska's side with the puppies. They had become sturdy little guys. Active in muscle and teeth. Then one day I noticed that they did not seem to be eating. It hit me that they could be sick. But their bellies were fat and full. Finally I noticed how Laska, after she had been fed, would run back to the young ones. They were already eight weeks old, and their mother had almost completely weaned them. Like a hurdler, Laska would jump over the fence around the pen. Legs astride, she stood over the young ones. But they weren't interested in her nipples anymore, and clamored around her mouth. I was shocked to see Laska vomit up some of her meal for her puppies. Greedily they pounced on it and gulped it down. Laska was obviously pleased with herself, you could see that in her face. In turn, she gobbled up what the puppies had left in their food bowl.

Now I knew why the pups had no appetite, and I began to make sure that they had eaten well before Laska could visit them. So much for my friend Schmöger's claim that there was no mother's love among animals. According to him, all attraction was just the instinct to nurse!

One day it occurred to me that my hens weren't laying well. I discovered the cause of that very quickly. I saw Laska take an egg in her mouth and race back to her children. Carefully she laid the egg on the floor in front of the puppies, who examined it curiously and then began shoving it back and forth, not really knowing what to do about the hard shell. Suddenly the egg was gone. I lifted up the dog crate, and there were 32 good eggs. Many years later, I observed another bitch take over a litter the moment the real mother, who had been leased for just one litter, had to leave. With no urging, she jumped right in with the eight-week-old pups and gave them nourishment in the same way Laska had. The nursing instinct had nothing to do with it.

Bad Days For Breeders And Puppies

Treating a dog for worms is an important matter. Some breeders aren't happy unless they can repeatedly deworm their animals. But if the puppies are fed properly that's not necessary. Puppies are not weak because they have worms; it's because they are weak that they have worms. If that is not the case, however, a good strong worm treatment can do wonders. New medicines have eliminated the problem. One only has to watch that the puppies remain otherwise healthy. If it is a matter of only tapeworms, sometimes a sudden change in diet will remove them.

During the war years, when neither vets nor medicines were available, occasionally just a coincidence helped me. Once when cooking beet syrup I fell asleep from exhaustion and awoke to a ruined syrup and a room full of smoke. I had to throw pot and all out the window. Another time I ruined a batch of celery salad. Even though it was wartime, I felt that neither was edible. But my dogs thought otherwise. They devoured the syrup and spoiled salad with great joy. The result was amazing. Their worms abandoned them in great heaps upon the ground.

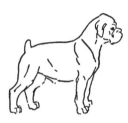

The experienced dog person recognizes the sweet, chloroform-like odor that comes from the mouths of puppies with worms. Worm-free puppies have a breath that is somewhat like the smell of fresh coffee beans.

In general, it's fresh air, sunshine and cleanliness that are the best medicine for a kennel.

There was another dark day for me in a litter's early stage, one which my husband often pointed to as evidence that dog breeding wasn't my forte, and that came with the ear cropping. That has been a hot potato for over fifty years now. In Germany and America the ears are cropped. In England and many other countries it is forbidden.

It is not just a matter of senseless fashion that led to it. There was a practical side too. Nor is it a coincidence that only the fighting breeds have cropped ears. The reasons were the frequent injuries to the ear lobes, along with the subsequent difficulty in healing ear wounds. Actually, Boxers do not have much of a problem with the so-called "ear worm," in contrast to many of the breeds whose ears stand naturally and seem to be often plagued with this middle-ear infection. But when we talk about the beauty of a cropped ear, we usually run into the old premise that what is natural is always the most beautiful. Is that really true? At the very least, one has to remember that the cropped ear is healthier than the uncropped. And the appearance of the cropped dog is more alert and friendly. The beautiful line of a noble neck is emphasized by the cropped ears.

And yet anyone who spends some time in England very quickly grows accustomed to the uncropped Boxer. If it should ever be that Germany and America cease this cosmetic surgery, the true friends of the Boxer will be able to endure it. All in all, whether cropped or uncropped, the advantages and disadvantages even out. So let each national club set its own standard.

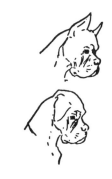

The surgery itself is less harmful than imagined. Today it is always done with the animal under anesthesia. You could compare it to the removal of a tooth. Of course, that's not a pleasant experience either, but with today's science the cropping operation has certainly lost much of its earlier horror. What's most important is that it is done by an expert. Unfortunately, many of our veterinarians today lack that necessary experience.

It seems to me that cropping is often more trouble for the breeder than the puppy. Once the operation is over, the puppies' eating is as normal as before. I have never known any puppies to lose their appetites because of the operation. After twenty-four hours, the shock and pain disappear and normal play returns to the litter. If the ears have been first properly bandaged, then those unpleasant bumps against them are almost impossible. After two weeks, at most three, all is healed, scarred over, and the dark day of cropping has been forgotten.

The last hill had been climbed. Laska's puppies were now "ear-finished" and ready for sale. But what beginning breeder can stand to see the little darlings depart? In the course of those first three months, the puppies themselves helped create a desire in us to see them go on to further training in someone else's good hands. Ben stayed the longest. He was going to get me my first-prize trophy. My critical nature, however, kept finding more and more faults in him. Thus I could not escape the impression that at least two grades difference lay between him and his father, Rolf von Vogelsberg.

My husband suggested I was always unsatisfied and would find faults in any dog, but I stuck by my guns. You can only be a good breeder when you are able to keep an

open mind and not be blinded by love for your own products. You must be able to see—and admit—their faults, or you can not avoid them in the future. Eventually, Ben found a fine home with a countess. She wanted a beautiful, well-trained dog, and Ben filled her wishes completely.

I began to suspect that it would not be easy to breed the ideal Boxer. Who knows how long it would have taken if I had not been lucky? Over and over I have learned that knowledge and superiority will not do it if you have bad luck. But there isn't any such thing as eternal good luck either.

My First Victory

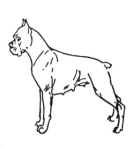

My friend Schmöger, for instance, was plagued with bad luck. One day he told me I really did not have to take in bitches whose breeding days were over. My optimism often let people take advantage of me in that respect. Now I had a chance to get the great champion, Urschi von Hildesberg. She would be one of our best, but she had already missed on her last three seasons. Schmöger confessed that Urschi was a great buy for a bitch with over forty first prizes behind her, and her owner was one of our finest fanciers. Despite that, he suggested that I also take his little Bilma. This bitch was small, but had a beautiful head. If I would breed her to Rolf, I could make the lease payment to Schmöger with a male puppy from the litter. He was positive I would get an all-brindle litter out of that match.

Of course I was interested in such an offer! My kennel population had already grown quite a bit. It made me well known. Once a friend came to Fürstenfeldbruck looking for me, but no one could help him. When he mentioned that I had a kennel, however, a little guy piped up, "Oh, you mean that girl with the Pugs!"

So Bilma joined my kennel. She was a canine

personality in every way. It was not easy to get along with her. She was never pleased, it seemed. That led to trouble between her, Laska and Urschi. If we took her out for an evening walk, she would nose around in all the dark corners, often finding couples doing a little necking. Then she would bark at them until we personally came over and took a look.

Soon Bilma began to expand, eventually measuring well over three feet around. As with Laska, we fretted about the coming big day. In the meantime, I kept busy at my trade. I wanted to try my luck again at the Glass Palace with another dog sculpture. But my living dogs took the largest portion of my time. Bilma's whelping time approached. She wasn't bothered in the least.

One beautiful fall morning, Laska romped with her playmate Champ Urschi in the yard. Old Traudel lay sunning herself in front of the door. Into this idyllic setting came the mailman and dropped off the newspaper in the mailbox. Bilma heard that. She pushed down on the door handle and trotted out. Traudel was in her way, so Bilma just ran over her. That angered Bilma's special enemy, Urschi. In a flash, the two tore into each other. Of course Laska couldn't just stand by. She jumped into the brawl, and then old Traudel came in to help her.

I was horrified because Bilma was in full pregnancy. But my experiences with Pluto had taught me a bit about handling fighting dogs. Immediately I pulled out Bilma and put her in the house while the others continued to fight. With my husband's help, we managed to separate the other three ruffians, and for punishment we tied them up right next to each other. They could think over their crimes together. In such cases, if the sinner were unrepentant, we used the hated muzzle, but those three knew what they had done wrong. When I would release them in two or three hours, they would be subdued and submissive.

First I had to convince myself that Bilma had not been injured. I opened the door cautiously, but Bilma was nowhere to be seen. How could that be? There was no other exit. All the windows were closed, so she had to be somewhere in the house. We looked under the bed, in the cellar, all in vain.

Eventually my husband became impatient—as do all men when they are hungry —so I set the table. But I had my ears and eyes open. Suddenly I heard a familiar sound, just a little whimper. Where? In the bedroom! But we had searched there. No mistaking it though, the sound came from there. I rushed in. There was a slight rustle in the wardrobe, which was closed. I had shut it myself. No matter! I pulled open the door, and there lay Bilma, comfortably placed on a pile of clothes. She had three puppies with her, and judging from her size, she was not finished. In a little while, the whole closet was full of puppies. Only when the eleventh arrived was she finally finished. With our lack of experience, how would we ever be able to make the selections? We planned to call Schmöger the next day. But could we leave eleven puppies with the mother until then?

Meanwhile, I had released the three sinners. With some warnings and a wave of the belt, I put Urschi and Traudel in the kitchen. Laska, however, kept sniffing around the bedroom door. That gave me an idea. I fetched a puppy and held it to Laska's nose. She immediately began to lick it, and when I started to leave she took him gently out of my hand. She had not been bred during her last season, and now was the time she would have had the puppies. Could she help raise Bilma's puppies?

We really had no choice but to let Bilma stay in the wardrobe. After all, she had picked it for her little home. Nor was it difficult to entice Laska back into her old whelping box with the extra puppies. She gladly accepted them. Within two hours she began producing milk. I informed Schmöger of all that, and urged him to come by and choose which puppies should be culled. But he wouldn't hear of it. As far as he was concerned, everything was in order. Bilma had six and Laska had five. He told me that was quite acceptable, and I ought to be happy about it. Basically, I had a different view. Yet, at that time there were no regulations forbidding more than six puppies for a dam. So we kept them all, and they seemed to thrive on the arrangement.

In this litter—whelped on September 28, 1912—lay my first Sieger. A golden brindle with a little spot of white on his chest. After eight weeks, Schmöger came by and made his pick: the only fawn male in the litter. He named him "Debbes," which was supposed to mean "the best." But his master had bad luck again. The best became the worst of the lot. For an encore, I also gave Schmöger the only fawn girl. He sold her, and later I ended up owning her again. She became a wonderful show dog, a fine mother, and one of the dearest bitches I have ever owned. But she left us too soon. Even today, some forty years later, when I think of her painful end it breaks my heart. We named her Derby, and she belongs to those Boxers that I will never forget. The great Sieger in the litter was Dampf. He earned honor for his name, because, like the lead character in the story, "Hans Dampf in allen Gassen," he triumphed everywhere.

Dog Training?

My mother's ambitions encouraged us to drop our lease and build our own house. It would be a large studio with all the other living quarters and all the comforts. How little did we know of the world in those days! The most practical thing at that time would have been for us to buy a farm. But we had grand ideals. Besides, who could have known what fate awaited Germany?

We bought a lot in the village of Emmering, in the district of Gemarkung, near a bridge. It was about an acre large, with a thick grove of beech trees. On a beautiful fall day, we went to Munich and withdrew a large sum of money. When we returned, I wished to stop and take a picture from our own land. Rolf and Laska were along and romped around in the fallen leaves. Although the light was

not quite right, I took a photograph anyway. Then we went on home.

Once at home, I immediately realized my purse was missing; apparently I had lost it while taking the picture. All of the money we withdrew in Munich was in it. My husband tried to calm me down. He rightly said that no matter what, it could not be found that night. We could do nothing other than wait for morning. But until then I could neither sleep nor eat. Toward morning I lay in a half slumber, dreaming that I was in a pile of hay and leaves. Suddenly, Laska stood before me. From the right side of her mouth hung my purse. I rubbed my eyes—but it was only a dream.

Rest was no longer possible. I quickly made some coffee, and was pleased to see that my husband was also up now. We took Laska along, although my husband thought that made no sense and she would only disturb us. For some time now, I had been training Laska. I had trained her to jump, to fetch, even to track down a hidden purse, but I had not worked with her for over a week. Maybe something was still left over from then.

So off we marched. Our destination was the place which was my last hope to find the purse. When we arrived, Laska, in contrast to me, was cheerful as she could be and kept smiling at me with her half-white muzzle. I gave the order, "Laska, find! Lost!" She responded immediately, wagged her tail, and began searching. Back and forth she ran through the leaves. It's pointless, I said to my husband. I really wasn't sure where we had been, nor was Laska, most likely. And where she was now, behind those bushes, we had definitely never gone.

It seemed best to me to call her back. If she continued to search and found nothing, it might ruin her joy in tracking forever. But my husband was more confident. She would return by herself when she didn't find any-thing, he said. And she did return. She stood between the bushes, looking at us and wagging her tail. "Laska!" We both shouted. Hanging from the jowls on the right side of her face was my purse.

Since then I have never again said there is no personal reason to train a dog for performance competition.

Champion Rolf Von Vogelsberg

I just cannot go on without giving Rolf von Vogelsberg the praise he so richly deserves. In many respects, Rolf's youth resembled my Pluto's. Rolf's breeder was the veterinarian Brechtel from Codalzburg. Sold when only half grown, Rolf came into bad hands. He was given too much freedom and was soon on his way to becoming a regular bum when Dr. Schülein saw him on the street and immediately offered a low price for him. Dr. Schülein knew dogs very well. He could see what a valuable Boxer Rolf was.

But Rolf gave his new owner some problems too. He was a poor eater, and at shows was often described as too lean. Two weeks before a show, his master would start giving him afternoon snacks of four or five pieces of cake. That was the only way to get him up to form. He showed first in Darmstadt in 1910. Right away he went to the top. In Dresden, that same year, he took the Sieger title, and followed that up with victories in Würzburg, Nuremberg, and Chemnitz to get his championship. More shows brought victory after victory. When he returned from his service in the war he was eleven years old, but he still took his fifth championship.

Dr. Schülein purchased him when he was two. Dog shows were the doctor's hobby, but he never had enough time for it. A lot of things were missing for a good dog environment. When I bought Rolf, he had just turned three. He was always a bit slim, but for his time he was a big Boxer, with a deep chest and a noble demeanor. Some breeders complained about him as a stud dog, saying he often failed to impregnate, and when he did his pups were often too unruly. I wanted to change that.

Dr. Schülein told me that Rolf had thrown up a small stone about the size of a walnut. Veterinarians told him the stone probably had been in the dog's stomach for many

months, causing the production of excessive stomach acid. The dog's appetite improved after the stone was gone. After Rolf came to us, it struck me that he could use a deworming. At that time there was an excellent medicine called "Walker's 60-Minute Cure." For years I used this, and I don't think anything since then has been better. Its success was just amazing. Never had I ever thought that a dog could have that many worms! From that time on, there never was another complaint about Rolf's weak fertility.

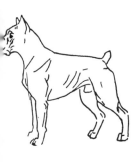

Since the beginning, the Boxer breed had been divided into fawn and brindle. Although the two groups had been interbred, there were still some faults and features that seemed more prevalent in one group than the other. Fawn Boxers were superior in structure. They had straight backs and good rear angulation. But the brindle Boxers were more noble and had better heads. Their poor structure, however, was a disadvantage, as they stood in the ring with their backs hunched up and poor rear angulation. Rolf von Vogelsberg was the first brindle with beautiful angulation. Yes, his back still hunched a bit, but he had the glorious head and neck of his color. And he was one of the biggest Boxers of his time.

Boxer breeders tended to divide along the same lines of brindle and fawn. Today, the red-fawn Boxer is still more popular, because the brindle—especially if plain—appears rather homely. But there are many who all of their lives have remained true to the brindles. If someone had asked me in those early years which color I preferred, I would have immediately answered brindle. Since then, fate has educated me a bit. Sure, I am still loyal to the brindles, but I do not judge a Boxer now on the basis of one color or the other.

At that time, shows and breedings were dominated by Rolf von Vogelsberg. To the very end, he remained undefeated by a brindle. The fawn Boxers were led by Remus von Pfalzgau. He was also an outstanding dog, but in May, 1912, he met his fate. He was badly defeated, leaving the ring in third place. At that time, I resolved that my dogs would be retired before they were forced out of conten-

Champion Rolf von Vogelsberg, the
Stockmann's first prepotent sire

Eight-week-old puppies out of Sanni and Kobold vom Dom

tion. Remus had taken care of his future, in a way. His son, Milo von Eigelstein, took over his father's top ranking.

Rolf was only undefeated in his color. In competition for the Rotating Trophy *[Wanderpreis],* when brindle and fawn competed for best dog, quite often the fawn topped him. First it was Remus, then Milo. How much the personal preferences of the judges for fawns played a role in that, is difficult to determine. In two aspects, Rolf beat out all his competition: he outlived them, and he became a major influence in the breed. There isn't a Boxer today that does not have Rolf for an ancestor.

In contrast to Pluto, nature's boy, Rolf was a pure aristocrat. Rolf was with me longer than Pluto, he was faithful and depended on me. It was a joy to go out with him. He survived his adolescent time, and not a trace of it remained in him. And he never caused me grief. But still, at no time was he as close to me as Pluto had been. I loved Rolf and was proud of his accomplishments, yet I never reached the same relationship with him that I had with Pluto.

Even in the dog game, all that glitters is not gold. When I joined the Boxer Club, I was young and not unattractive. In addition, I was from the Baltic, then a part of Russia, so I was also a foreigner. Mother had urged me to keep my maiden name as a part of my married name, thus I am officially "Friederun von Miram-Stockman." My first artistic successes came under that name.

That was something new in the realm of dog sports. Fact is, I was able to buy the two best brindle Boxers, Champion Rolf and Sieger Urschi, because I had a reputation of being rich. There was even an attempt made to elevate me to the rank of a Russian Royal Princess. How little I cared about that! My ambition and pride arose only from my Boxers, and that is the way it has remained to this day.

But I soon learned that there was another side to that coin. If you wish to become unpopular, just buy a beautiful dog. Young and full of ideals, I had spent a great deal of money for my Boxers. It was a great personal sacrifice for me. So now I wished to confirm the good results of my efforts by exhibiting in the ring. Moreover, both Rolf and Urschi were in their prime.

Then I began to notice how the atmosphere around me became unfriendly. Every victory of my dogs had to be purchased with the antipathy of those whose dogs placed behind Rolf and Urschi. Gradually, I began to realize that it was no special distinction to buy beautiful dogs and use them to take the prizes away from others.

It had never occurred to me to buy Rolf to make money from him. I wanted to have the joy of owning him, and to use him in my breeding program. Of course, I would be pleased if his stud fees helped pay a part of his purchase price. But there was no sympathy for that view at all. People constantly complained that the stud fee was too high. And every loser-offspring would be blamed on him, although the bitch played a role equal to his. I made Rolf available to all breeders, regardless of circumstance, but even that was supposed to be wrong! Some even uttered nonsense about "unfair competition."

In order to stimulate entries and enthusiasm, I donated a bronze Boxer statue to the Bavarian group of the Boxer Club for their Rotating Trophy. I had believed they would be pleased to receive it. But the result of my efforts were exactly the opposite. At the next show in Stuttgart, both judges and breeders made bitter comments to me, because as a young beginner I had presumed to donate a trophy for Bavaria by myself. And the North Germans felt they had been slighted to the same degree that the Bavarians felt insulted!

Actually, that type of thing has stayed the same right down to the present time. Nor do negatives and positives always balance out. Human inadequacies lead one to just want to turn the back on those people. But then there are the Boxers! And when my love for them is put on the

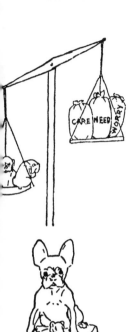

scale, all hostility disappears. There only remains our animals, with their honest eyes and joyful tail-wagging.

In The New Home

At first everything seemed to be wonderful. The Glass Palace had accepted another work of mine: a statue of a French Bulldog, which became the best seller of the season. What a help that was for my depleted dog budget! And it was an artistic success to boot. In that direction, I had more plans. I wanted to become a dog photographer, so I purchased a 13 x 18cm reflex camera. It was the best on the market then. We also built a large kiln in the basement. I thought the bronze castings were too expensive and wanted to make my own ceramic works. Everything seemed wonderfully hopeful.

Finally we moved into the new house. Big rooms and beautiful furniture greeted us. All of which would prove very useful later. In contrast, our dogs were not happy with the new circumstances. The first night, as we finally settled into bed, exhausted from the moving, the dogs began a maddening chorus of howling. They felt lonely and abandoned. We had to get up and console them.

A big surprise awaited us the next morning. Four of Laska's puppies, which I had kept in a kennel, had disappeared. The whole lot was surrounded by a wire fence. At that time, I had not yet learned what a dog can do when it decides it is absolutely going to leave. It took us three days before we had all the dogs back with us. Especially the bitches seemed most irritated and upset. I just did not know that dogs often react to a move in this manner. About two weeks passed before our four-legged friends fully adjusted to the new location. Whether the dogs liked their new kennel, I can't really say. I do know that if I were to do it over, I would build the kennel differently, and for about half the cost.

In the middle of May, there was another show in Munich. A large group of North German fanciers, judges and breeders—among them the owner of Milo von Eigelstein—had promised to visit me on their way down to Munich. For that reason I decided to wait at home, and my husband took our entries to Munich.

Dogs Are Pack Animals

Of course, everything had to follow a system at our place. When my visitors finally saw that most of our dogs were running free and playing with each other in the yard, they declared it was impossible for so many Boxers to do that together without eventually starting a deadly fight. I did not agree with that view then. My argument was that dogs were pack animals, and they had to subordinate their individuality to the group. But the "old boys" disagreed, and they had paid their breeder's dues and spoke from many years of experience.

Over the many decades since then, my view has proved to be the correct one. I could not prove it then, but those who visit me today are amazed and pleased by the pack they find here. The animals get along with each other because they must get along with each other. Their free life prevents them from becoming dull, bored kennel dogs. They learn quickly to follow orders, for it would not work if they didn't.

My best helper now is the pack leader, a powerful fawn male, calm but far superior to the others in strength and intelligence. He is a many-time great grandson of Rolf von Vogelsberg. There are about ten generations between them. This dog keeps over twenty dogs and bitches under control inside the fence.

Of course, the absolute top dog must be the owner. And when there is a dog that simply will not fit in, then it must be separated from the others. Two males of equal strength will fight to the death. The weaker gets the death sentence. But is it any different with other pack animals, or even with humans?

I paid my dues here too. Sometimes there was a bloody sacrifice. And most of the time it was my fault it happened. But would things have been different if they had been penned up all the time? There are always accidents. For sure, when two kennel dogs meet each other a catastrophe is almost unavoidable.

The visit from the North Germans left a lasting impression on me. Above all, I had the feeling that even long-experienced breeders did not always see things straight. How else could they have overlooked the young Dampf, Rolf's son?

Munich 1913

I met my husband and the dogs in Munich. We had not shown Rolf, but his successful son, Schelm vom Angetor, instead. Even as a puppy, Schelm seemed destined to beat his father in the ring, but it had not happened yet. I came to own him by coincidence. His previous owner was Josef Widmann, a longtime Munich butcher, and certainly one of the most decent and honest of all dog fanciers. And in the coming years, he stood by me again and again during my breeder's crises. We even planned once to have a kennel together, and I would be in charge of caring for the dogs.

He proposed I take Schelm in return for some puppies later. Of course, it should be mentioned Schelm had become a bit too much for the old gentleman. The unruly Schelm gave him no end of grief, and every show degenerated into a battle between Schelm and his master's umbrella. Naturally, such activity either led to the anger or amusement of everybody at the show.

So I took over Schelm and tried to talk some sense into him. In Munich, Schelm had his work cut out for him. A new star had risen in the north. Judges' reports praised this brindle male in all aspects. According to them, the new star's head, neck and back were superior to any previous brindle. They meant Rolf when they said that! So we put up a Rolf son against the new star in Munich. But in the ring, it became soon apparent that Schelm could not best this male. Oh, if only I had been there with the father! With his charming nobility, his size, his power, Rolf would have triumphed even under a North German judge.

I had never seen the new star, Heinz von der Elbe. When I entered the show grounds, I saw a tall man standing off to the side, and he had a brindle Boxer with him. One glance and I knew that had to be him!

People in the sport of purebred dogs are like a big family. Despite our human weaknesses, we are tied together by a common love of this hobby. The experienced fanciers know each other. Some twenty years later at a show in Vienna, I again met this gentleman who had owned that new star. He asked how long we had known each other, and I actually could not remember. But he knew exactly. It had been at that very show in Munich in 1913, where we had first met. He told me that our meeting then was still very clear in his memory. The North German judges had overpraised his dog in 1913, but the Bavarians had also criticized his dog too strongly. Among the North Germans, there was a feeling that the South Germans ruined anything sent to them from the north.

It had been a cool reception for him in Munich. For that reason, he had stood off to the side with his dog. Then he saw me enter. He watched as I moved through the crowd, eventually coming over to his dog. I came close, petting and calming his dog. Turning to an acquaintance, I remarked that this was clearly the best dog here and should be the Sieger today. That made a deep impression on him. He knew who I was, and he also knew that I would be showing the main competition to his dog. Understandably, he had assumed that I would share the opinions of the other Bavarians. But my unprejudiced objectivity remained with him all through the next twenty years.

I could only say to him that I just did not remember

those events as well as he did. But I was certain I did not deserve any admiration. I have always tried to judge the dog. It's all the same to me, no matter what the owner means to me. If I'm in the ring with my dog, however, then I look at the others in the ring as my opponents. That does not mean I am blinded by love for my dogs, although I love them all with all my heart. It is that attitude which has brought about my success. And I always find joy in the fact that I have never felt jealousy.

When I see another fancier with a dog I wish I owned myself, then again and again I have managed to breed to that dog and—if luck is with me—get an offspring that is even better! Fairness is always the best rule in life.

Back home, my husband noticed that I was not saying much. He asked me if Schelm's defeat—he came in a far-back second—had upset me. But that was certainly not the case. Even this show had taught me some things. I now told him I wished to sell Schelm as soon as possible. With his too-long back and short muzzle, he was not up to his father Rolf. Schelm did not seem to have Rolf's type, and because of that his victories did not really please me as they should have.

Furthermore, I did not wish to exhibit Rolf any more. I no longer wished to hear that my victories only came from dogs I had purchased. Young Dampf, a pup of our own breeding, was going to represent our kennel in the future. He might not have the glorious head of his father, but in the ring Dampf knew how to make something of himself. And Urschi could always join in, until we could replace her with one of our own breeding.

Mainz 1913

Then some other things happened. We were showing four Boxers in Mainz a month later, and things went quite well. Schelm took first place among the brindles. He had finally learned to behave himself in the ring, and the judge

fell so in love with him that he gave me an offer to buy him, which I accepted.

Dampf now began to show his colors. In the fall of 1913, he brought home two firsts and a second from Karlsruhe, and in November he did the same thing in Berlin.

Meanwhile, there was another addition to our family: March 14, 1914, our daughter was born. I didn't have it easy in those days. There was no help available, and I only had an elderly lady in the house with me. Our artistic endeavors were not going so well either. For those reasons, I began thinking about cutting back on the size of my kennel. Of course, exhibiting took a lot of money and time too.

Hans Dampf The Sieger

Once again the show season began. Hamburg put on a big title show on March 22 and 23, 1914. A Sieger title would be presented. I could not make it, since our daughter was only three weeks old, so my husband made the trip alone. There was quite a bit at stake. The local club was giving a special prize of 250 marks each for the best dog and the best bitch to get a third certificate. Urschi already had two certificates. If she won another, they would have to give her the prize.

My husband received very explicit advice from me. He took three dogs, and each one had to be handled differently. If someone offered him a good price, he could sell two of the three. I insisted that Derby, Dampf's fawn sister, must remain in our kennel no matter what the circumstances might be.

Then I sat at home and waited. From hour to hour, I kept imagining what my husband would likely be doing. Finally, the train bringing him back arrived in Bruck. In a few minutes he would be here. Then I caught a glimpse of him coming home through the bushes along the shortcut.

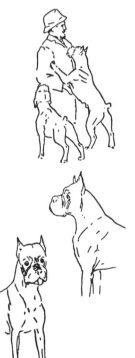

Next to him a red-fawn coat. That would be Derby. Then a small, dainty brindle dashed into view. That was Urschi. But where was Dampf?

I hardly let my husband get a word in edgewise. When I asked where Dampf was, he replied, "Sold!" Right then I knew that Dampf had taken a Sieger title. Just what I had thought all along! But my husband told me it was not a foregone conclusion. Six brindle dogs stood for the final round, and each owner believed the title was his. Dampf had some very tough competition, but in the end he was victorious. My husband congratulated me on my first homebred Sieger.

He received a purchase offer for 1300 marks right after the show. And since he knew how much we needed the money, he decided to sell our first Sieger.

I knew he did the right thing, but I still felt a pain in my heart. So much trouble, so much work and love—all for a handful of money! But I consoled myself with the thought that Dampf was actually no real improvement over his father. He was certainly a beautiful fellow, but I was convinced that I could breed even better Boxers.

We humans have our illusions. If I could have seen into the future, I would probably still have sold Dampf. But my heart would have been much heavier.

Eventually, my husband was able to tell me of the problems he had in the ring with the three. Derby constantly jumped up on him, but Dampf was on his best behavior. Urschi made it to the last round of competition for the money prize, but then she let the tip of her tongue show. As long as I had owned that bitch, she had never shown that fault. And after the Hamburg show, she never showed it again. Under the circumstances, the judge had to believe she was a born tongue-shower, so he gave the certificate to the other bitch, who couldn't hold a candle to Urschi. In the end, that prize was never given. It was a victim of World War I and the later inflation.

On The Eve Of World War I

It probably will not amaze anyone, when even the course of the First World War comes back to me in terms of my relationship with my dogs.

There was a sense of this great coming disaster in the air. Every Boxer breeder felt its influence. Milo and Rolf had been withdrawn from the ring. Rolf was still lean, and no one could have guessed his age. In contrast, Milo aged prematurely. He was a small dog in comparison to Rolf, but he had more than enough substance, which Rolf lacked. Nor did Milo reach an old age. He passed away during the first year of the war.

Our last show, where we all were happy and full of hopes, was in Ulm on July 26, 1914. Of course, the big winners were missing at this show. I had planned to buy a bitch there, one that would be a good breeding partner for Rolf. Just as I was ready to seal the purchase, an unusual stirring began among the crowd. Fliers were being distributed. A few days earlier, the Austrian Archduke Franz Ferdinand and his wife had been assassinated by a Serb. Austria issued an ultimatum to Serbia. Serbia refused it, and with that came the declaration of war by Austria. Germany declared itself united with Austria.

This news shook the very ground on which we stood. Days passed before I fully realized what had come down upon us, but everything was overcome by the threatening realization that my husband would be called into service, and I would be left alone with a small child and the whole pack of dogs. Why would I need an expensive camera now? Who would have the time and interest to have a dog photographed? And what use is my kiln now? Would anyone even buy ceramics? The fuel for the kiln never crossed my mind until later. Oh, if I only had the money now that we spent on all of those things!

But it would get worse. Of course, many young women had husbands who were called up. But not many were completely alone, as I was. Most of them had

relatives. When Russia entered the war, all traffic to the Baltic areas from the west stopped. It was the iron curtain for me, because all of the people who were near and dear to me were now cut off.

When my husband, after several weeks, got his call, I felt totally alone. But was it really so? Didn't I have a darling little girl and lots of hungry Boxers who would be faithful to me? Attempts to get special wartime rations failed. People with their own house and a pack of dogs received no help at all.

In the early morning about 4 A.M., I went with my husband to the train station. It had now become fall. A beautiful starlit night. It was such a difficult good-bye, but we had to bend to the inevitable. As his last parting words—the same that he would repeat some thirty years later in even more difficult times—he told me, "I know you can do it!" It was not some banal comment, but an honest conviction from his heart.

I left the station slowly. For a long time I watched the train's taillights, then I made my way home. My confidence was gone. Seldom had I ever been so confused as then. Then suddenly a meteor flashed across the sky. A streak of bright light and then it was gone. Was it perhaps a greeting from Heaven itself? In any case, from then on I knew that I would indeed get by, although just how was unknown.

At home four Boxers waited to receive me. They also had an unshakable faith in me. Should I disappoint them? And in the bedroom I found my little daughter, a rosy little thing, lying in her crib and smiling. How could I feel lonely, when such dear forms of life needed my help?

New Duties

Some time later, a gentleman stopped by to visit. He was a native of the Baltic and now came from Sweden. He brought me greetings and a little package from my mother. In a letter, she put me at rest about her situation, and expressed her belief that I would survive the difficult times of the war. When I was alone again, I opened the little package and found an antique silver powder box. It was filled with gold coins. It seemed almost like a dream!

And so another page turned. Neighbor ladies, women in the same situation as I, came by to visit. I received my first letter from my husband. He had been shipped from Munich to Augsburg, but it would be weeks before his training ended. Now and then he might be able to visit me. Some friends even arranged a monthly subsidy for me from the Artists' Guild in Munich. All of those things made me aware that other people were also thinking of my welfare.

During this time, an idea of mine began to develop into a specific plan. When my husband came home on his first leave, I laid out these long-planned thoughts for him to consider. I would turn our property into a farm. My belief was that the production of food for humans and animals soon would become one of the country's most important needs. Our impractical kennel would become an agricultural building.

I had already leased over four more acres of meadow and purchased twenty hens and three goats. Fodder for these animals, as well as food for our dogs, had already been laid up. Of course, I had to release my old servant Elies. She did not like farm work, and she never had worked out a very good relationship with the dogs. But a tavern in our neighborhood had been turned into a reserve hospital, and the young soldiers there—mostly farm boys—were happy to help me out. The neighbor ladies took turns helping care for our little daughter.

My husband was more than a little amazed, when I showed him how far I had gone toward realizing those plans. When I walked back to the station with him, I took along Laska and Rolf. While we waited for the train, he seemed worried about me, and a bit skeptical too. That's when I decided to play my last card. I told him I had already talked to the mayor about arranging an agricultural furlough for him. He was speechless. The train arrived, and as it pulled away I began to fear I had actually frightened my husband.

Certainly it was not easy. I had to juggle everything, just to keep my head above water. I wrote articles for the dog magazines, painted, and even bought a book with the promising title, "How can I write for a movie?" I even tried that—without success, of course!

Taking pictures of soldiers turned out to be the most profitable of my enterprises. Usually, my husband took the pictures, then sent me the film and I developed it. We had to overcome some difficulties to do that. Film quality deteriorated during the war, and sometimes we had to do a little dealing under the table to get the supplies to satisfy our customers' wishes.

But who had it easy during those war years? Many men were drafted and did not know what to do with their dogs. Once again, I was able to help. Many pets were boarded at farms, where they could at least get something to eat. But sometimes doing a good deed requires a double sacrifice. One of those boarding dogs, a bitch that I had taken in, attacked and killed a beautiful daughter of Rolf— she was my favorite—while I was away for a few minutes.

Everything began to change. Our very lives became affected by the war. Over and over, our dogs set the pattern for our existence. That was the way it had to be. Dogs and people remained inseparable, no matter what the future might bring.

Winter came with shorter days, longer and more lonely nights. They assigned my husband to a reserve unit near Augsburg. Every day he expected to be called to the front lines. Occasionally he visited us on a Sunday.

Perhaps it was just as well that I had little time for reflection. My shoulders carried a full load. Above all, I constantly had to search for dog food. I pedaled over ten miles to a butcher just to get half a bucket of intestines. Eventually I began to go through the garbage cans outside

Philipp Stockmann with two of the Vom Dom Boxers in WWI

Philipp Stockman, right, at his training center

Boxers being trained at the military center in Berlin

military barracks, hoping to find scraps for the dogs. Really hard times still had not arrived, and sometimes I found whole loaves of bread. Because my bicycle was still in good shape, my search area was quite large. Later, that changed. Worn out tires were replaced with braided feathers. Tarred rope also worked, but riding my bicycle eventually became a real torture.

Home and child, dogs and farming with goats and chickens—all required.care. I was not really used to hard work. Cleaning the stalls was very difficult for me. A real farmer would have chuckled about that, but I hated it.

Boxers Become War Dogs

One day I could hardly believe my eyes when my husband showed up without having told me that he was going to get leave. I never actually noticed that it was he, despite all the barking and his rambling through the house, until he came to bed. But what he told me then popped my eyes wide open.

A commander of an infantry battalion in Belgium reported to Munich that his patrols behind the front lines were being shot by partisans. He believed this unfortunate situation could be ended if the troops had some well-trained aggressive dogs. Munich headquarters then turned to the German Boxer Club. The Boxer's talents for this kind of work were obvious.

Our friend Schmöger immediately supplied six dogs. They were transported by special car to Belgium. In a very short time, they determined that casualties had almost disappeared among those soldiers who had a dog on patrol with them. All of the regional Boxer clubs now began a large effort to produce capable Boxers for the military. My husband had been transferred from the reserves to the national guard, with orders to organize the training and placement of these dogs.

Of course, in many ways that was personally more

pleasant for him. We both continued to be amazed—and pleased— at how much our lives had become entwined with those of our Boxers.

The next morning my husband began making contact with Boxer owners. It was a much different method than what later developed during the Second World War, when everything was organized, dogs were registered and taken. Then the dogs disappeared, and very seldom did the former owners ever hear a word more about their animals. It was calculated, loveless, cold and gruesome, as was everything else about that horrible war.

In 1914, everything was more humane, and thereby more endurable for both humans and animals. My husband trained a small staff out of people who had affection and understanding for dogs. There were many Boxers that had been left somewhat homeless after their owners were drafted into the service. Often the wives worried about how to feed those dogs. Other Boxers were available because the food shortage forced owners to reduce their kennels. Quite a few of those Boxers were the darlings of their masters, but patriotism and the feeling that the dog might save the life of a husband or son came first.

I remember one of those, a dandy Boxer boy named Polly. His mistress brought him in, wearing a black, filled blanket that had pink ribbons tied to the corners. She also brought his special comb, brush, and bowl. The elderly mistress expressed a wish that Polly would be able to save many German soldiers from death and accidents. For that reason she willingly gave up Polly, although her heart was obviously broken. Her sad good-bye touched everyone.

And Polly turned out to be a good soldier! He was one of the most reliable and intelligent of the dogs. It was a great pleasure for me to relate that later to his mistress. But the little package I received containing the rosy ribbons, the comb and brush and bowl?—Somehow that disappeared without a trace before I talked to her.

Also, we should mention Blitz von Hirschpark, who resembled Polly in many ways but was not so spoiled.

Blitz was a master at climbing and jumping. He could jump through a hoop, clearing seven chairs in a row. One time he climbed right up a ladder to corner a burglar on the roof.

Traudel, Laska's mother, and Freya von Hildesberg, the mother of my Siegerin Urschi, were among those in the first shipment. It was hard for me to say farewell to those dogs.

My husband took ten Boxers with him. I was convinced he had made himself personally responsible for those dogs, and he was determined to see they worked out as well as possible under very difficult circumstances. My greatest hope was that he could watch over our two wonderful bitches. But the only one to survive the war was old Rolf. He had gone into the service a year later in 1916, as the special companion of my husband.

I don't believe the dogs were at all homesick. They definitely ate better than they would have at home. And there was always a special relationship between handler and dog, genuine comrades in every sense of the word.

Although many dogs never returned, one has to remember the war lasted four years, and many were already between four and six years old when they began their service. Most dogs do not live any longer than that. And one has to remember also—war years count double for dogs and men.

In mid-December, I received news that my husband's unit would be moved to the front. My last assignment was to bring our youngest war dog, the six-month-old Lump vom Dom, to Augsburg. People still had not begun to see the tragedy of the war, since it was all so far removed. Some even joked about it, in an attempt to push away the thoughts of a terrible future. Both dogs and men were decorated with flowers when they shipped out.

They did not want wives at the train station. Farewell scenes were not desired. But since I had a dog to deliver,

I was able to get through. Anyway, I was long used to saying good-bye.

The local Boxer club in Munich supplied sixty dogs for the war. All were donated unconditionally to the army. The club provided a leash and collar for each. Until then, the military had never been interested in using dogs for war service, but many lives were saved when they did. What was interesting was how this first use of our Boxers eventually led to other breeds being used. Before the war was over, a very large canine force had been developed.

In silence, I returned home. Like almost everyone, I consoled myself with the thought that this war could not last long. With my daily tasks and worries, artistic activity was just not possible. Any high and mighty plans had to wait until the war ended. One day followed another, all the same. Even Sundays were empty and lonely.

Boxer Experiences In World War I

My first letter from the front was a great event. He wrote about their trip through the many German cities, all fully decorated for them. Everywhere cheering crowds greeted the trains. Who didn't believe there would be a quick victory? Our Boxers were a tremendous hit. If the train stopped, the cars would be filled with gifts and snacks. The biggest share was always received by the first cars, and often the last ones received slim pickings. Somehow, that image seemed to fit those war years that lay ahead.

At first, Boxers did regular guard duty in the occupied areas behind the lines. Their main duty was to prevent prisoners of war from passing on any information to civilians, especially about the amount and type of weapons. In no time at all, the dogs had it down. Whenever a civilian approached the prisoners, the Boxers moved in and watched every move. Usually that was all that was

necessary, for the dogs did not look any too friendly when on duty.

Of particular interest is how the dogs reacted under wartime conditions. They had a very difficult duty in the region of Flanders. The civilian population there engaged in spying and smuggling. Although they had made a great effort to control it, the military had not been successful. So a canine unit commanded by my husband moved in. On one of the very first night patrols, a soldier-handler saw some suspicious figures in the bushes. When they noticed the soldier, they withdrew and cursed at him. According to regulations, the dog had to be leashed because it had just arrived. So the soldier answered the curses with some blind shots into the bushes. More curses, whereupon the soldier released the Boxer.

Immediately, the Boxer leaped into the brush. In just seconds, the woods were full of shouts. Quickly a second patrol came over. A search of the woods turned up the culprits. The first one had a bad bite on his upper arm; the second had a facial injury; the third had a badly chewed rear end. Later investigation revealed that the first had tried to use a club on the dog, and the second had tried to shoot it. When the third saw his friends being overcome by the Boxer, he decided to climb a tree. But the dog pulled him down. All three were lying on the ground when the patrols arrived, and the dog stood calmly among them.

Normally, if the dog or soldier were not directly attacked, the dogs did not bite. Today, dogs are trained to attack the arm, but at that time the training procedure was to attack with a leap to the back of the neck. It had the advantage that a dog could disable four to six people in a very short time.

A year and a half later, while on leave, my husband gave me a very informative description of his work with Rolf von Vogelsberg. Usually he made his rounds with Rolf alone. At those critical places, which both knew, they would often stop for an hour or more. Most amazing was how well the dog withstood some harsh conditions. At

home, Rolf had always loved the area around the stove, but on the front it was ice cold. Yet he turned down an offer to lie on my husband's coat or even a blanket when he was on duty. As much as the dogs loved being inside the guard house, when they had outside duty they refused any type of shelter. Rolf always lay down on the ground, somewhat away from his master. It probably allowed Rolf to be more alert and hear better.

Anything suspicious would be first noticeable by the movements of his ears and tail. If it were a German patrol coming, then Rolf would wag his tail. But if the tail stood straight up and the hair on his back also went up, those were clear signs of something suspicious. Usually he would growl so softly his master could only sense it by laying his hand on Rolf's head. Dog and master were such a team that my husband would often lie down beside Rolf, just to be able to tell from which direction the dog sensed danger.

Soon the first smugglers' forms would begin to appear in the darkness. Some distance behind followed others. They wore shoes with rubber or felt soles, so they could move without sound. The first one seldom had anything, and the second carried very little. Those following carried almost all the booty. My husband would wait until he could see that Rolf was only looking at those who had passed. That was how he could be sure no more were coming. All it took then was a nod at Rolf, and the dog bolted after the smugglers. Starting at the back of the column, he leaped on each man and threw him to the ground. Then he would circle back, and woe to anyone who tried to get up. Rolf made it very clear they were to stay down until his master arrived and took them prisoner. Of course, Rolf also helped bring the prisoners back to camp.

It soon became apparent the dogs were more feared than rifles. When prisoners were marched back to camp, Rolf made sure none went out in front and none lagged behind. They weren't even allowed to turn around. If one moved too slowly, Rolf would give him a push in the back with his nose. Obviously the dog made them all very uncomfortable. In this manner, my husband arrested over two hundred smugglers in one month.

Boxers also turned out to be wonderful message carriers, because they very seldom barked. That feature was useful in patrol too. If a dog barked at things, the patrol would be useless.

One time, one of my husband's Boxers barked while on patrol duty. They had just checked a guard station, and then had to follow a narrow, icy foot path. On the left lay a creek bed with steep banks, and on the right was deep snow. Suddenly the Boxer stopped. His tail was straight up, and he stared into the bushes next to the creek.

My husband just could not believe that an enemy had come so close to the guard station. So he gave the dog a little pat and commanded him to go on. The dog's immediate answer was a powerful bark. Right away a voice from the bushes shouted, "Mon dieu, mon dieu, prisonaire!" My husband found him in a small cave, covered with brush. Later they learned that the young man had been wanted for a long time, and was a rare case where he made his smuggling excursions alone rather than with a group.

At first, the military often discussed how the Boxers might react under fire. Boxers were trained at that time to attack the person who fired the shot. When one of the handlers actually did the shooting, the dogs were at first confused. One even tried to pull down his handler's arm. But once they were instructed where the enemy really was, the dogs attacked that target. Usually by the second time out, no Boxer was confused by shots from the handler's weapon. When ordered, the dogs would head out in the same direction as the handler shot.

Without much trouble, Boxers also became used to artillery fire. Old Blitz, who had never been under fire, came over one day with his handler to visit my husband. Without warning, a mortar shell fell nearby, and Blitz received a small wound on the rear from a piece of shrapnel. That made him furious. He ran over to the shell crater looking for the enemy. More shells followed, and

Blitz kept running from one crater to another, until he realized how stupid it was. Finally he returned to his handler—luckily unhurt—and a half hour later was lying at his master's feet snoring as only a Boxer can, while the mortar shells continued to come in.

Barbed wire barricades did not stop Boxers. Actually, the dogs were a great help in finding passages through the barbed wire at night. The paths were very difficult to follow in the darkness, but the dogs always knew which was the right path. Many times the handlers on patrol would have lost their way in unknown territory had it not been for those reliable Boxers. They only needed to travel the path once. After that, they never forgot the route.

The Boxer As A Herding Dog

One time a herd of four hundred cattle had to be guarded near the front. Attempts to steal such animals at night were common. The German guards requested that Polly, who was one of the most reliable dogs in the company, be assigned as a watch dog over the herd. From that day on, all cattle rustling stopped. Polly soon became known as the best of their herding dogs. He drove the cattle to water and then back to the meadow. He always watched out for his herd. The twelve guards declared that Polly was more help than another two dozen guards.

And Polly had never been around cattle before. He came from Munich, where he always wore a black blanket-coat with pink ribbons when the weather was bad.

After the cattle command was replaced, Polly returned to his old company. He had to run ten miles just to reach the train station for the trip back. But on the very day he returned, Polly disappeared. When my husband learned of it he immediately called the company with the cattle and asked if the Boxer were there. Of course they thought that was impossible. On the next day, however, they notified my husband that Polly had indeed come back. It seems that suddenly a Boxer showed up, circled the whole herd, sniffed all the guards, but would not let himself be captured. He then jumped into the guards' trailer house and wouldn't let anyone else in. Only some advice from an animal-loving soldier that the dog had to have been in this area before, saved Polly from being shot on the spot.

When a man who had been with the former guard unit showed up, he and Polly had a great reunion. On the advice of my husband, Polly was assigned to that soldier. And that proved to have been best for all.

Rolf's Blood Lives On

So passed the first year of the war and half of the second. For both my husband and me it was just one day after another. Besides everyday concerns, I tried to keep our war-ruined plans alive. Our breeding was a part of that. Of course, I did not wish to make money from my dogs, but they should pay part of their upkeep. The war turned that into an illusion as well.

Rolf's complete record shows he did stud service thirty-three times, fourteen of which had been with our bitches. The Munich breeders themselves demonstrated that the prophet has indeed no honor in his own land. Only one breeder from Munich used Rolf. That had unpleasant results later, but by then it was too late to change.

Rolf had bred thirteen of our bitches. Their offspring were good, but not the Sieger of my dreams. Rolf's last entry—which was our fourteenth bitch bred to him—reads, "28 April 1916, Champion Rolf von Vogelsberg bred Bella von der Elbe, same owner."

Who was Bella von der Elbe? I owned her, thanks to one of those many, but yet odd, coincidences or twists of fate that have occurred in my life. At the time, one of the most excellent bitches in Germany was a red-fawn with white markings, Zilly von der Elbe. She was a show dog, the pride of her owner. The best breeders in Germany all wanted to get a bitch from Zilly, but her owner was in no hurry to breed her. He enjoyed taking her from one show to another. When she finally was bred, only one female pup was in the litter.

All the top breeders wanted that little girl. She went to the Falkenhorst kennel, which also owned Champion Milo von Eigelstein. But the puppy never fulfilled their expectations. She had neither the size nor nobility of her mother, and remained all her life a rather uninspiring and unexciting dog. It was hard to believe how much of a furor her birth had caused among Germany's best Boxer breeders.

It had become almost a custom for conscripted owners from good kennels to bring their dogs to me for safe-keeping while they were in the service. One day I received a letter from Zilly's breeder. He offered to give me a two-year-old daughter of Zilly, and a younger sister of the bitch whose birth had been so awaited by all breeders. He, too, had been called up for service and was willing to give up "Bella," just to be sure she was in good hands.

From experience, I had become a bit smarter about this. Most of the Boxers offered to me as gifts were not all in order. Besides, I had plenty of problems just trying to feed my own dogs. Still, it seemed to me as though this bitch just might be the last chance for Rolf. For that reason alone, I accepted her.

At first, Bella did not fit in very well. As I took her out of the crate she came in, I was disappointed in her stretched-out head and light coat. But you also could not miss her nice height and enormous deep chest. And she was already in season. I could take her to Rolf right away. One of her first deeds was to steal a hen and destroy some fifteen eggs that were ready to hatch. Then a few days later she killed my nicest young goat. Those were irreplaceable losses.

It has always been my belief that good luck has to be paid for somehow, and bad luck usually contains the seed for a happy event later on. It may not always balance out, but in the case of Bella the happiness she brought me later easily paid for her earlier bad deeds. After the usual nine weeks, on June 27, 1916, Bella whelped a litter of eight puppies. I selected four boys and one girl. Actually, given the hard times, I really had not wished to keep a girl, but she was the very image of her father Rolf von Vogelsberg. So I kept her too. I certainly didn't know then that "Rassel"—as I named her—would be the foundation bitch of all my present Boxers. Of all Rolf's children, it was she and her half-brother Champion Rolf von Walhall, who made their father's blood immortal.

Rolf was eight years old in 1916, when he went to war with my husband. His most important descendants were the following:

> Siegerin Betty von Goldrhein
> Sieger Dampf vom Dom
> Schelm vom Angertor
> Champion Rolf von Walhall
> Siegerin Rassel vom Dom

The last two have achieved a place in the history of Boxer breeding. There are no Boxers, either in Germany or outside of Germany, that do not have these two in their pedigrees.

After Rolf left for service, all I had surviving from him were his two daughters, Derby—Dampf's sister and my darling—and Rassel. I might have tried to place Rassel, because the times were so difficult for keeping dogs, but then Derby became mortally ill. Only death could free her from her suffering.

Derby died during the infamous ice-cold winter of 1916/17, and I wanted her to have a real grave. I wrapped her in a blanket and put her into a new sack. Those were

expensive items at that difficult time. It had been so cold the ground was frozen rock-hard for more than three-feet deep. So I was not able to dig a grave. Instead I laid Derby to rest at the end of the garden, under a large beech tree. Despite Pluto and Laska and Rolf, all of whom I loved dearly, she was the dearest Boxer that I had ever owned up to then.

Along with me, little Rassel also seemed to feel the loss of Derby. Day after day, through the bitter cold weather, she would go out to the dead Derby and keep a death watch. When finally warmer days came, I dug a deep grave for Derby. After that, Rassel made the connection between the mound and her lost friend, and continued her watch by sitting on the grave.

Time crawled by. It seemed to me as though the war years were not just twice as long as a normal year, but ten times. My husband's first leave came after twelve months, the next after another sixteen months. Trench warfare had set in, and the initial enthusiasm disappeared. At the front, canine units and canine schools now appeared. At home, our main problem was how we could continue to feed our dogs.

There was no way for me to be scientific about what I fed. I judged things by primitive standards. First of all, did the dog like the food? Secondly, was it nutritious? Did the animal maintain weight? Did it get leaner or heavier? That was what counted the most. The first guideline for feeding was always a systematic, careful observation of the animals.

Of course, I hardly had to worry about the dogs not having an appetite or getting too fat. They ate everything, even boiled turnips. Sometimes their bellies stuck out like pregnant cows, but they never seemed to get full.

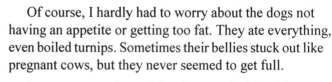

In more recent times, it has become fashionable to recommend feeding dogs a much larger portion of vegetarian food. But one shouldn't be deceived by this. The dog is by nature a carnivore and will remain so, if he is to be kept healthy and active. In the long run, meat is the cheapest nourishment. After all, the vegetable substitutes and fillers also cost money, but above all they are lacking in necessary supplements, such as liver oil and other vitamin carriers.

Necessity Can Change Anything

This old truism became apparent to us in those war years. To feed our animals, we would buy old dogs from the farmers, shoot them, then feed them to our own kennel. Despite their great hunger, our Boxers needed time to overcome their natural aversion to that. But when it was cooked with a lot of spices, they eventually accepted the meat, and then came to relish it. We could always see a noticeable improvement in their physical condition after eating such food, but, unfortunately, there weren't many of those opportunities.

If anyone today reacts in horror to such methods, then they should remember that without them there would hardly have been any Boxers left for postwar breeding. Would Amundson have reached the South Pole if he had not fed his strongest sled dogs in the same way? Sadly, gone were the days of my happy childhood, when in my dreams I would say, "Illa, please feed my dogs."

Everything was sacrificed for our dogs. Even the milk from our seven goats went mostly for dog food. I bought what I could on the black market, but it never seemed enough. Once I sold a puppy, the weakest and most meager in the litter. Six weeks later I took it back to do some corrective work on the ears. When I looked at that puppy then, I was astonished to see the little guy weighed half again as much as his litter mates in my home. After that, I did anything and everything possible to keep my dogs from starving.

The war was not completely successful in destroying the sport of dogs. Yet in order to keep the older ones, necessity required me to sell all my younger dogs. With

some concern, I placed an ad in one of the dog magazines. I did not have much hope for success from the ad, but the result was amazing. I received sixteen inquiries. One person wrote, " I will give you twenty marks more than your highest bid." Within a week, all of my puppies had found homes.

There were even some shows during the war. One took place in Mainz in 1916. I stayed home. In 1917, I decided to go to a show in Mannheim. I returned with two first prizes. All three of the dogs with me had taken their classes. But shows without competition don't have much attraction.

Since life was now so depressing, it is understandable that people wanted an escape. They wanted to forget for a while. In a modest way, some of the dog-show newspapers began to reappear. Various editors made contact with me. Patriotic breeders, who had sacrificed for the war, also sought to reestablish prewar relationships. Under the ashes the coals were still glowing.

But none of us had any idea what lay before us, otherwise our optimism would have been greatly cooled.

Milo Von Eigelstein's Descendants

Rolf von Vogelsberg's most significant offspring for the Boxer breed have already been mentioned. Therefore, it is only fair and right that some attention be paid to those of Milo von Eigelstein—the champion of champions, as his owner called him. Milo's descendants, who embellished the postwar years, were as follows:

Champion Remus von Pfalzgau

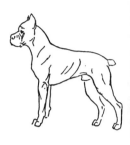

|

Champion Milo von Eigelstein

| |

| Sieger | Sieger |
| Omar v. Falkenhorst | Treu v. Kurland |

| |

| Sieger | Sieger |
| Pascha v. Neuenburg | Tasso v. d. Spree |

| |

| Belfine v. Isarstrand | Sieger |
| | Harras v. Sachsenwald |

By far, the best of these descendents of Milo was Harras vom Sachsenwald. Sadly, he died when only two and left no offspring. Nor did his father or grandfather leave any descendants of significance. Probably it's just as well that nothing from them has come down to our time.

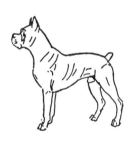

Harras seemed to have all the requirements to become a great sire, but it was not to be. Thus, the grandson of Rolf von Vogelsberg, Sieger Egon vom Gumbertusbrunnen—who had been beaten by Harras—became the leading stud dog of that time. Eventually, Egon's half-brother, Moritz vom Goldrhein—also a grandson of Rolf— challenged him for that position.

Milo died too soon, and just a short time later his owner had a tragic death. And Milo's fine sons have disappeared without renown. The name of Milo von Eigelstein might have disappeared completely from our pedigrees, were it not for his grandson, the postwar Sieger, Pascha von Neuenburg. Pascha produced a beautiful little daughter, Belfine vom Isarstrand, who produced a blood line with Egon von Gumbertusbrunnen that is still in some pedigrees today. In any case, the above named descendents of Rolf and Milo were the foundation of Boxer breeding from 1916 to 1921.

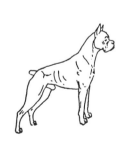

It was very difficult in those years to move ahead with any breeding program. There were hardly any stud dogs in all of Bavaria. Milo's descendants were all in North Germany. Only by accident did Omar vom Falkenhorst come to Bavaria. Once again, I was left entirely dependent on my own resources.

The Black Boxer

The history of the black Boxer reaches back to the first stud book begun in 1904. Among other entries, there was one for the black Boxer dog, Graf Blitz von Graudenz, whelped 8 August 1899. Parents were Michel's Max and Lore von Eisleben. Blitz was shown and won trophies. That the dog became controversial was probably to be expected.

I met black Boxers through their originator, Mr. Schachtner. He had bred them well, but knew little about good sportsmanship and stirred up opposition just by his personality. The extinction of black Boxers has to be laid at his feet. When I met him, I had not been in the sport long and had just purchased Rolf von Vogelsberg. Mr. Schachtner asked if I would be willing to breed Rolf to two of the black Blitz's daughters, Biola and Aster von Graudenz. That was something new, and I eagerly agreed to do it.

When I later met my friend from the Boxer Club, Mr. Schmöger, I mentioned the black Boxers. He advised me to keep my fingers out of it. In his opinion, there were no blacks, because if you took them out into bright sunlight you could see they were either dark brindles or brown. But I told him that Biola and especially Asta were indeed an intensive black. Schmöger claimed, however, that neither one was then a real Boxer. I disagreed.

But I had to admit that neither one of the black bitches was a quality animal, yet I was still intrigued by the idea of breeding to them. And I told Schmöger that. Whereupon he became very angry. Finally, he told me that Lore von

Eisleben, the granddam of both black Boxer bitches, had been a Bulldog bitch. During an exhibition she came into season and was accidently bred by a Schnauzer. Even the breeder would not deny that. Schmöger's position was that black was not a color natural to the Boxer breed, and because of that the Munich Boxer Club would not recognize it.

With that, he had thrown down the gauntlet. I would have picked it up, even if it weren't my best friend who threw it at my feet. They were going to find out I could finish a job that others might have broken their teeth on. Of course, I was taking on some things that I was not quite up to yet.

A little later, I purchased a bitch from one of Schachtner's black litters. She was not cheap, and her quality was so poor that I could not use her in my breeding program. Since the bitch was alert and courageous, Schmöger helped me find a good home for her, but breeding her was out of the question. Her cost had to be counted as a loss. Schmöger was smart enough not to give me any more orders, so the matter of breeding black Boxers in Bavaria seemed to be closed.

I was not the only one who liked the black color. Edmund Halter, a breeder from Allgäu, also had a black bitch bred to Rolf. The result was a litter of beautiful black animals, better than ever shown before. From that litter, the best was Flock von der Adeleck. Flock had a successful show career. And it was Flock who revived my old desire to breed to a black Boxer.

A special Boxer show had been scheduled to take place at the Nymphenburg Castle in Munich. Exhibitors were coming from distant places, and it was very difficult then to find any housing in Munich. Mr. Halter wrote to me and asked if I could put up Flock for a few days. I agreed, and that put me to thinking. Up to now, black bitches of terrible quality were mated with the best stud dogs. How would it work, I thought, if a high quality bitch—such as Rassel vom Dom—were mated with the very nice Flock? And Rassel was in heat right then. My old ambition came alive, and besides, I wanted to show Schmöger a little stubbornness, come what may!

I had promised to bring Flock to the show. He was going to look as beautiful as possible, so I trimmed his long nails and brushed him. But the result did not satisfy me. Schmöger was not entirely wrong, the coloring on Flock's flanks was not as deep as it ought to be. What could I do about it? Next thing I knew, there was a can of black shoe polish in my hand. I began brushing some of the polish into his coat, more for fun than anything, but the more I did it the more it pleased me. Flock looked brilliant, brilliant in the true sense of the word. He actually glittered. I was positive everyone would be astounded.

When I arrived at the show the next day, the first one to run up to me was Flock's owner. He was just speechless over the appearance of his dog. His wife, he told me in an almost regrettable way, had never been able to do such a wonderful job grooming Flock as I had.

I was in a really good mood. Spring was here, and I was wearing my only nice dress. It was made of cream-colored Russian silk. I knew the black Boxer would have twice the impact beside me. And he walked right beside me, as I paraded him around to meet all the Munich Boxer prominences.

Flock's owner was supposed to take him into the ring. But when the owner approached me, he was horrified to see the left side of my nice silk dress had black smeared all over it. My sins had come back: it was the black shoe polish! I had no choice but to turn Flock over to his master, and I asked Mr. Halter to loan me his coat, which I then draped over my left arm. All I could do was stand quietly off to the side.

I have no idea if anyone else had noticed my blunder. It probably would not have hurt me even if they had noticed. Coloring a dog usually made no difference anyway. It would have probably all gone under the category of "make up," as the Americans call it. But it bothered me a lot, and in fact it was the first and last time I ever tried such a thing.

Actually, it all seemed to go as I had planned. I only wanted three puppies, no more. A brindle had already been promised to a buyer. For myself, I wanted to keep a pair. I thought a lot about which one should have the white markings, decided on the male, and the girl for my breeding would have to be coal black.

When the sixty-third day came, Rassel actually delivered two boys, a brindle and a black one with white markings. Exactly as I had dreamed, only the little girl was missing. But on the next day, even that came true. As long as I have been breeding, I have never been so accurate in predicting a litter. Shouldn't that have been a good omen for my black Boxers? Unfortunately, it didn't turn out that way.

I named the two Ulla and Utter. Ulla was an attractive, noble, small Boxer lady with a model head. Utter, on the other hand, was a powerful, striking dog. Because I could not exhibit them, I spread the word about them through pictures and reports in the dog publications. I had not planned to sell them, but the originator of the blacks, Schachtner, sent me a very good offer for Utter, so I sold him. It seemed to me that Schachtner would have better financial means and connections than I, and he would be able to promote them better. It was not until much later that I learned his ruthless manner ruined it for all the black Boxers.

The End Of The Black Boxer

In the fall of 1918, my husband had another furlough. He was scheduled to transport some recruits up to the front, but it never happened. A general collapse of the German troops brought the war to an end. We all breathed easier, but the circumstances of the collapse and the armistice created discontent. Still, the worst peace is always better than war. We were determined to end what had oppressed us for four years. A new beginning was what we longed for, one that was better than ever before.

In 1919, Munich began gearing up for a show. My old Rolf had returned home. He was now eleven years old, but he survived the war in good shape. He was still noble and lean, not an ounce of flesh too much, and his head was still ideal, something only his daughter Rassel had attained. But he was weary, like an old man who, because of the horrors of war, had lost his zest for life.

This Munich show was especially hopeful for me. I wanted to exhibit Ulla and Utter—and I had received permission to do so from the club—as two excellent black Boxers. The only real competition was from the fawn dogs. With some hesitation, I entered Rolf in the open brindle class. Utter was in the same class. In all, I had seven Boxers from my kennel entered.

When I looked at the catalog, I saw that Rolf and Utter were the only entries in their class. If I did not take in Rolf, then Utter would have to receive the first place, and with it also the Sieger title. Utter was such a beautiful animal they would never dare to withhold first place from him. It would be a great victory for the black Boxers. But an uneasy feeling seemed to be warning me not to do that.

The fawn dogs, who always go first, had already entered the ring. They were a bunch of pathetic witnesses to a lost glory. Best of the lot was a Milo grandson, Alexander von Deutenkoven, a promising young dog that has unfortunately disappeared from Boxer breeding without leaving a single noteworthy descendant behind. Next to him was another—but older—Milo son, also a war veteran, and in third place stood the aristocratic competitor, Rino von der Elbe. At one time, Rino was Milo's strongest competition. His former owner had been an Englishman who would never have sold him for any price. But when the war began, Rino stayed behind in Germany. Now this old, tired dog stood in the ring, only a shadow of his former beauty remaining. The judge's report on him stated, "For his age, still an excellent dog. But just as he was once defeated by Champion Milo, now he must stand behind Milo's son and grandson."

Then it was time for the brindles. I picked up Utter and entered the ring, alone in the class. I sensed that the atmosphere was not right. But it was not until much later that I learned the club had made the judge swear he would not give first place to a black Boxer. A large audience was present. No one could deny that Utter made a noticeable impression on all who were not part of the breeders' clique. This powerful black dog, with his white markings and white collar, almost seemed to be flirting with the spectators, as he showed himself in the ring. The Munich breeders silently stared daggers at us.

All eyes turned to the judge. I noticed that he could feel the atmosphere too. He approached me, praised the dog, remarked how pretty and tall he was, pointed out that the back seemed a bit longer than needed, but the head was typically noble. But he would not recognize the color. In the judge's opinion, for Utter to receive first place he would have to be all black. Since that was not the case, he withheld the first prize. At first, I could not comprehend what the judge was saying. There were no color restrictions at that time.

My first reaction was to refuse to show Rolf. But could I deny that old faithful companion his well-deserved last victory? Thus, I brought Rolf in the ring. He received first place, with an "excellent" rating, and then he won his fifth Sieger title. The judge wrote, "Still the beautiful Rolf."

In order to emphasize his decision on Utter, the judge did not give him a second place behind Rolf, but awarded the dog third, with the rating of "very good." In his final report on Utter, the judge wrote, "For fans of this black color, probably a beautiful dog. But he will have no success in the ring."

With that, I had received my notice. I had gambled and lost. Not because the exhibits of my breeding had not met the standard, but because of other people's

unsportsmanlike tactics. It was little consolation that Rassel also won a Siegerin title. Her half-sister Morna vom Dom followed, and in third place was the little black Ulla, who simply could not be denied an "excellent" rating.

Human nature never changes. After years of war nothing had changed. Weren't there more important things than a squabble about black and white colors for Boxers? I agree that white Boxers are not desirable and should be restricted. But that was hardly a reason to give blacks a death sentence. Perhaps a more determined effort from me might have been successful. But the controversy was being fought with means that were repugnant to me. Furthermore, it had become clear to me that other things also threatened Boxers.

The years right after the war were no better for us than the war years themselves. Germany faced a total economic collapse, threatening the very existence of hundreds of thousands of people. We had to make a serious decision too. Should we maintain this lifestyle in the future, or should we give up on dog breeding?

Boxers Turn Me Into A Farmer

The necessity for a decision soon became clear to me. What a joy it was to learn that my mother, still in good health, could come to us from the Baltic. She had survived very hard times. Now we could work out our future together. It was obvious that the kiln had not been successful, and it would be impossible for me to find the money to put it back into operation. And my reflex camera had been superceded by the smaller hand-held models. Anyway, where were the fanciers who had money for photos of their dogs?

My husband searched for work, but without luck. The many former officers always had preference in hiring. Everything seemed so hopeless. The only way out seemed to be what I had thought of doing during the war years.

After all, we had to live and earn money somehow, and I did not wish to give up my dogs.

My mother had trouble accepting my views on how our lives should go. She had hoped a conversation with the famous Munich Professor Doerner, her friend of many years, would turn things the way she wished. But when she told him about how her daughter planned to abandon her art and sell the nice home, all so she could buy a farm—even he could think of no good reason not to do it. He regretted that I could not remain true to my original profession, but, in good conscience, he could not suggest another course than what I had chosen.

Hard times lay behind us; an uncertain future was in front. Once we made our decision, everything happened rapidly. There was hardly any time to work out details. We had searched for a buyer for months. It seemed hopeless at first, but suddenly some prospects appeared, people who had made money during the war, and I had my buyer. The sale was contingent upon our moving out in two months. We had only that long to find another home.

Fortunately, excessive speculation with farm land had resulted in restrictions. Farms could only be purchased, when the buyer could produce proof that the farm would remain as such and be used only for agricultural purposes. After endless running around, I finally was able to get an official declaration that I intended to maintain the farm's agricultural purposes. So my struggles during the war years to keep alive our dreams were not all in vain.

A New Life

So often it seems that big mistakes in life later turn out to be useful. Our villa and furniture, once far too expensive for our means, now brought in a very nice price. Selling off the furniture was how we managed to save our property during the collapse. After the sale, everything had to be

done quickly. Every day the value of the mark dropped more. With the help of a realtor, we had purchased a farm in the area around Altötting-Mühldorfer.

There was some kind of farmer holiday going on when we arrived at Altötting to close the purchase of our new home. Despite being late fall, the sun shone, and all the bells were ringing. Would this finally mean that I had found my place of peace?

At first, everything went wrong. It soon became apparent that I had used my esthetic sense to select a farm, rather than any practical sense. Our neighbors believed every person who had owned that property was mentally disturbed. And besides, the house was supposed to be haunted. Finally, everybody who had lived there had been horribly ruined. I consoled my husband by telling him that the spook would soon take off, once we brought in the dogs. Of course, it wasn't that easy.

First we were visited by a kennel owner's worst devil. Our dogs broke out with a skin infection. We had no idea where this infection had come from. For months, I fought against it, but everything seemed useless.

Ulla had whelped a nice black litter. Rassel had a brindle litter from the fawn Munich Sieger. I wanted to keep a male from each litter, and both seemed to be very nice, promising animals, but even they became infected. There were no regular medicines, and no veterinarian available. Finally, for a high price I managed to get a sulphur-based medicine. It did no good, and the puppies died of sulphur poisoning.

I had been happy about the prospect of finally getting enough milk for our dogs from our own barn. Even that wish went unfilled. Oh, yes, we had four nice calves, but only one cow gave milk. And from that milk we were all supposed to live! Seven costly goats which I brought along all died. The cause of all these losses was unknown. Superstitious farmers told me goats were evil but very useful animals. They attracted diseases and other evil spirits which would otherwise have gone to the cattle. We were supposed to hope that the deaths of the goats would break the evil curse upon our old farm.

In the very beginning, we never noticed anything wrong. When we moved in, we found everything gone that wasn't nailed down or attached, including all food supplies. Then we learned that the rationing offices for the area were at least seven, in some cases over fifteen miles away. The church, the school, and even the train station were three miles away. And the place where I could get horse meat for the dogs was eight miles distant. My only means of transportation was a bicycle, and in another five months I expected my second child. I knew that all forms of life entrusted to me had come in pairs, and I wanted to remain true to that in our family.

From that time on, the Boxers had to compete with the horses for my attention. Just knowing that it would now be possible to have horses was a great help to me in overcoming the other problems in farming. The one I bought, however, only looked good. She was a very pretty little mare, but when starting to go uphill she stood stock still, and going downhill she ran. Eventually we traded her for a cow and a goat.

A little later I was traveling through Mühldorf, and there was a horse market. After some bargaining with a horse trader, I purchased a pregnant mare. A beautiful sorrel, almost the size of a pony but well constructed. Again, it was love at first sight! I had enough money with me, so I bought her. Proud as a king, I led her by the reins for the nine-mile trip back home.

This time it wasn't a complete disappointment. Of course, she was not really pregnant, but she was an honest, strong, hard-working horse. Soon thereafter, another dealer brought me a brown mare of about the same size. She was not as pretty as the other, but she too was a good worker. These two horses helped us to overcome the distances and to work the fields. They were also used to pull the machines for cutting and turning the hay.

Our farming neighbors, who only used big, heavy horses, just shook their heads. But they did respect us!

Our numerous worries and the shortage of feed, pushed the dog game somewhat to the side. Immediately after the war there had been extensive slaughtering of old army horses, and that helped ease the meat shortage for the dogs. Then, with the help of a veterinarian, I was also able to get plenty of meat from those animals condemned with foot-and-mouth disease.

An emergency in the cow barn put me in contact with a man the farmers called a nature healer. He also purchased disabled animals for rendering, dressed out animals, dealt in horses and cows, and did a few other things. We did not want to have anything to do with him at first, but in the stall the man had definite abilities. So we made a deal with him. I would deliver dead horses and cows to him, and he would supply me with meat. If there were too much, then—like the Indians—we cut it into strips and dried them. In that way, we had the basis for keeping our breeding program.

The First Postwar Breeding Results

Of course, all of that work demanded a great effort from us. But it was the only way to keep the pack together. From then up to now, that meant thirty to forty dogs. And they all knew their own names. Strangers often have a hard time believing that. Every dog loved us and was, in turn, loved by us; each one had a separate character and a unique personality.

Champion Rolf never made the move. A few days before, he collapsed. His heart was very weak, and we had to put him to sleep. Most likely, he never would have survived the hardships of moving. Now all of my hopes rested on Rassel. I bred her to a Rolf grandson, Rolf von Ismaning, out of which came a litter of five: four girls and one boy. I sold the male puppy, and I placed a white check bitch with the nature healer. The other three daughters of Rassel I kept. Zita was the image of her mother, and nobody—except me—could tell them apart. Zenta was a dark brindle, had a very nice head, but nothing special in her coloring. Zwibel [which means onion] took a lot of laughter because of her name. She was a light fawn bitch with white markings, looking very much like Rassel's mother and grandmother. Which one of these three would inherit the wonderful breeding potency that Rolf had?

These were difficult times for us. My mother had not felt up to the move and remained in Fürstenfeldbruck. We had so many chores and worries, that I never even found the time to give our son a proper birth. He was already looking at the new world and being fed, when the midwife arrived. Four days later, I was back in the field. Looking back, I have to say I never thought anything of it.

Eventually my husband pointed out to me that for several years now, I had lost my enthusiasm for showing dogs. It sounds strange, but that was a sacrifice I forced on my dogs. They certainly did not deserve such treatment. Rassel had her three daughters with her. Ulla was now in Sweden, as was also the black-blooded brindle, Sara. I had closed the book on the black Boxer. Understandably, that seemed a sign that I no longer had a will to fight and compete.

Our new location did not really have a kennel layout, and there was a shortage of cash and material. Rassel seemed so sweet, I didn't think a kennel was necessary. I expected the same character from her three daughters. Of course, I misled myself, as experienced breeders often do when judging their own animals.

My dogs had an unusual habit then. All day long they would lie around in the sun, lazy and indifferent, but about five in the afternoon they disappeared. Around dark they were back, lying around as though nothing had happened. When I checked into it, I found out they were roaming many miles away. They had been seen chasing rabbits. I was certainly concerned, but I just could not

bring myself to put them on chains. So—one day it happened. Zita and Zenta ran over the hill. Half an hour later, Zenta returned, but the beautiful Zita—the image of her mother—disappeared forever.

It hit me like a blow from a whip, when I received a telegram three days later from an unknowing North German wood dealer, "Will buy Zita for 5,000 marks. First litter by sire of your choice belongs to you."

I had no other choice but to start breeding again, yet all seemed so hopeless. Despite many attempts with dogs from all over Germany, Rassel never conceived. The stud dogs of that time were all worn out.

Milo's descendants aged rapidly, like their father. They would play a significant role for maybe two, at most three years, and then be finished. Our friend Schmöger had a Milo grandson, Pascha von Neuenburg. Pasha became a police dog, and with the help of two other Munich friends, Schmöger succeeded in getting the Boxers officially recognized as service dogs. One has to give my old friend credit. Until his last breath, he kept his love for Boxers and did many good things to promote the breed.

Several times I mated Zenta with Pascha von Neuenburg. But who was able to get a useful litter from that sire? And meanwhile, inflation continually eroded the mark's value, until it was almost worthless. Two thousand or five thousand marks were now just a handful of paper. In order to prevent Zenta—who had become a fertile bitch—from having the same fate as Zita, I gave her to friends in Lower Bavaria, but even she could not overcome the inadequacies of the contemporary stud dogs.

A DOG FOR 2,000,000 MARKS

My husband often urged me during this time to visit a show. So I decided to enter Rassel, who was still a beautiful bitch, in a show in Ulm. While there, I received an offer for her. Two gentlemen, one being a successful trainer, were founding a breeding and training kennel. They wanted excellent breeding stock. Although I told them that Rassel had missed conception two times, they pressed me to sell her for two million marks and two puppies from the first litter she produced. Several things went through my mind. There were bitches that had not conceived even with Sieger Moritz von Goldrhein, a grandson of Rolf. And then there was the fact that Rassel, too, had taken to hunting in the evening. So I decided to take the offer, and I became a double millionaire.

I felt bad about Rassel's departure. My loss was soon brought to me in harsh terms. During the train trip to Munich, I lost my hat. The other fanciers kidded me about it, but a true dog lover doesn't let such things matter, whether one's clothes are torn or covered with dog hair. Neither should hair messed up by the wind, or the smell of dogs make any difference. But we have our weak moments, when things get on our nerves and we are tempted to fight back. That's the way it was with me then in Munich.

I made up my mind to buy another hat. Right away I found a shop, and it did not take long to make my choice. When I asked about the price, I was told it was two million marks. I was too timid to just walk away, so I paid exactly as much as I had taken for my Rassel! All the way home I thought of Rassel's sad eyes in Ulm. I was so ashamed of myself for what I had done. Silently I put the new hat in the closet. Since then, I have never again worn a hat.

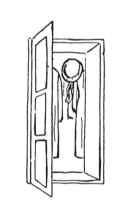

Actually, Rassel had a good home. But she never conceived again. One day, the wood dealer who had offered to buy Zita reported to me he had seen Rassel at a show. She was one of the top animals, and her head was the best of all. But then one afternoon Rassel did not return from her walk. The same fate came to Rassel—a fate I had tried to protect her from—as had befallen her daughter Zita.

Inflation was grinding down all of us. We were too small an operation to survive it. An eye injury from the war made it difficult for my husband to practice his trade. I was nearly breaking down from the load on my shoulders. Unfortunately, it did not really help when my uncle—the same one who had owned the Dachshund Bill—purchased a small farm close to ours. He did not get along with my husband, so I ended up in the middle between two people that I loved.

There was no shortage of good advice, but from advice to help is a long step. Nor was I able to accept our friend Schmöger's offer. He wanted me to take over the salaried position in the Munich Boxer club. If I had done that, everything we had done up to then would have to be put aside. And wouldn't there have been a constant suspicion that my dogs were receiving preferential treatment in the ring? Lastly, why did we sell the villa, if we were not dedicated to this kind of life?

Zwibel, The Boxer Bitch

One day my uncle pointed out to me that our farm would have to change, if it were ever going to be profitable. He recommended an expansion of our dog breeding and a specialization in horse breeding. Both of his suggestions seemed well-founded to me.

But I only had one bitch, Rassel's daughter Zwibel. She was a direct grand daughter of Rolf, light fawn, very tall, noble, and had nice lines. Her head needed a little more type, as is often the case with the noble ones. Rolf's heritage was in this girl, but I did not know it then.

An outbreak of rabies now brought three long years quarantine restrictions. All dogs had to be controlled and muzzled. For that reason we had to restrict our breeding program.

I had never really felt very close to Zwibel. She had always been a rather distant animal. Many times, however, I could not help but admire her. One day she and I drove into Neuötting. There, in the middle of the street, was a big dog fight. A large hunting dog had jumped on a Russian Greyhound. They rolled around in a cloud of dust. A passing German Shepherd decided to take the opportunity to join in. All around them were screaming people, all

afraid to break it up. Like a bolt of lightning, Zwibel jumped into the fray. First she clamped onto the Shepherd's long ear. He let out a scream, jerked loose and disappeared immediately. Never a lazy one, the Boxer bitch then upended the hunting dog, his feet now pointing straight up. Whereupon the Greyhound leaped up, and took off running as fast as a Greyhound could. Zwibel just stood on the street calmly, legs somewhat apart, and looked rather astounded at how many people had gathered around her and were now applauding.

Another time, I pedaled into Neuötting to get some meat from the horse butcher's shop. Their were two entrances to the store. Zwibel knew that she had to remain outside, even when I took the bicycle through the courtyard to the second entrance. After I had made my purchase, I returned to my bicycle and was surprised that my bitch was not there. I had forgotten that I left her outside the front entrance. For a moment I was even a bit angry because I thought Zwibel might have taken off for home. Yet I was sure she would not just leave me completely in the lurch

Zwibel was not home when I arrived, nor did she show up later. Haying prevented me from returning right away to Neuötting. Finally, three days later I returned and found Zwibel sitting exactly where I had left her at the front entrance.

The people in the shop took a happy breath and asked me if I had not received their card. Zwibel had been guarding their door for three days. She let anyone go in, but would not let anyone come out. An attempt to drive her away with a riding crop failed. She became angry and seemed ready to attack anybody who threatened her.

Later, the veterinarian across the street, who knew Zwibel well, came over and tried to lure her into his apartment with treats. Nothing worked. So the vet gave them some good advice. Let her sit there until I come back to get her. And that I did. But Zwibel didn't give me the joyous welcome one would usually expect from a Boxer. She had done her duty, and she had waited for me.

Now I was supposed to do mine and pick her up. As far as she was concerned, everything was in order!

One time Zwibel's true value became apparent. We had a cow in the barn that was for sale. A buyer had been found, but he was late. Since the rabies quarantine still existed, and we had to work in the fields, we left Zwibel in the barn. Following the custom on farms, the barn was not locked. That way the stranger would be able to look at the cow even though we were not there. Of course, he did not see the dog lying in ambush. When he came to leave the barn, Zwibel gave him a hefty bite in the rear. Because of the rabies danger, that was especially embarrassing. She should have been muzzled.

I bred Zwibel four times, and each litter miscarried. Despite that, I wanted to try one more time. The young Munich dog, Buko von Biederstein, was highly praised at that time, so I chose him for the breeding, which took place in November, 1924.

An Intermezzo With Horses

On that occasion, I became acquainted with a man who was truly a jack-of-all-trades, and he was successful in everything. Of course, he was also a member of the Boxer Club. In addition, he owned a hotel, a sausage factory, a rock crusher, and he was also interested in taking over a farming operation. In the course of a skill-fully directed conversation, he aroused my interest in breeding trotters. Race horses had become almost a mass madness at that time. I decided to sell the mature timber on our acreage to raise some cash. He handled the timber sale, as well as the horse purchase.

On an ice-cold December day, we drove to the location of the trotting mares. My heart went immediately to a dark sorrel mare. She was supposed to be pregnant, but didn't look it. Her mother had been a Vienna Derby winner, although she herself had never run a race. For that reason, I hooked her up to the sulky and was able to convince myself that she was uncommonly fast. I bought that horse.

The second animal I chose was a tall brown mare that was obviously pregnant. Although she had run in races and won with good times, for some reason she had lost that ability. Supposedly, she would not let herself be hooked up to anything again. To me, the most important thing was that she was pregnant. I didn't plan to race her again anyway. Besides, she was relatively cheap.

But my broker was not entirely happy with my choice. He introduced me to a light gold sorrel mare. She had run quite a few races and was the youngest of the lot. Furthermore, she was supposed to be pregnant. A beautiful animal, but also the most expensive. I just could not bring myself to buy her. I stuck with my Libelle, the sorrel, and Fledermaus, the brown one.

Everything was signed. I was to receive the papers later. These were Austrian trotters that had been smuggled over the border—so I was told—and for that reason the papers would be late.

On December 24, I went to pick up the horses. I left early in the morning for Munich and planned to be back for Christmas Eve. That is one Christmas Eve I will never forget. We loaded the horses into the boxcar in the morning, and I should have been back in Mühldorf in the afternoon. Unintentionally, the car with me and the horses ended up sitting on a dead track. Only after hours, did I succeed in getting anybody's attention. We talked and argued, and finally decided that the car would be attached to a freight train late that night. Until then, I felt as though I were sitting on hot coals.

Around ten that night, we pulled into Mühldorf. How happy I was to hear my husband's voice! Now I would not have to tramp the eight miles back to our farm alone with these temperamental horses. We arrived about midnight. By the time we had taken care of the horses, Christmas Eve was over. Our little boy lay all rolled up like a little dog, sleeping next to Zwibel under the table. And the

servant, who was to take care of the boy, slept with his head upon his arms next to the undecorated Christmas tree.

The next day my uncle inspected the horses. His opinion was important to me. Libelle pleased him right away. Fledermaus, on the other hand, did not get his approval. She was a tail-swisher, he said, and they are not worth anything. He did encourage us with the hope that she might have nice foals.

Soon after, I decided to test whether Fledermaus could be used to pull. She let me harness her with no trouble at all. Then I led her out of the barn and put the blinders on her. Last of all, I quietly hooked her up to a light cutter. I then climbed in, took the reins and called out to the servant to remove the blinders.

Away she went!

Over hills and across valleys, it went fine, although I could feel that she had taken the bit between her teeth. At first, that never bothered me. But then her speed became terribly fast. We were nearing a small village, where a wedding was being celebrated. Should I be seen there with this runaway nag? For the sake of my prestige, that did not seem like a good idea, so at the first chance I hopped off into a snow drift, nice and easy and painless. Then I walked into the village, told some farm boys that my horse had run off while I was hooking her up, and offered a good reward to get her back. An hour later she was brought back to me dripping wet. My uncle really gave me a lecture.

Fledermaus went through many hands. And every owner gave in to her. When she had a little brown daughter—a spitting image of her mother—she turned out to be the same kind of tail-swisher.

A Trotting Race

My trotting chapter did not close with that incident. I wanted to redeem myself for the disaster with Fledermaus. At the time, they had winter sleigh races in the village. The only horses that could not compete were those that had already won a race. To the victor went a flag, and if it were a really good race—sometimes a trophy. Both prizes were highly sought. I wanted to enter Libelle in one of those races. The veterinarian who was the race director warned me against it, but I had made up my mind.

The day arrived. Luckily, both my husband and uncle were away. I drew number one. That lessened the danger of being surrounded by other sleds. Above all, the butchers—who owned fast horses—seemed to regard me as serious competition and gave me some dirty looks. I didn't pay any attention to them.

Fourteen racers took off at the sound of the starter's shot and the drop of the flag. Along with three or four others, I stayed in the front group. Libelle was really running. Then suddenly a driver came up alongside us, and tried to spook Libelle with his riding crop. Others joined in by shouting at me. But she didn't react the way they had hoped. When the first swat hit her, she leaped up and sprang to the side. We were off the track then, but we had a clear field in front. Thirty or forty yards across crusted snow was nothing for Libelle.

The race director lifted his hand in warning, but my horse was already back to a trot. I had no idea who was behind me. In fact, I never even noticed I crossed the finish line until I stopped. Of course, there was a tremendous controversy. The audience was definitely on my side. The race officials denied the protests of my competition. I had won by half a length. My prizes were a beautiful silk flag and a pewter beer stein. I escaped from all the excitement as quietly and unnoticed as possible.

Only after getting home did I have a celebration with

my four-year-old boy and a young hired hand. I had no idea that the controversy over my victory in Neuötting caused a later riot in one of the taverns. Naturally, my husband and uncle learned about this triumph. The local newspaper reported it with huge headlines. My pride won out over the not-unjustified complaints.

That was the high point of my trotter breeding. Not only did recognition come from the race, but also a lot of practical help. Most important was that I was able to sell Libelle for a good price, which helped protect me against great losses. I had produced two purebred trotter foals. They also brought very good prices. But all of those financial successes that I had gained during those days never meant a thing. When the inflation finally ended, we realized that the ground upon which we had built was solid. Many things went wrong, but we still managed to survive.

Ivein Vom Dom

The best thing from the trotter experience was that it put some encouragement into my life. And when Zwibel followed those significant days with a gift of her own—three little Boxers—it was a much larger step forward than I could judge at the moment. Once again we were on the way up!

Zwibel had been a victim of the times. Because of the quarantine, she could not make any more excursions with me. She developed the same vice of hunting that her mother Rassel and sister Zita had. Secretly, she would pursue that vice, and no human could have been any trickier about it than she was. If I took her out in the field with me, she would lie harmlessly and sleepily around in the shade, while I worked nearby. But no matter how closely I watched, suddenly she would be gone. After an hour or two, she was back lying in the same spot. I never actually saw her come or go. If Zwibel had not always come back dripping wet, I might have questioned my own eyes. Could she have been so smart that she took a cold bath before she came back from the hunt, just so she wouldn't be panting and overheated? She wouldn't realize that being wet would give her away.

When she became older and was unable to leap our highest fence, her vice took another form. She became a brawler and eventually a murderer. For her second murder—it was of her most valuable kennel mate—she received the death sentence. She had reached eleven years and whelped eleven litters, which was a record no other bitch of mine ever matched.

But of all her litters, none was more important than the one in those difficult, critical days. Actually, the only one of great importance was the little red-fawn boy that lay in that litter. We named him Ivein. Here is what the pedigree of this Boxer, whose descendants were of much more significance than those of Rolf, looked like:

Ch. Rolf von Vogelsberg
|
Ch. Rolf von Wallhall
|

Ch. Moritz v. Goldrain	Ch. Rolf von Vogelsberg
Sieger Cäsar v. Deutenkofen	Siegerin Rassel vom Dom
Sieger Bucko v. Biederstein	Zwibel Vom Dom

|
Ivein vom Dom

Ivein was whelped in January 1925, along with two sisters. The year before, Boxers had been recognized as service dogs. This official recognition gave us much hope, and today it is taken for granted. Probably the best part of it was that the Boxer began to receive much better training. The burdensome fighting, so typical of Boxers, began to ease up. And our hobby, before mainly conformation showing, was now greatly enriched through obedience

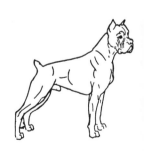

training. An early dream to make the Boxer competitive with the German Shepherd, however, did not come true.

The Shepherd will remain the primary working dog. His thick coat makes him much less sensitive to the effects of bad weather than the Boxer could ever be. In addition, the Shepherd is less bother to feed. A Boxer is like somebody from Munich. His food has to be heavy and good. In contrast to the Boxer, the Shepherd is a fast learner. Even in the hands of an unskilled trainer, the Shepherd can still be easily trained. Those are undeniable facts, which make the Boxer unsuitable for many purposes that the Shepherd can fulfill.

Still, with his short coat the Boxer is the finest gentleman among dogs. He values good food and demands civilized treatment. He bonds quickly with his master, accepts his leadership easily. But the Boxer does not take a harsh hand or an injustice very well. It's like this: Boxers have their own thick skulls, and each one is a unique personality. Their true calling is to be a home and family dog, a friend of children. His coat is easy to keep clean, and his calm behavior makes him well-fitted for life in an apartment in a large city. The Boxer likes to go for a swim, even more for a ride in the car. It doesn't mean a thing to him to trot twenty-five or thirty miles behind a horse, or a car, or a bicycle. I always had my Boxers with me behind my bicycle or cart, but today the high point of high points is a ride in the car. As a protector and a fighter, the Boxer is unsurpassed.

Before the war, we trained both Laska and Rolf. After that, our farming left us no time, although Ivein would have loved to go through such training.

Even as a little guy, he quickly stood out above the others. Once again, I looked at the head of my dreams. Always tall and strong for his age, he also had beautiful dark eyes. Characteristically, he had inherited much from his mother, but at least I was successful in turning him away from any hunting instinct at an early age. Still, I had luck even in that. Twice, when he was a puppy, I grabbed

Ivein vom Dom with
the angora cat

Ivein vom Dom with
his beloved horses

him as he started to chase a deer. I was able to punish him on the spot. Later, it was enough if I just took along a little belt on our walks. When he picked up the scent of an animal, or perhaps saw one, he would raise his head, but he caught on quickly that I would not let him chase. When a startled rabbit once actually ran right between his legs, he just watched and then kept walking.

Against his joy in fighting, I was less successful. He was eight months old when they lifted the rabies quarantine. I proudly took him for his first walk. At first everything went well. Both of us were happy about the return of freedom. Then a dog barked from behind a six-foot-high wooden fence. Ivein froze for a moment, then in one spring he was up and almost over the fence. At the last moment, I managed to grab his back legs and pull him down. But from that moment on, he saw every strange dog as his enemy.

Even as a pup, Ivein was his own man. Hardly eight weeks old, he was already biting hard while playing. If he got a little cuff for that, he would erupt into a rage. The little guy's hackles would go up, he would shake with anger and then start biting. But if he were calmed with a soft word and petted, he would become as gentle as a lamb. Yet he couldn't stop fighting.

Ivein took over Zwibel's place. He was well raised, and I had him well under control. He had never threatened me. He was so well trained, that if I had the cart I could give a command, and he would move behind and trot with his head right next to the axle, come what may. While doing this, Ivein was bitten three times by a big fawn tavern dog for no apparent reason. The fourth time we went past, I sped up the horse to get by as fast as possible. I never saw the tavern dog. But then I heard a terrible yelping behind me.

Thinking the worst, I whirled around and saw Ivein dragging this big watch dog along like a sack. I leaped out of the wagon. Ivein had him by the neck, and it looked as though the other dog was unconscious. He had some bad neck wounds, but came to right away, so I took him to his worried owner. The innkeeper naturally complained, so I asked him why he had not restrained his dog from attacking my youngster the three other times. It had been a fateful encounter for both dogs. After that, Ivein became the dictator of all dogs in a very large area, and his opponent later died of the wounds, after weeks of sickness.

Ivein's adventures and heroic deeds exceeded even those of Pluto. He was one of those rare tall, strong Boxers with unlimited power. Any game that required full use of such abilities, soon became a passion with him. If I wanted to make him really happy, I would sit down on a sturdy chair, take hold of a broad leather strap and hold it out to him. He would chomp down on it and jerk and pull me—despite my rather substantial weight—and the chair completely across the room.

His favorite activity was jousting with the pack. Our kennel had grown back to its usual large size. When he played, Ivein never would bite a young dog, but he also would never play with a young dog if it were a male. He watched over all male puppies until they were eight months old. At that age, the young male would get instructions from Ivein as to who was boss of the kennel. Ivein would find some petty reason to grab him by the neck and force him to submit. The young dog never received a wound or injury from that, but from that moment on he was Ivein's subject. If Ivein were so inclined, this young vassal could later join in on the pack-game.

Ivein would then stand in the middle of the yard, often with a stone or stick in his mouth, and the other animals would gather around him. Legs apart, head slightly bowed, Ivein watched. Suddenly the pack would attack, and in such a way as though they really wanted to fight with Ivein. One would leap at him, and he would whirl and shove it back. Of course, it was only play-fighting, but certainly an instinctual practice for the real thing. They could play like that for hours. If he became thirsty, he would walk over to one of the reserve water barrels, grab

the planks covering it with his teeth, pull them aside and lap up the water.

He was my constant companion, no matter where I went. Usually he stayed right beside the wagon. If a dog appeared I would slow the horses to a walk and shout, "Ivein, hup!" With a powerful leap, he would be in the wagon, and I could always depend on him staying there until I said, "Now go!" Then he would jump down from the front of the wagon, between the traces. Not once did he ever hit the traces or injure himself by doing that, although I never slowed down before he jumped .

To give him more opportunities to get out and around, I resorted to a muzzle. But what good is a muzzle? Near the school where my children went, there was a big, piebald dog. Everybody was afraid of it. The owner had been ticketed many times, because the dog had attacked both adults and children. The village lay rather high, and you had to follow a winding road to get to it. There was always a steep bank along one side. As I rounded one of the curves, up popped that big checked dog in front of us. Ivein, despite his muzzle, jumped him instantly. Both rolled around in the dust. Ivein couldn't bite, of course, so he boxed. He kept banging the other dog with his muzzled head. The other, bigger dog kept jumping up and would then get thrown down again. So it went, until finally both of them went tumbling a good one hundred feet down the steep bank. I watched when they hit the bottom. Ivein lay on top of his enemy. Then he jumped off and started pulling at the muzzle with his front paws. The other rascal grabbed the opportunity and ran, ran, ran.

Another time I went with a friend to pick up dog food. I had been told the farm had a vicious dog. When I arrived, I carefully tied Ivein to the wagon's rear axle, so he had almost no slack. The other dog was nowhere in sight. And then, suddenly, up leaped this huge Shepherd-mix and charged us. He saw the tethered Ivein and jumped him. I could not really see what was going on under the wagon. But we did hear a dog begin to yelp its head off. Of course, I was afraid it was Ivein.

The farmer ran over and grabbed his dog by the tail and started pulling. Then the yelping under the wagon became even worse. Finally, I was able to get around to the other side, reach under and let Ivein loose. Now we realized it was not Ivein doing the screaming. He had clamped his teeth on the other's ear and would not let go. Only after I pulled so hard on his choke chain that he could not breathe, did Ivein let go. Since the farmer was still pulling on his dog's tail, Ivein's sudden release caused the farmer to land flat on his back. The Shepherd-mix took to his heels faster than his owner had ever seen before.

That was Ivein! And there was a lot more. He remained so faithful to me that not even a bitch in heat could get him to leave me. Nor would he stay with a bitch if I were not there too. I can only remember one exception. Once I wanted to mate his mother, Zwibel, with a promising young dog. The dog was with me for just one day, did his job and was picked up by his owner. Then I noticed that Ivein was missing. A little later, I was told he was in the next town with a Zwibel daughter who was in heat. I picked him up, and when he looked at me he seemed to be saying, "If you won't let my harem stay faithful to me, then I know where I can get even." Never again did he ever leave us for even an hour.

It wasn't so lonely for us anymore either. We were frequently visited by Boxer friends. A friend from Munich often visited us, and he would take Ivein for walks. Ivein liked to go with him, but only on our property. There was no way to get that dog to take one step outside the borders of our farm. I was always puzzled just how the dog knew where those boundaries were, but he did know them.

In the winter I often watched Ivein, as he sat near the hearth. We used briquettes, and sometimes a glowing piece would tumble out of the firebox. Some ashes were usually lying around the stove. Slowly Ivein would rise, walk over and use his nose to push ashes over the glowing piece. He was a rare, unique dog. Ever since him, my fawns have been on an equal footing with the brindles, whom I had spent half a lifetime admiring.

When he was old and dying, Ivein still tried to keep his son Sigurd from fighting with his grandson Zorn. They always separated and walked shyly off to the side when he intervened, though either one could have beat him with no trouble at all. In the end, my wish that he would remain with me as he grew old and finally died was granted. One thing Ivein could not stand was showing. He cared as little about outward appearance as his owners. Several times he was rated "Very good." Once he received "Excellent." In contrast, his genetic potency was outstanding. I have consoled myself a hundred times with the fact that you can produce an occasional Sieger with patience, money and luck. But they alone will never get you a prepotent sire.

The New Boxer Dynasty

Ivein convinced me he could be the basis for a new Boxer dynasty. It was most important to me to find the right bitches for him. Ever since Zwibel's mating with Buko von Biederstein—Ivein's father—I had only used the top dogs with her. But I had never produced anything equal to Ivein. Buko's father, Cäsar von Deutenkofen, was at the time second only to Champion Egon von Gumbertusbrunnen as a prepotent stud dog. The following pedigree is of those dogs who were contemporaries of Ivein and his competition in the ring.

These bloodlines in the following table show all the dogs were descendants of my Rolf von Vogelsberg through his son Rolf von Walhall. They are the dogs that dominated the shows and breeding from 1928 to 1930. Among the fawns, Sieger Hansel von Stolzenfels passed the torch to his half-brother, Edler vom Isarstrand. He was pursued by the small, typey Edler vom Isarstrand, who had been given a clear road by the withdrawal of five-year-old Buko von Biederstein, the father of Ivein. Just why I stuck by Ivein, although he could never have bested these elite dogs in the ring, is something I can not explain. A breeder has to have a sixth sense, otherwise it just doesn't work.

Gelb = Fawn   Gestromt = Brindle

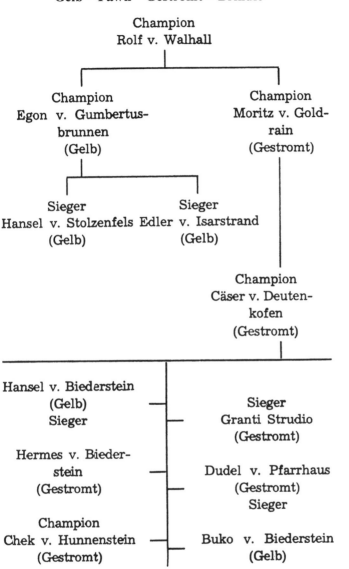

Champion
Rolf v. Walhall

Champion
Egon v. Gumbertus-
brunnen
(Gelb)

Champion
Moritz v. Gold-
rain
(Gestromt)

Sieger
Hansel v. Stolzenfels
(Gelb)

Sieger
Edler v. Isarstrand
(Gelb)

Champion
Cäser v. Deuten-
kofen
(Gestromt)

Hansel v. Biederstein
(Gelb)
Sieger

Sieger
Granti Strudio
(Gestromt)

Hermes v. Bieder-
stein
(Gestromt)

Dudel v. Pfarrhaus
(Gestromt)
Sieger

Champion
Chek v. Hunnenstein
(Gestromt)

Buko v. Biederstein
(Gelb)

My search for Ivein's partner was for a bitch with the blood of his grandfather, Cäsar von Deutenkofen. A small, compact, very typey bitch named Bellinde Hassie, a granddaughter of Cäsar, was my choice. That mating

produced only three puppies, but at least two were males and the other a girl. We named them Sigurd, Schach, and Sausel. Finally, we lucked out and got the Sieger I had waited for all of those hard years. Sigurd became the foundation of a new dynasty and ruled for five years as an unequaled stud dog.

But all good luck has a down side. The puppies had hardly been whelped, when Zwibel killed their mother Bellinde. Zwibel had also killed another young bitch a year before, and that had hit me hard. But this time the sorrow was even greater, because Bellinde had become our favorite. We put Zwibel down because of that. She was eleven years old, but how much damage could she still do? We buried both Zwibel and Bellinde in the same grave. I hurt just as much for one as the other. There are tragedies in animals' lives, just as in humans'. Nor did I excuse myself for what happened. I had broken a basic rule by putting more than two adult dogs in the same run. Their grave served as a painful reminder of that.

Sigurd Vom Dom And Dudel Vom Pfarrhaus

In contrast to his father, Sigurd loved the show world. He was a natural showman, and his body was a perfect model. Front and hind quarters were correct, and his outstanding head rested on a powerful aristocratic neck. He was not the same type as Rolf, but instead was the ideal Boxer, one in which strength, quickness, and nobility all blended together.

When just nine months old, he created great excitement at a show in Munich. On May 13, 1931, I took him to the Vienna Sieger show. When I received my hotel room, it was number thirteen. Had I been superstitious, I would have left immediately. But I stayed, and the show was a great success. Sigurd brought home his first title: Vienna Sieger, 1931.

Then came one win after another. Experience has

Young Sigurd at fourteen months

Adult Sigurd, one of the most prepotent
sires in the history of the breed

taught me that a dog isn't a real Sieger until everybody is cursing him. But that was hardly the case with Sigurd. He was needed, and people demanded him. He was not totally without opposition. But those efforts went the same way they had in my trotting race with Libelle. Sigurd remained the Sieger without peer!

Ivein had some really nice descendants. The best were Sigurd and the International Siegerin Pia von Isebeck. There can only be a few Siegers each year under the German system of judging. But that's not so important. Much more significant is the overall quality of the whole breed. And in that respect, Ivein and Sigurd performed a great service. Sigurd's most significant descendants were the following:

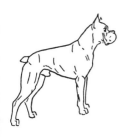

> Champion Xerxes vom Dom
> International Sieger Zero vom Dom
> International Sieger Fachinger von Neu-Drosedow
> Champion Just vom Dom
> Champion Corso vom Uracher Wasserfall
> Sieger Yva von Marienhof
> and
> Zorn vom Dom, with his sister
> Siegerin Zeila vom Dom

Fate is fickle, even in the world of dogs. The only one not to get a Sieger's title or a championship, the one who always had to line up behind his brother Zero—but who always was in the top group—was Zorn vom Dom. But without doubt he possessed the qualities for a greater Boxer than Sigurd.

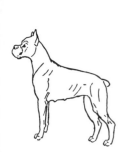

I had chosen Dudel vom Pfarrhaus as a partner for Sigurd. She was a daughter of Cäsar von Deutenkofen and one of the sweetest Boxer bitches that I have ever owned. Today, her light-brown eyes, which shone with a love of life and mischief, would probably be questioned. She was a courageous bitch and an excellent mother. Dudel and Sigurd were a great love match. She bit at every male as long as Sigurd belonged to me, and Sigurd had no interest in any other bitches when Dudel was in season.

With Sigurd, I never achieved the kind of relationship that I had with his father, Ivein. He had to be kenneled much of the time. For a while, it was too dangerous for me to allow Sigurd and Ivein, both powerful dogs, to be loose together. They were much too valuable for me to take any chances. Under such circumstances, personal contact was difficult and thus suffered.

Sigurd's genetic potency was unique. He put his stamp of quality and type on the puppies of every bitch he bred. His most successful descendants came out of his relationship with Dudel vom Pfarrhaus. Those were children of a true Boxer love affair.

There is still a little story told about Dudel. She wasn't yet a year old, when we took her on an afternoon stroll through our meadow. While there, we heard hoof beats, and up galloped our six-month-old foal to beg for some bread and sugar. The animal ran right up to us. Dudel thought we were in danger, so she immediately fastened on to the filly's rear quarter. The reaction was also immediate. The foal kicked, and Dudel went flying high in the air. Dudel stood up, shook the dust off herself, and then leaped right up on the horse's back and bit into its mane. The little filly panicked. She raced away with Dudel firmly attached on top. But the ending was not quite as dramatic as the one in Ferdinand Freilingrath's *Desert Ride*. Eventually, Dudel got bored and just slid off sideways. The horse galloped away, and Dudel returned to us, proud as she could be that she had saved our lives. In appearance, Dudel was only a little above average, but she had such charm that wherever she went she won everyone's heart.

Sigurd had the traits of a genial Munich citizen. There isn't much I can write about his private life, since he was mostly busy with his harem. Once we went to a show in Berlin, and there were taxis parked all along the side of a wide street. At the time, that was a rather unusual sight for us. Sigurd stopped in front of the first car. He had ridden in one for a short distance the day before. Apparently the taxi

driver understood what Sigurd wanted. He popped open the door and shouted, "Climb in, fatty." You didn't have to say that twice to Sigurd. He climbed right in, and I had a very hard time getting him back out. Oh my! All of the other drivers saw that episode, and each one now offered the same invitation to Sigurd, and every time I literally had to pull him out. We ran the gauntlet of some twelve to fifteen taxis!

Sigurd was very vain. He loved to be photographed. He would sit there, still as a mouse, until the camera clicked. Then, with one leap he disappeared.

At that time, I was responsible for the illustrations in the *Boxer Blätter.* In order to keep getting fresh and humorous material, we began photographing Boxers that had been dressed up in funny costumes, and we managed to create a number of specific types that seemed to match the various personalities of the Boxers. These pictures were published all over the world. It was the first—and the last— time I ever dressed up a dog for a picture.

Sigurd was my dream come true: A winner beyond comparison and without rival. But over and over, a little question nagged at me: Shouldn't he have been a brindle?

Sigurd's Descendants

Among the top dogs that came out of the mating of Sigurd and Dudel, one has to mention first the three-leaf clover of Zero, Zorn, and Zeila. All three were brindle. I sold Zero, who was the largest in the litter, to a friend. That dog had a great show career and eventually became a World Sieger. Zeila also became a Siegerin. In 1933, three of my Boxers won Sieger titles at the Frankfurt show— something no one had ever achieved before.

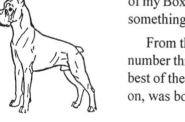

From the very beginning, I picked for myself puppy number three, the dark-brindle Zorn. He looked to be the best of the lot. But this animal, from the time of his birth on, was both a bad-luck kid and a special character. He was living proof that Siegers can be made, but not prepotent breeding dogs. His brother Zero became the great show dog. It should also be pointed out that Zero came into the hands of people who had means and influence. Certainly, it would have been difficult for me to have had such success with him.

But I know today that I had the right feelings for a dog's breeding capabilities. And Zorn was the quality stud dog! He had a beautiful head, and along with it he had the talent to show how beautiful he was. I was convinced of his genetic strength to improve the breed, and I allowed him to be used often for breeding— so often that I almost became irritated about the number of unknown bitches being brought to him.

His grandfather Ivein had been a real gentleman. Not really overbearing but instead friendly, although self-confident and sure of his goal when he serviced his harem. Yet he always seemed to have more interests than just the girls. It was different with his son Sigurd. He was a born pasha. If the beauty of the day didn't want to do it his way, he would grab her by the neck and shake her almost to the point of unconsciousness.

But Zorn, in turn, was quite different from his father Sigurd. In general, he did not care for the girls. Little dark brindles seemed especially despised by him. Many times you could not get him even interested in such a type of bitch. His taste ran to light fawns, the bigger the better. The fatter she was the more he loved her. Because of that nonsense, over the years a bit of a hostility developed between him and me.

When a bitch was brought to him, he would stand off to the side and stare at her. If she weren't too interested in him and maybe growled a bit, he would turn around and be on his way. But if the bitch showed a friendly face, then he would glance at me. He always knew immediately when I was angry with him. And if I did become angry, that was it! He would dash to the nearest corner of the building, leave his liquid calling card on it, and then off he

went. When that happened in front of the bitches' owners—many of whom had traveled long distances—it was very embarrassing for me. But when he put aside his inhibitions, he could be a good stud dog and a first-class genetic carrier.

In Vienna—when Sigurd won his first Sieger title—he also mated with the brindle Siegerin Uni von der Würm. Uni was a great granddaughter of the small, aristocratic bitch, Belfine vom Isarstrand. She was the last bitch with Milo's blood. From that breeding came Esta von der Würm. She would also become the foundation bitch of a new generation. My husband picked her for our stud fee.

Esta was a wonderful girl, the image of her father, but brindled. Unfortunately, she became so undershot that both her teeth and tongue showed. Many times later I wished I had such a bitch as Esta, but without that fault. Esta's grandfather was Belfine's beautiful son, Edler vom Isarstrand. He had been a one-time Sieger, and was one of Ivein's strongest competitors. But he was not very successful for passing on his characteristics. If that breeding in Vienna had not been successful, the last trace of Milo's blood would have disappeared from Boxer history. But this blood line blended itself in, and a dog was born who left all others before him in the shadows: Lustig vom Dom.

Lustig vom Dom

Is it possible to be so lucky you could win the grand lottery two times in a row? Again and again, we see a novice have the success that longtime breeders have sought in vain. But it is not the rule. The lucky beginner soon learns no one can count on good fortune continuing. Perhaps there comes a time when success is deserved but does not happen. Often this type of breeder gets angry and quits as soon as an expected win doesn't happen. There is no such thing as constant good or bad luck.

Mostly, my good and bad luck was mixed. To achieve a

Lustig vom Dom, right, at seven weeks old

Zorn, left, and Lustig vom Dom

deserved success, I had to fight for a lifetime, using love, patience, sacrifice, and—if my husband were right—with a sixth sense for breeding. For those reasons, I believe that my successes over many decades were more than luck.

At that time, I mated Esta von der Würm with her half-sibling Zorn vom Dom. Esta had a glorious litter. I left her five boys and one girl. Two of the boys were fawn, all the others brindle. One of the fawn dogs had a white marking on only one side of his face and a large white stripe going up the forehead. When I looked at him, I told my daughter to call a friend and tell him I had a cheap puppy for him.

Three days later, the golden fawn daughter of Sigurd, Goldi von Pfarrkirchen also whelped a very attractive litter with four dogs and two bitches. Like Dudel, Goldi was also one of our favorites. Outwardly, she was very much like the unforgettable Derby.

Goldi fell ill just twenty-four hours after whelping. She left the litter box, lay down on the cold tile and refused to eat. She had an unquenchable thirst. A visit from the veterinarian achieved nothing. I pleaded with him to save Goldi. I would have rather lost Esta and her whole litter!

All of my efforts failed to save her, and she died a painful death. Goldi was no longer there, but her puppies were. There was nothing else I could do than turn over her six puppies to Esta.

Of course, with twelve puppies I had to bottle feed too. Esta, with her excessive underbite and long tongue, was pushed to her limit. She had trouble keeping them dry. But all of the little guys were fine—round as noodles, with good appetites. You could see them growing. And there among those puppies, like some kind of animal miracle, a golden fawn boy with white markings and a coat like silk began to develop in a wondrous way. It was the despised "cheap" puppy. Because he always seemed so happy [*lustig*] he made you forget your troubles, we decided to call him Lustig vom Dom.

Lustig brought great honor to his name. There were people who wanted him when he was just eight weeks old, but I turned down all offers. As a little fellow, Lustig still had a fault. Boxers with white markings usually are born with a flesh-colored nose. When they are two or three days old, some black spots begin to appear there and soon enlarge. Eventually they merge together and the nose becomes pigmented. The process can go fairly quickly. But it went very slowly with Lustig. His nose became mostly black, but a small butterfly of pink remained. Because I was so in love with the dog, I told myself I would not sell the happy puppy as long as the pink spot was there.

Sigurd Goes To America

In the meantime, I had another temptation. I received an inquiry from America for a fawn Boxer Sieger. At the time, the only fawn Sieger for the last three years had been Sigurd. The brindles were dominated by his son Zero. Sigurd was now five years old. At that age, even good dogs can be hard to sell. If all went well, he might have another three or four years of stud service. And I always needed money. So I made my decision to sell him. The separation wasn't easy, but, when all was said and done, I still had my great one: Lustig!

When my husband returned from a trip abroad, I surprised him with what had taken place. I had sold Sigurd, and I had bought a motorcycle that would climb the hills. We had a short argument, and then it all passed over. The motorcycle had fulfilled one of my long-held desires.

We never heard a thing about Sigurd for a whole year. It seemed as though he had disappeared from the earth. Dog breeding can be a strange thing. Long before any birth, the pedigrees are studied, and the appearance and backgrounds of the prospective parents are compared and judged. Then the selected pair are bred. It's almost as though precious seeds were being planted in the earth. The expectant mother is fed the best food available. The days and hours are counted, until the little ones come into the world. Their lives and welfare are constantly watched over.

Finally, they must learn the same as children to behave themselves and to obey.

With pounding hearts, the breeders take them to the shows. And there they find love, admiration, and also envy. Thus the animals become a part of their breeders. They are like their children to them, sometimes even more so because they are a type of art work and the breeder is the artist. Then in the end, some stranger comes along and offers you a handful of money. In this case, the money is like Judas' pieces of silver. But what can the breeder do? Breeding has become a passion, generations grow up, puppies need food—all that costs money!

The responsible breeder should always make sure that the dogs are placed in good hands and keep track of them. One year after Sigurd's sale, an American lady asked us about a Boxer she wished to purchase, and I took the opportunity to inquire about Sigurd. I learned he had continued on his Sieger course. And he had become the most popular Boxer stud dog in the United States. For Christmas, this lady sent me a large package full of dog magazines that had articles about Sigurd. What a joy that was!

The motorcycle was a great help. Now there was no distance too far for me. Occasionally it was even possible to take a little vacation. Even my husband liked to go riding around the country with me. But not all was simple pleasure. Most of all I missed having my canine companions. With sad eyes, they stood at the door and watched as I took out the gas bicycle. Without a doubt, they must have really hated that thing! They used to circle me excitedly, when I brought out the old bicycle and they thought that my trip might permit them to run along.

There was nothing I could not transport now. A couple hundred pounds of grain, huge buckets of blood, I even took a she-goat to a billy-goat for breeding without incident. It was wonderful as long as the weather was nice. Unfortunately, I also had to travel in all kinds of weather, during rain, storms, and snow. Ice crystals often pounded my face. My worst enemy was bare ice.

Once I was hauling a huge wash tub with blood in it. The motorcycle went into a skid on bare ice, and a great amount of blood ended up on top of the white snow. I didn't have to worry about that, but some jokers put up a memorial marker with a description of the accident on the edge of the road. It was not until spring, that the bloody spot finally disappeared.

Dog Sports In The Third Reich

National Socialism, the "new order," brought about the *Gleichschaltung,* or forced coordination, of even the dog game. All aspects of life were aligned with the goals of the party. Part of that meant some dubious elements were installed in the top positions of society. Very seldom can you replace quality with uniforms. Despite that, many fanciers put their faith in the new regime.

But my dog star sent me a timely warning, which I understood clearly. There was a Nazi radio dealer who had told us stories about how he and his comrades had been fighting the Communists. Such stories reminded me of what our guard dogs had done during the war. I told him about that and how dogs might be used for protection in this case. At the time, I had a six-month-old son of Ivein, who was quite capable of becoming an aggressive guard dog. I gave him this dog. Our son took the animal to Mühldorf to see how it worked out. In the beginning everything went fine. Then things began happening. Shortly after the Nazi takeover on January 30, 1933, the radio dealer's wife cheerfully told my son that their troubles were now over.

A few days later I received a hastily written note from the dealer himself. He wrote that he no longer needed a dog, and I should come pick it up because he and his

family had moved to Munich. They had locked the dog up inside a garden shed.

Naturally, I went there immediately. I released the poor animal, who had gone several days without food or water. It took weeks for him to recover fully.

Certainly, I know that a large political party like the Nazis cannot always be held responsible for the actions of its individual members. But as events progressed, it repeatedly became clear to me that animal abusers are not good for people either.

The Nazi-installed head of the Boxer Club soon had to step down. In barely one year, he spent over 12,000 marks of the club's funds. After that, things went back to normal. But, of course, it was only the calm before the storm. Life did get a bit easier, however, and the sport of dogs flourished everywhere. For the fanciers, the International Sieger Show in Frankfurt in 1935, was the high point of this epoch.

Lustig vom Dom had now become the undisputed Boxer leader. But he was still two months too young to win the International Sieger title. So the fawn-dog title went to a son of Sigurd, Fachinger von Neu-Dresedow. Another descendant of Sigurd, his grandson Dorian von Marienhof, was still too young to take the brindle title, so it went to Sigurd's son, Zero vom Dom. As expected, Lustig vom Dom took the title of Most Beautiful Boxer.

Then among the top brindle bitches was also a Sigurd daughter, Iva von Marienhof, and the fawn-bitch International Siegerin title went to Ivein's daughter, Thea von Isebeck. Almost the whole Boxer elite at that show came from my breeding. It was one of those few truly happy years that have been granted me.

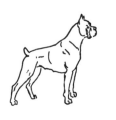

During that time, I had some success in letting various animals species mingle together. Many funny—and often touching—stories came out of that. For the sake of animal psychology alone, it's worth keeping some of them alive. For that reason, I'll relate a few now.

Monkeys, Deer, Foxes, And Badgers

At the head of the line would be our Rhesus monkey. He had a very close relationship with Lustig vom Dom, and often used Lustig as a riding horse. When we went out to the fields, and the dogs ran along, the monkey could not keep up. So it would leap on the back of the nearest dog. If he felt a little sassy or sensed danger, he would move up on Lustig's neck, press himself down between the dog's ears, and bare his teeth. We had three monkeys, one after the other, and all three died of tuberculosis.

For a long time we had a roe [*Reh*] deer. It had been found injured in the woods. That animal nursed so willingly on our bitches, one would think it quite natural. In the same way, it ran around and played with our dog family. Sometimes an elderly farmer near us will still tell the story of a miracle he had seen at our place. He saw a deer grazing peacefully in our meadow. Suddenly a whole pack of dogs came bearing down on it. The deer raised its head and then bounded away in great leaps, but it did not go far. Unexpectedly, the deer stopped, turned around and walked back to the Boxers. The pack stopped running too, and they all walked peacefully together back to the house.

The little roe deer stayed with us for a long time. When it grew older, it seemed to prefer the nearby woods. Only when the cows were being milked, did it sometimes appear for a bowl of milk. Then the visits gradually came less often. Once, after several months, we saw it running across the meadow. Everybody shouted, "Rehlein!"

It stopped, stared at the dogs, and then slowly went back to the woods. At night it slept by a little wooden house near us, where an old lady and her grandson lived. Then it disappeared for a very long time. But the next summer we saw her again with a little fawn. The dogs never tried to bother them, yet the doe would only stand on top of the hill and watch us below. She had made her decision to stay in the familiar woods.

I did not have much luck in breeding and raising red

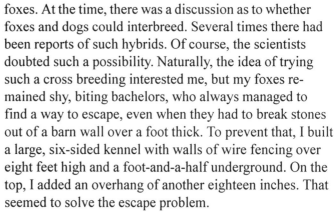

foxes. At the time, there was a discussion as to whether foxes and dogs could interbreed. Several times there had been reports of such hybrids. Of course, the scientists doubted such a possibility. Naturally, the idea of trying such a cross breeding interested me, but my foxes remained shy, biting bachelors, who always managed to find a way to escape, even when they had to break stones out of a barn wall over a foot thick. To prevent that, I built a large, six-sided kennel with walls of wire fencing over eight feet high and a foot-and-a-half underground. On the top, I added an overhang of another eighteen inches. That seemed to solve the escape problem.

Then very early one morning, when I went out to the kennels I saw a fox inside the Boxer puppies' kennel playing with them. As soon as he heard me, he was gone in a flash. Later I found a tunnel from the fox's kennel to the puppies' kennel. The fox had dug it. As sorry as I was to do it, I still had to seal off the tunnel.

I had some even stranger experiences with these wild bachelors. In the beginning, only one old fox was in the kennel. Then one day a farmer brought me a young one. It was half tame. In order to stay friendly with it, I did not want to put it in the kennel. But despite my cautions, after a short time the young fellow disappeared, escaped! We searched the grounds for three days, looking for him. On the fourth day, when I went out to feed the other fox I was amazed to see that he had company. The little one had climbed over an eight-foot fence, and then dropped down into the kennel. Had he been attracted by the scent of his own species? Usually foxes are not pack animals but solitary. Unfortunately, both were males, so I ended up with two bachelors living together.

Still, I had this notion of a cross breeding. I went to the Spitz club and received a little white bitch: Katey the fox-bride! My assumption was that a Spitz would be easiest for mating to a fox. So Katey was put in with them. But it didn't work out the way I had planned. Katey became the tyrant of the kennel. I tried over and over to change that, but she made the two foxes keep their distances—espe-

Lustig vom Dom examines another house pet of the Stockmanns

The Reh deer which lived at the Stockmann farm until fully grown.

Two five-week-old
puppies, a fox
(left) and a Boxer

Lustig and Zorn vom Dom, with a monkey on Lustig's back

cially around the food bowl. If I had not finally intervened, the foxes would have starved to death.

Then I tried to have a Boxer bitch raise a four-day-old fox puppy. I thought that might produce a tame fox. But this experiment failed too.

Our pet badger, Madam Stups, should also be mentioned. She came to us very young and became much tamer than the foxes ever did. To tell the truth, she was the sweetest and funniest animal we ever owned. And she got along very well with the dogs. Her play with them was a bit rough sometimes, because she seemed instinctively to know just where the dogs' most tender spots were—for instance, the tender flesh between the toes—and would attack there. Her teeth were snow white and extremely strong. Although she was very mischievous, she made us laugh many times.

At night, she loved to steal our blankets. To do that, she waited patiently until she could catch hold of a corner. She would grab it with her teeth and then rapidly roll around on the floor. In no time at all, she made a long sausage out of the blanket and then ran up and down the stairs dragging it. If it had been your blanket that was stolen, you probably first noticed it when you woke up freezing.

No other animal ate like Madam Stups. She could not resist turning over the pigs' buckets, just to pick out the most tasty morsels. She did the same thing with the dogs' food. But her favorite treat was bread with strawberry marmalade.

Madam Stups was house broken, walked on a leash, and obeyed quite well. When we went for walks, we often took her along on the leash. Not many of our neighbors even knew what a badger was.

One time Madam Stups came upon a flock of geese. The big birds spotted this hunter and began running and honking. It took just one shout and Madam Stups was back with us. Yet she did not always do what we wanted. Like her kind in the wild, she was a nocturnal animal. Two

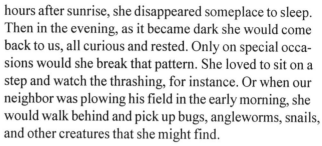

hours after sunrise, she disappeared someplace to sleep. Then in the evening, as it became dark she would come back to us, all curious and rested. Only on special occasions would she break that pattern. She loved to sit on a step and watch the thrashing, for instance. Or when our neighbor was plowing his field in the early morning, she would walk behind and pick up bugs, angleworms, snails, and other creatures that she might find.

Madam Stups never stole any poultry from either us or our neighbors. But a catastrophe happened when a distant farmer threw a dead chicken on top of his manure pile. Stups picked up the scent of that carcass and ate it. That was not enough, however. She then went into the chicken house and took four nice fat hens. Since she was already full, all she ate from the four were their intestines. She wasn't a bit careful, so of course she was seen and recognized. We paid the farmer, naturally, and then securely penned up Stups. Two days later she was back in the same chicken coup! This time there were sixteen victims. That cost her her life. Our local newspaper once again had something to write about. The article was titled, "The Blood Test." But despite it all, we—even the dogs— mourned Madam Stups for a long time.

Besides the playmates for our dogs, there were many others, including Angora cats, ravens, magpies, jackdaws, and white rats. This was a quiet peaceful time. My artistic interest began to revive. But it was only the quiet before the storm.

A Catastrophic Year

Lustig was the sunshine of our home. Again and again, I claimed that I would never be parted from him. In no way, did I suspect how soon our separation would actually take place. Since Sigurd's appearance in the United States, the interest in Boxers had greatly expanded over there. In particular, there were some very wealthy fanciers who now wished to purchase the most beautiful animals in Germany.

They began to outbid themselves. Undefeated Lustig drew all kinds of offers, but I stayed firm and refused them all. Then came 1936, a disastrous year for us.

A beautiful young brood mare, on which we had placed great hope, died while foaling. Carefully, we raised the foal with cow's and goat's milk. But a foal needs three or four gallons of milk a day, and we just did not always have that much surplus on our little farm. Finally a neighbor helped too. When they finished milking they would set a bowl of milk in front of our door, and the little foal would soon appear, stick its nose in the bowl and gobble it up. If the bowl were not there at the expected time, the foal would knock on the front door with its hoof, until it got its milk.

But that was just the first setback. After a wonderful spring, we had a horrible summer. Rain drenched everything. Grain rotted in the fields and potatoes in the ground. We had no hay, yet there was plenty of green for grazing, more than the livestock could eat. Suddenly a terrible disease broke out among the cows. First it hit a rather distant farm, then it hit us and soon spread to the whole district. A veterinarian said the cause was poisoning from rotten meat or contamination from manure piles. His diagnosis became a sentence for us.

It was a short step from spoiled meat to our dogs. Sure, we could not deny that we often picked up meat from the rendering plants. But an analysis of the dead cows' stomachs revealed nothing to confirm the veterinarian's diagnosis. Furthermore, the illness appeared in other regions where our dogs had no contact at all. The matter was never really explained.

It was bad enough that we lost all of our cattle, had a harvest destroyed, and now had nothing left. But we also had to stand by and watch one or two dead cows a day being dragged out of our neighbor's barn. The wives stood around crying, and the men kept glaring over at us. Among them were those who had helped supply our motherless foal with milk. To replace the foal's mother, I had purchased an old, large workhorse. We also owned an old mare that suffered from asthma. Both horses escaped

the disease. I used them for work, and I also allowed my neighbors to use them.

The neighbors had not lost as many cows as we had, but they were much more dependent on them for draft animals. Whether or not I was responsible for our common misfortunes did not matter, I felt I owed them our help. So we helped where we could. And it was great consolation to me that this help was recognized and appreciated. Our district agricultural director also helped us. We received milk stamps and groceries, even a little cash. I alone had to care for my five dogs and the orphaned foal.

But that was not the end of the business. One day the district veterinarian showed up. He gave us a long lecture, the gist of which was that our dogs had been the cause of all the sickness. They supposedly had carried raw meat around the area, and through that meat the cows became infected. I argued in vain that the dogs only received cooked meat and were always fed in the barn, and to avoid any fighting among the dogs, I was meticulously careful that no food was ever carried away. Also, I mentioned that in many oriental countries dogs are used as health police.

As I said before—all of that was useless. Somebody had to be guilty, and this time it was me and my dogs. Before it was over, I was happy they had not ordered me to be punished. I was forbidden to feed any more meat from animals that had died naturally, rather than had been slaughtered. And I had to chain up our dogs or else fence in our property.

Looking for dog food was nothing new to me. Again and again, I had managed to solve the problem. When I told the owner of a slaughter house about it, he offered to supply me with as much cattle blood and intestines as I wanted.

Chaining up my dogs was the other question. Did I want to have a pack of dogs chained to their kennels? Never! So there was only one answer: To fence in our property. The fence would have to be sturdy and surround the whole complex. I did not really have any objections to that, but where would the money come from? Except for two old mares and two goats, we had nothing. For us to exist, we needed more livestock.

Our agricultural director then pointed out to us that there were loans available to needy farmers at a low interest rate and long terms. He encouraged my husband to apply for one. The National Department of Nutrition [*Reichsnährstand*] administered the loans. I was not all in favor of this, but we really had no other choice. So one day two typical Nazi-types showed up. And what did they see? Rotting grain in the fields and a few little potatoes rotting away as they floated in water that had seeped into the potato bin. Our visitors were not any more pleased with the scene than we were.

When they walked past the dogs' kennels, they wrinkled up their noses. The round fox kennel, where two veterans from my attempts to cross species still remained, produced some disgusted glances. Finally they came to my empty livestock barn, with the two goats and the two tired old mares that did the work for three farms. In front of the stalls lay some green fodder, since it was right at feeding time. When the animals heard my voice, there arose a loud whistling that pricked up the ears of the two Nazis.

Lastly, two well-fed guinea pigs showed up in the barn door and then trotted over to the pile of green fodder and began to feast. The party officials just had no sympathy for that sort of thing. They left with the advice that they would be in touch with us. "Heil Hitler!" was the last thing I ever heard from them on our property.

Of course they turned down our application. In their justification, they had to point out that people who had five dogs, two foxes, and then guinea pigs to boot, could hardly be in great need. They advised us to replace our animals with a pair of draft cattle.

I confess, there are very few times when I have been so

outraged as I was when I read that notification. And I did not try to hide my feelings. But that did not help our situation. Thus, it was a tremendous relief to us when our credit union declared itself ready to loan us 2,000 marks. Of course, we had to find someone to vouch for us. I thought that would be a mere formality, but it turned out to be almost impossible. It did show us how the doors of the well-to-do are bolted shut when someone in need comes around. We became filled with bitterness and disappointment. But then we did find help. My mother and our old friends had not been told of our misfortunes. When they finally heard of our problems, there were more than enough people to stand up for us. So we received our loan to bridge us over and, above all, to fence our property. I tried to make our dogs secure and patiently waited for the sad hour of departure that was coming soon.

Lustig Goes To America

Winter had come to Germany. Icy winds swept powdered snow into deep drifts. Our farm, Reich-Schmitt lay just half-ways up a high hill. Whoever wanted to get to us had to go through the village first, cross a small bridge and then again go up a steep slope. Up there the world seemed to have died out, especially at the Reich-Schmitt farm where we lived. One day our daughter saw a car coming toward our place. At first, that struck us as humorous and foolish, because the steep road was covered with glare ice. But somebody really wanted to reach our place.

With hesitation, the visitor entered the large family room. You could see he would rather be somewhere else when our five Boxers rose and gave him a good sniffing over. His companion was a taxi driver we knew from the village where the train stopped, who had brought him here with his taxicab. After the introductions, the man got right to the point. He asked us straight out if Lustig vom Dom were for sale. We hesitated somewhat at first, and pointed out that any final decision would depend greatly on what was offered. Thereupon, he told us he already understood we would want a figure with at least five figures. We, in turn, assured him there was no urgency in the matter. He wasn't in any way impressed.

He made us an offer of 12,000 marks for Lustig, and asked frankly if we would sell him for that. Of course, he pointed out it was a very large sum for a dog, for a living animal that tomorrow might have a bad accident! At first we said nothing and silently looked at each other. It was a very difficult decision, but in the end was there any other choice but to accept?

The man put pressure on us. He told us he had been commissioned to buy Lustig for a friend in America, and he was well aware his offer for Lustig was a fortune.

If we had been true farmers, we would have gotten half again that much. But we were almost stupefied. All of the needs and worries of the time passed through our minds. Neither my husband nor I said a word, but we each knew what the other was thinking. Finally my husband declared that we would accept the offer. My daughter and I said nothing, but the visitor still had something to say. He asked the taxi driver to leave the room. Then he took 1,000 marks from his wallet and laid it on the table. That was the down payment, the rest we would receive when the dog had been delivered to him.

But the broker wanted to make a little more money. He laid another 1,000 marks on the table and asked us to agree that the purchase price would be listed as 14,000 marks. We gave him a receipt for the 2,000 marks, and agreed to sell Lustig vom Dom for a total of 13,000 marks, payable on delivery to him. With that, the dice had been thrown.

The visitor took his leave, and we sat silent in the room. Each of us felt as though one of us had been sold. I couldn't sleep the whole night. A thousand thoughts raced through my grieving mind. I even seriously considered

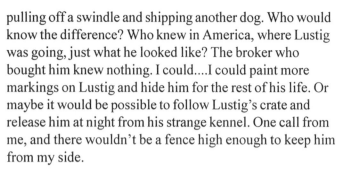

pulling off a swindle and shipping another dog. Who would know the difference? Who knew in America, where Lustig was going, just what he looked like? The broker who bought him knew nothing. I could....I could paint more markings on Lustig and hide him for the rest of his life. Or maybe it would be possible to follow Lustig's crate and release him at night from his strange kennel. One call from me, and there wouldn't be a fence high enough to keep him from my side.

I knew those were just pipe dreams. But somehow, they seemed to console me, even though it was very clear fate was stronger than I, and when all was said and done I would have to bend to it. For the moment, however, it was terribly painful. I never suspected, of course, what fate really had in mind. Only many years later did I learn what Lustig had truly meant for me.

At first I wished never to see Lustig again. I never wanted to see him in some stranger's hands. And we certainly did not want anybody else to learn what we had received for him. Envy should not be the cause of hostility between us and our neighbors. But that had been the wrong way to think.

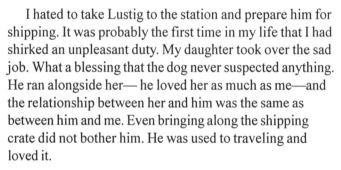

I hated to take Lustig to the station and prepare him for shipping. It was probably the first time in my life that I had shirked an unpleasant duty. My daughter took over the sad job. What a blessing that the dog never suspected anything. He ran alongside her— he loved her as much as me—and the relationship between her and him was the same as between him and me. Even bringing along the shipping crate did not bother him. He was used to traveling and loved it.

Of course, they were somewhat of a sensation at the depot. Sending a dog COD for 11,000 marks had never happened before. When my daughter said a last good-bye to Lustig through the bars of his crate, he took the leash hanging from his collar into his mouth and seemed to plead with her, "Please let me go back home with you." My daughter cried and cried. We had shipped many dogs, but never one like him.

On the trip back home, it was pitch dark. Several farmers were ahead of my daughter and so deep in conversation they never noticed who was behind them. Was it really true, one asked, that the Stockmanns had sold a dog for a fortune? Nobody actually believed it. Then someone mentioned the taxi driver. He had to know! Ever since the cow business, we had been careful never to talk to anybody about our financial affairs, but we also made no attempt to listen when others talked about us. Now my daughter had become an unwilling listener, but she was not hearing something scandalous about us.

All of the talkers were genuinely happy about our success. They mentioned that Reich-Schmitt had been a thankless piece of property, and that for many years we had been plagued with terrible circumstances. But despite the word of the taxi driver, they were still not sure we had been so lucky. So my daughter, as sad as she was, cheerfully joined in the conversation. She realized neither the cab driver nor the station master had kept their mouths shut. That led her to tell the whole story, and the farmers—who always had liked her—were grateful for her openness.

In the meantime, I had sat at home, about as far down in the dumps as you can get. I denounced myself as petty and cowardly. Finally my husband lost his temper and told me to stop torturing myself. For consolation, he told me I could now trade the motorcycle for the car I had wanted so long. I needed that to find new sources of dog food.

Then our daughter arrived. She told us about her conversations with the farmers, and that seemed to break the spell over me. It began to appear that the sacrifice we made with the sale of Lustig would not be in vain. Would life start getting better now?

As a postscript I might mention that I never saw Lustig again. But my husband did! One year after Lustig went to America, my husband accepted an offer to judge in the United States. His assignment was at America's greatest dog show of the year—the Westminster Kennel Club's show. Lustig took the well-deserved Best of Breed. He had

already won his American championship. He ended his show career after that. In America, he will remain immortal, because the Americans value tradition much more than we do.

Eleven years later I stood before Lustig's grave. It is a moment I will never forget. A beautiful wrought-iron fence surrounded a grassy area, on which thousands of violets were blooming. In the center was a large rough-cut stone with a memorial tablet attached to it. On the tablet, in large golden letters, stood simply the name "Lustig."

One should remember that in America the cemeteries are particularly somber by German standards. In the cities, sometimes wide streets go right through the "final resting place." There aren't many flowers, and there seem to be no restrictions against the outside world. Tombstones are not always used, and some of those are often tasteless. So I was moved even more when I was led—quite unexpectedly—to that beautiful and emotional memorial to my dog. While there, I received a copy of Lustig's death notice with his picture on it and the following words:

International Champion Lustig v. Dom of Tulgey Wood

A.K.C. No. A 149 471

Born: 28 December 1933
Died: 14 June 1945

At the time he was shipped, in early 1937, he wore on his identification collar the simple inscription:

"ICH BIN DER HERRLICHE LUSTIG"
[I am the magnificent Lustig]

Those of us who have known and loved him for the last eight years of his life, know how much he deserved that description.

Lustig's Descendants

Lustig was no longer in Europe, but his descendants ruled over all the shows. The first to name would be his younger brother Utz vom Dom. He resembled Lustig, somewhat lighter in color, not quite as solid in his back, but tall and noble like his brother. Later, he also went to the United States and played an important role there as a sire. In Germany, he always had to fight for first place with the Sieger, Kyrras von der Blütenau, a red-fawn son of Lustig with markings like his father.

Kyrras won again and again because of his better manner and temperament. When the war broke out, Kyrras soon left Germany—as did his sister, Liesel von der Blütenau. Both went to America too.

Also, I ought to mention the powerful son of Lustig, Ernst Lustig vom Zollernhof. He was a Sieger many times over and was of the same quality as his father. Due to a leap out of a window, he broke both pasterns, but patient care led to a complete recovery. Ernst Lustig remained in Germany and passed on many qualities from his father, Lustig, to his descendants.

The big, flashy, red-fawn Lustig son, Ajax von der Holderburg, also played a prominent role, as did his litter mate, Arno von der Holderburg. Ajax was a first-rate sire. He was very important in keeping Lustig's blood alive in German Boxer breeding. Undoubtedly, his greatest son was Droll vom Taubenhänsel, a flashy golden brindle.

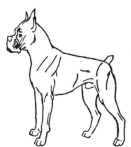

All of Lustig's immediate offspring were just a notch behind him in quality. But the grandchildren moved back up to Lustig's level. Arno von der Holderburg, sired a red-fawn son, Carlo von der Wolfsschlucht, and that Boxer ruled the fawns for years. When the war ended, eight-year-old Carlo also made the trip across the Atlantic to America [with the later Boxer handler and judge Larry Downey]. His brindle half-brother, another fine dog,

turned out to be sterile. The war, with all its side effects, had worked to his disadvantage.

There was also the North German brother-trio of Brillant, Bastel and Budden vom Elbufer. The two best of them went to America. But Brillant turned out to be sterile, and then died from either poison or a heat stroke while at a show in America. Bastel did not enjoy success in the United States. He was too massive for the American ring. Budden, who was the largest of the three, but the least attractive, stayed in Hamburg. His bloodline is very good and has survived some close inbreeding. All of the North German Boxer breeding, and the best of our present Boxers, go back to him.

Among Lustig's sons were also the two brothers, Zünftig and Volkmar vom Dom. Both were first-class dogs. Unfortunately, Zünftig was quite light in color, although long-legged and elegant. Even though he was sold when young to an Englishman, he did leave behind a few nice offspring. But he played a major role in British breeding. When the war began, Zünftig was sold at a Red Cross benefit and went to America. His owner there said of him, "For every person there is one special dog. Zünftig vom Dom was mine."

Of all Lustig's sons that could be top-ranked, only Danilo vom Königsee remained in Germany. He was a brindle, and at the shows he took over first place from Sigurd's grandson, Dorian von Marienhof. Dorian had also gone to America, where he and Utz and Lustig dominated all Boxer breeding. Danilo's sons and grandchildren survived the Second World War in Germany. Thus, all pedigrees of our present top Boxers in Germany go back to Lustig through his sons, Danilo vom Königsee, Budden vom Elbufer and Zünftig vom Dom.

Before World War II

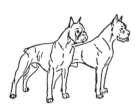

After Lustig's departure, we still had almost two more years of a quiet and bearable life. I bought my long-

The classic photo of Lustig vom Dom in a typical German Boxer stance. Lustig came to the United States in 1937

Lustig and Zorn vom Dom

desired car, built up our farm and tried to give new life to my Boxer breeding. But I could not get over the loss of Lustig. It was just too great. So I tried to buy other breeding stock, in order to start a new line.

Then there were other blows. The eight-year-old Zorn, Lustig's sire, had to be destroyed because of cancer. Even more difficult for me was the death of Zorn's mother, Dudel vom Pfarrhaus. She had two difficult operations at Munich's veterinary college, and each time I brought her home cured. But finally I had to part with her too.

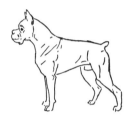

As Dudel lay dying, her little brindle granddaughter, with Dudel's dark-gold coloring and a wonderful head, lay in the kennel. She had Dudel's temperament and manner, but was almost too clinging. When I came out to the kennel, she would go right up the fence like a monkey and leap into my arms. I swore I would make her Dudel's successor when Dudel was no longer there.

Streaks Of Fire In The Sky

Now it is necessary to talk of dogs that played no significant roles in the show world. We often felt a special relationship to those animals. Perhaps because they only seemed to exist to be our darling pets. They did not have to go from show to show, trying to earn us money; their existence only required them to give us pleasure and be breeding stock. Actually, in those days just before the war, there was not much opportunity for sport and shows.

The day after my husband left on his America trip, we had a strange experience. That night our neighbors excitedly called us outside. In the sky, great flames seemed to move back and forth and white streaks shot though the red glow. It was a fantastic, never-before-seen spectacle. My farmer friends were almost in panic. Did it mean war, destruction and maybe the end of the world? I turned on the radio and listened to a report about a rare display of northern lights, visible across all Germany.

As I listened, the light decreased and this unusual brightness disappeared. A dark smoke-like bank of clouds spread across the sky, leaving us in deep darkness. Was it all not really a symbolic preview of what stood before us?

And Once More War

The sport of dogs in Germany, after the Nazi takeover, had been attached to the huge National Organization for Sports. Later, they decided it would fit in better if it were classified as a part of the small-animal breeders' category. Finally, they decided to take the Organization for German Dogs out of the Small-Animals Breeders' Organization and make it an independent group. This Organization for German Dogs was under the authority of the Army High Command.

Our dog magazines were full of official notices and regulations of all kinds. In particular, they instructed us that there would be no more large exhibitions of any kind. But little shows were permitted. Obviously, their plan was to use our dogs for military purposes. They issued a regulation that in dog breeding, at least one of the parents had to have a Schutzhund degree.

When the war began, there was an actual registration of all dogs. Those animals that passed inspection received rationing cards for their food. The ones that failed were forbidden to breed—and received no cards. During this national registration, some 32% of the Boxers passed examination—they were in second place among all breeds.

The sense of panic among dog breeders was much the same as in 1914. Many dogs were placed in other homes, but many were also just killed. Since I remembered clearly the circumstances of the First World War, I did everything I could to warn and encourage my dog friends. Sometimes those efforts were successful, but I was not able to stop breeders from sending their good—and in many cases their best—dogs to foreign countries.

After many of the first dogs that they drafted ended up being destroyed because they could not make the adjustment to military life, the army decided to approve more dogs for breeding. They ordered all suitable bitches to produce at least one litter a year. One could now keep seven or eight puppies, and the breeders were assured that the military would pay them good prices for all the eight-week-old puppies they wished to sell.

The big attraction was mainly the cherished dog's ration card. Although the rations were small, you were still able to get enough to have a basic supply of feed. When circumstances became worse, we protested. Their answer was that the food ration card was only intended to be a supplement. The dog owners would have to find their own primary food supply!

Thus began a type of bartering in the rural areas, whether we wanted it or not. People began squabbling and finding fault with each other, the farmer with the city-dweller and vice versa. In the end, we all had to suffer and adjust to the miserable conditions as well as we could.

I tried everywhere to buy leftover feed, garbage, fish and similar protein-like foods. Occasionally, the farmers would sell me stillborn calves. I was not actually allowed to take those, but I would do anything for my dogs. Their pleading eyes led me over and over to push all caution aside.

Our little farm was completely overburdened. We had five refugees from the Baltic living with us. All had to be fed somehow. But our acreage could only produce a part of our needs.

Worries About A Horse

Once again another calamity struck us. It began with the horses. I had produced two young, beautiful fillies by breeding my wheezing old mare. They were now three and four years old. Quite unexpectedly, the older one began foaling. Somehow we had not been aware of the breeding. The foal did not come out properly and died. We finally had to use force to remove it from the mare. The mother was so exhausted from the ordeal that she died two days later. So I applied for an allocation of an army horse. After much running around, I did get the permit for a horse. It was supposed to be a nice gelding, four years old.

When I took the animal out of the barn to bring him home, I was shocked. My daughter was with me, and she asked what was the matter. I could not really explain, but the horse almost seemed as though it had been revived from death. Around this dead-looking animal's eyes were swarms of flies. Something was definitely not right. I went back to the dealer. He only assured me that the horse had been properly released to him and seemed to eat very well. On the horse's hips were freshly-healed scarred areas. According to the dealer, four weeks in the meadow and the horse would be like new. If only I had followed my instincts and never brought that old nag back home!

I remained suspicious. Three veterinarians looked at the horse. Nothing! Two weeks later our pretty young filly became ill. Again, I turned to the vets. They wrinkled up their foreheads, and in three days our little mare was dead. In desperation, I wrote to my old friend, Dr. Wagner, at the stud farm in Neustadt, near the Dosse river.

He wrote back, "Your horses have an infectious anemia. The black one has a less deadly form of it, and he brought the disease to your farm. Send a notice immediately to the district veterinarian, because only then will you be eligible for compensation from the Diseased Animal Fund. Observe all precautions. The disease is very contagious and deadly!"

Once again the same district veterinarian, who had made life so difficult for us because of our dogs, came out to our farm. He was upset because he himself had not diagnosed the disease. Blood tests were taken, temperatures were taken, and afterwards the results were not

clear. I had to take the horse's temperature twice a day and watch him carefully. Then the vet went on vacation, and our horse continued to grow sicker and sicker. It stumbled back and forth in the stall and sometimes collapsed. Now I understood why there were scars on its hips. On its belly, a large open tumor began to develop. But I was forbidden to destroy the animal. I had to wait. Finally, the poor thing died, and I immediately called the animal coroner and asked for an autopsy.

Weeks later I was told that air raids had stopped the autopsy. The actual cause of the illness was never officially determined.

Under the circumstances, I never received any compensation. The district vet could have been a great help to us, but as far as he was concerned the matter was now closed. For the next two years, I was forbidden to have any horses. That was a hard blow, but we managed somehow to survive without a team of horses.

Dog Breeding During The War

Officially, dogs were declared necessary for the war effort. We even received gasoline rations because we bred dogs. Of course, there was no gas. Then the Fatherland decided it needed the battery and tires from our car. So those had to be removed, and we were paid about one-third what they were actually worth.

In the meantime, we switched our farm operation over to oxen. That had not been easy to do. One of the oxen had to be smuggled in by our daughter. A Boxer breeder in Austria helped her, and with "corrected" export papers they brought the ox to Braunau, and from there over the bridge to Simbach. It was over twenty miles farther to Reich-Schmitt, and my daughter walked the whole distance leading that ox.

Those problems on the farm always kept us worried. Whatever happened outside our actual area, we only

learned from the radio, My husband believed everything the military reported. Enthusiastically, he accepted the official line being fed to the German people. It would have been unthinkable for him to have listened to a foreign broadcast. Thus we never knew what actually was going on. I turned my whole interest to the farm, my family, and to my dogs.

We needed to get some form of transportation, so I applied for a permit to get a bicycle with a trailer. Because of the bad luck with the horses and our requisitioned tires and battery, they granted my request. There was no way to tell where that bicycle was made or by whom. In any case, it was an impossible vehicle. We called it "the deer," because it was terribly high and had handle bars that turned up like a deer's antlers. And the seat was so narrow only those who had starved could use it. Still, I breathed a sigh of relief when the bicycle became mine.

Once again I had some way to haul dog food. Twice a week I rode a fifteen-mile route to a packing plant, where I would pick up some one-hundred to one-hundred-fifty pounds of meat to feed the dogs. The trip over had some very steep sections, so those days when I did not go were like holidays to me. Even on the hottest days, or during snow storms and glare ice, I pedaled back and forth without fail.

Now my husband became more and more entangled in the confusion of political events. Those who lost their homes from bombing attacks, as well as the many refugees coming into Germany, had to be provided for and were his responsibility. Dissatisfaction and anger with him were often a part of that work. My daughter and I had to do all the needed work on the farm. Our son had been drafted into the army. Even as a boy, he had been a self-starter and a good-luck kid. We were convinced that he would survive the war. After all, he came into this world without the help of a midwife. And so—with faith in his lucky star— he came through it all. May his life continue to follow that course!

Dog Training

Despite the difficult circumstances of the times, my dogs were always a source of joy. Dog shows, of course, stopped completely. At night the enemy's planes droned on, as the cities were bombed and the raids grew more frequent and became more dangerous. Around us it was quite peaceful, but we could hear the bombs exploding in the distance and see the glow of the fires reflected in the night sky. There were now so many people at Reich-Schmitt farm that we actually had some free time for working with the dogs. That always made us happy. No matter how many dogs were in our kennel, none was going to go untrained. Dogs need a good upbringing as much as people. In the dogs' case, that meant first of all coming quickly to a call or a whistle.

Many dogs are naturals for training. Others have to be taught the basics. At the present time, there is a large body of literature to teach every trainer what is necessary. By the time the dog is four months old it should be house trained and know how to fetch and carry objects. For all of our dogs, that was just a matter of course. When about one year old, regular obedience training—the dog's college education—should begin. Everything then was based on later army service for the dog. The General Staff wanted to have fully-trained animals.

This training consisted of three parts:

1.   Tracking work.

2.   Obedience: Recall, jumping, heeling and staying.

3.   Protection work: Protecting the handler, pursuing and retaining the criminal, holding the criminal at bay while barking.

If these performance goals were reached, then the dog had passed the Schutzhund I test. Besides that test, there were also a level II and III. Each one of the examinations signified a higher level of performance. The tracking trail became longer, the number of objects to find increased, the protection work demanded more aggression and absolute obedience, the search for the criminal had to be done at full speed, the criminal had to be cornered without biting, the dog had to help in moving the prisoner— and many other things.

As a rule, my daughter and I did the training. Each of us had three or four dogs. We looked for those dogs that seemed to have the ability and temperament best suited for working with us. It was not uncommon for us to exchange dogs. Sometimes that went much better.

Every dog possesses a special character and a unique talent. That was apparent in our group of messenger dogs. A dog needed a special aptitude for that type of work. In order to train those dogs we needed two handlers. Each one of the dogs received his own courier dog's coat and a wide collar that had a message container attached to it.

One of the handlers would take the dog at least two-thirds of a mile away. The other handler remained standing in the original place during that time. After a short pause, the dog would be given the command, "Take the message!" and be sent on his way back to the other handler. If the dog really took off, it could be very funny. We waved flags to get the dog's attention if he went astray. Once back to the other handler, the message was taken and the dog immediately received several nice-tasting treats. After a ten-minute rest, the dog was sent back to the other handler. Later we would move the courier training to a hilly area. We also trained the dog to run through farm yards where poultry were present, and on the return trip some shots would be fired. None of that could bother the canine messenger. It was a job that had all kinds of challenges!

Many dogs ran with great enthusiasm. Others hated the training. At the time, I had a beautiful fawn bitch, Petra vom Dom. She loved to run, but trouble began if she came across a pair of farmer's wooden shoes someone had placed on the edge of the field while he was working. She

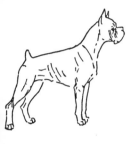

would pick up one and carry it the whole distance. Petra was really a rare animal. She was excellent in Schutzhund work, but she hated to be drilled in it. If you worked with her right before the test, she was excellent. But go to a second practice and she would begin to lag. By the third practice we were lucky if she did anything.

During that time, they changed the rules of the test. Many of the army dogs were being used to fight against partisans, and the army soon realized that fleeing partisans often threw mines and hand grenades behind themselves. If dogs were chasing them, then sometimes the animals swerved away to go after what had been thrown, snapping at it and even picking it up. If the explosive went off in the dog's muzzle, the dog was literally blown to bits. To avoid that, another exercise was added to our training program: the fleeing suspect would throw objects behind himself, and the dogs were forbidden to pay any attention to them.

We had a young Polish prisoner of war living with us, and he was excellent with animals. He played the villain in our training, and I have never had a better Schutzhund helper since him. After we told him what the new exercise entailed, we began the training. We put four or five dogs through it, each chasing him while he threw things behind that we had agreed upon. Once it was a pair of pliers, then his pipe, a piece of wood and other things like that. Every dog stayed the course and never was distracted by the object. They only saw him and not what he threw.

At the very end of the practice, we brought out Petra. She was eager and grabbed the helper right away. After she was commanded to release him, he then fled. Just then he realized he had no objects left to throw, so he jerked off his hat and threw it away! It was amazingly successful. Petra froze like a block of ice, astonished. She looked at the hat and then at the man. Astonishment was so apparent in her face that we almost collapsed from laughter. Petra's face seemed to say, "That's something I've never seen before. He took off his head, threw it

Wartime training on the Stockmann farm for the "man-work" part of Schutzhund training

Training for the tracking part of Schutzhund training

away and kept running!" It was just too much for her canine brain!

Our Lustig son, Zünftig vom Dom, was different from Petra. He hated courier training and only participated when forced. Then he would not run but simply walked at the slowest possible tempo. Before he would allow himself to be commanded to go, he could not resist sniffing around and lifting his leg a few times. That was his way of saying, "You can all kiss my. . . ."

One time he delivered the message to my daughter, the intended target. He was supposed to be sent back with a return message. Nearby, there were some curious children watching from a small farm yard. Zünftig was given the command to return the message. He started as usual by checking out the area and finally found what he wanted: the corner of a fence. But this time he was not as successful in doing his usual business. As soon as he lifted one leg the whole yard full of children roared with laughter. Zünftig glanced around and you could see that he was ashamed of himself. He took off running and finished his courier job quicker than ever before. Of course, his later journeys were never too fast, but at least he never lifted his leg again while on duty.

Our best worker was my daughter's dog, Quantum vom Dom, who was called "Hunks" [Gimpy]. The nickname came from the fact that she limped. As an adolescent, she somehow broke a bone in one pastern while in the kennel run. The break healed quickly, but all her life she had a slight limp. Yet she was an excellent jumper! A three-foot vertical jump or a leap over a six-foot fence were nothing for her. And for a Boxer, she was almost unmatched in tracking, just as she was an absolutely fearless Schutzhund dog. She earned a Schutzhund III title, a unique accomplishment in those days for a bitch.

Another excellent worker was the fawn Anka von Hoffbauer. The history of this dog was like a novel. On occasion I have written about her, and it would be too much to tell the whole story here. Anka was close to Hunks in what she achieved. She earned the Schutzhund

II title. But when all was said and done she lacked that indestructible temperament that allowed Hunks to excel in every tracking event, scramble over the highest climbing wall, and playfully leap over a ten-foot span.

Anka's real talent was in another area. She could not stand heat very well, but 10 degrees above (Fahrenheit) and deep snow drifts were her pleasure. And she too was an excellent tracker that excited every judge who ever saw her work. Yet, it was not a passion with her. She knew she would get a treat for every one of the hidden objects that she found. The reward was the only reason for working.

Dogs were not allowed to pick up the object when found. They had to point it out while lying, sitting or standing next to it. Anka always sat down next to the treasure, which looked so nice after her confident and precise search work. But if she had to search too long, she would start to cheat. Sometimes she just sat down for a little rest.

Above all, Anka was an excellent brood bitch. She went with me on my trips for dog food for fourteen years. Whether it rained or snowed meant nothing to her. Two times a week she trotted over thirty miles beside my cart, my only constant companion over all the side roads that I often had to use to avoid bombing raids and strafing attacks.

During winter I usually made the trip in the dark. Anka was always with me. Quiet and modest, she never left my side. At home you hardly noticed her presence. And even with all of that, she gave me a litter a year of strong, healthy puppies at a time when there was an unexplainably high death rate for puppies. High enough to take the joy out of breeding, even out of life. But Anka's puppies stayed healthy. When this loyal dog reached the advanced age of fourteen years and passed away—she just lay dead in her bed one morning—she had died as she lived: quiet and unassuming, without ever causing trouble or anger.

Unfortunately, Hunks died very young of heart problems. Only two of her children survived her. Of those, one male became a first-rate worker like his mother. He died from a bombing attack while he was protecting a damaged house from being looted. Hunk's other survivor was a daughter. Because of her, many Boxer grandchildren and great-grandchildren now live in England. My hope is that someday it may be possible for me to bring a trace of her bloodline back to Germany.

Besides Hunks and Anka, Rolle Firn vom Dom also played an important role. She was an elegant brindle animal, who I once thought would replace my Dudel. We called her Finni. Finni was a precious personality. Everyone who ever saw her, admired and loved her. In her own way, she had many charms. When visitors came she hopped upon the window ledge and eagerly began to clean the glass.

She was quite meticulous, starting in one corner of the window and ending in the other. Naturally, we were not too pleased with this passion of hers. Her tongue left streaks all over the glass. But that never bothered her. Of course, every stranger was greatly amused when she did that. And once when I tried to stop her a visitor calmly remarked, "How could anyone want to disturb a dog doing such a useful job!"

Finni was not very brave. Like her mother, she could not stand gunfire. But she had such unshakable faith in me, that she would overcome that fear and many times make as good an impression as the fearless Anka.

Since we had to train all of our dogs in those days, Finni had to take her turn. For a helper, we had a young girl, who had already handled one dog for us. But the dog had not been a good worker for her, so I placed him in a civilian home. For a substitute, I let the little girl go through our kennel and pick out another dog to train. She chose Finni. We were all agreeable to that—except Finni.

It was just amazing to see all the ways that bitch could find to offer her young trainer passive resistance. She always kept one eye on me —and then did exactly what she wished. The result was that I finally took over. When she started using the same trick with me, I gave her a good hard slap on her muzzle. It was the one and only slap she ever received from me. After that, everything went perfectly. She did her exercises with passion, and I never had another dog easier to train than she was.

Shooting over Finni was a project in itself. We realized it would be a difficult for her to handle. But the examination soon came, and gunfire was a part of the qualifying exam. She took it well. Our biggest worry after that was how she would do when the gunfire came during the retrieve over a hurdle. The handler would command the dog to heel and then throw a light object over the hurdle. Then he commanded the dog to fetch, and the dog would leap over the hurdle, pick up the object and return over the hurdle. It was while the dog was making the return jump that the shot was fired. Gun-shy dogs would usually drop the object, return without it or— if really frightened—just take off for the wild blue yonder.

Everyone was worried about Finni. One woman gave her a handful of tranquilizers. Another woman offered to stand way off to the side and point the pistol in the opposite direction when she fired it. Above all, they wanted to be sure that Finni had the object in her mouth and was already making the leap when the shot was fired. In that way they were sure it would go all right, Finni would pass, come back to me all proud and confident, convinced that she had completed all the tasks. But of course it didn't go that way.

The object flew over the hurdle, with Finni soon following. Then nothing happened. Far to the rear, the judge and another assistant plus the shooter just stood and looked. Why didn't she fire? Because Finni made no motion to pick up the object. And Finni never picked it up because she knew they would shoot then. She looked at the testers, and I could just imagine how she was shaking her head over their inability to comprehend what she was doing. In the meantime, the shooter complained because the shot did not go off. But that wasn't Finni's problem.

She jumped over the hurdle—without the object—and set herself down next to me, quite satisfied. The shot finally echoed around, much too late and unheard by most. Finni lost some points, of course, but no one seemed to realize she was just waiting for the shot that she knew was coming.

In the last exercise Finni had to do her "man work": protect me and seize the enemy when he neared. That went excellently. Then came the flight, when she had to pursue and seize the enemy. And there was also shooting with that. A head start was given the enemy, and then I released Finni. She really took off. Then came the first shot. It appeared as though she did not slow down, but she did not gain on him either. At that point the judge made a mistake. He believed the enemy was running so fast the dog could not catch him. I certainly knew that was wrong, because a dog can always outrun a man. Finni simply wanted to stay out of harm's way as long as those loud noises were going on. Only when I began to run in the direction of the enemy, apparently to catch him, did Finni run up and grab him. Thus she earned her Schutzhund title, a ration card, and saved her reputation. But the new title had other consequences.

They called up the dogs that passed for a state testing.. We had five dogs for inspection: Anka—who still had five-week-old puppies, Hunks, Finni, and Mirzel von Pfarrkirchen, a big light-fawn bitch that I had nursed back to health from a serious illness. She was very aggressive, but not of much value for breeding. Still, she was a very pretty Boxer. Besides those there was Heiner von Zwergeck, my later Zonal [postwar Western occupation zones] Sieger. He was the noblest and best bred by modern standards—an image of his distant ancestor, Rolf von Vogelsberg. Heiner was a strong sire. He was mine from before his birth, but a dog broker, one of the most evil figures of the time, almost swindled him from me. There was a long battle, which I eventually won. With great effort I took the run-down dog, raised him up and led

him to the titles of Vienna Sieger and Zonal Sieger. The Boxer Club also restored his certificate for breeding.

Heiner was a grandson of Lustig's sons, Sieger Danilo von Koenigsee and Volkmar vom Dom. You can see that through all generations I have remained true to my blood line.

The state examination was conducted in different ways. Usually we worked with the padded sleeve, the whip, some shots and some explosives.

Mirzel went first. She passed and received her breeding authorization. Anka was spared because of her puppies. Hunks never was in question because of her limp. Right from the beginning, Finni was too small and delicate, but she never faltered under gunfire. We felt proud of the results, because our dogs were the best attackers of all. All kind of dogs were at the examination, and the old superstition that mixed breeds are the best workers was basically disproven.

We returned home satisfied with our pack, and forgot about the whole call-up as our daily worries continued. Then one day—like a bolt of lightning from a clear blue sky—we received a summons. Within the next three days, Finni was to be delivered to the canine staff headquarters in Munich. It made me sick. Finni, with her charm and humor and her little rabbit heart? I knew she was not the kind of dog they could use. Ever since Lustig went to America and I had to put Dudel out of her misery, Finni was my dearest dog. No! I would not give Finni to them, even if they locked me up in a concentration camp.

But I had to take a dog to them, although giving up any of them would be painful. So the choice fell on Mirzel von Pfarrkirchen. She was best suited to the job. Besides that, she had a strong preference for men, a man's dog. She always had doubts about women.

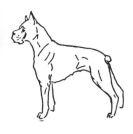

My daughter took over the difficult delivery. The military officials greeted her in a friendly way. Mirzel made an immediate hit with the soldiers, and walked away with them without even a backward glance. We felt bad about it, but it was the only way to save Finni. Such an atmosphere would have destroyed her.

My daughter asked them if we would ever hear about our dog again. The sergeant-major was friendly and promised to write us; my daughter left our address, but we knew such hopes were wishful thinking. Dogs that went into the military in World War II were never seen again by their owners. Between them and their former civilian life there was an iron curtain. It was different in the beginning. Short communications went back and forth between owner and handler. But this bit of trust was not rational, and under certain circumstances could develop into something unpleasant. The common good must come before personal feelings. That was their view.

Germany Collapses

Time passed. Two times weekly I hauled dog food, and from the constant overexertion I developed a painful and persistent arthritis in my knees. Once again, I had to apply for a horse. They promised me I could buy one as soon as a transport returned from the field. We searched for a long time to find a suitable animal, and finally we were lucky. We received a little mare. She was too light for farm work, but she served me well in hauling dog food.

Just to be able to see a pretty horse's head in the barn was a joy at any time, especially since the clouds of fate became darker and darker. Many times I had to dash into some farmer's yard or a building to escape the strafing fighter planes.

One day our first refugee arrived. Until then we had

been spared from providing quarters for refugees because of our dogs. More came shortly thereafter. Soon we had eight people in the house—all dog lovers who had much in common with us.

In the village, conditions required my husband to take over the duties of civil defense commander. It was a great sacrifice for him, as he already carried the beginning of a fatal disease.

Conditions began to deteriorate. Numerous times the flights of enemy bombers and fighter planes passed over our farm. There was no place to hide or go for protection in the countryside. At night the only thing we could do was pull the covers over our heads. The dogs' reactions to air raid alarms and attacks were interesting. Unless the dog were gun shy, it reacted exactly the same as its owner. Either it ran more or less rapidly to the shelter, or it just stretched out, lying around oblivious to it all. Those dogs that experienced many warnings knew immediately how their owners would react to the sounds of the planes' motors. Like most dogs, they had sensitive ears for engines. I knew one dog that had no interest at all in the sound of a motorcycle, but he could always recognize mine and barked at me because he hated my dogs.

For the most part, our Boxers stayed calm during the air raid warnings—with the exception of one young bitch. She wouldn't harm a feather on a bird's head, was always easy going, a fearless daughter of Anka. Yet when that first siren went off she went into a rage, attacked the geese and left a horrible blood bath behind. We did not notice what had happened until after the alarm had stopped. Of course, she was strongly reprimanded, and after that she became as calm and nice as before.

But our hopes proved wrong. With the next alarm, we saw her grab a goose by the neck. The poor bird thrashed around, and was unconscious by the time we rescued it. When the warning sounded again—and between alarms she had been quite normal—she leaped up onto the hayloft in the pig shed and stayed there shaking all the time. We watched her carefully. Obviously she was a

quivering bundle of nerves. Her wild eyes were almost popping out of her skull.

Then she saw a goose some ways off. Away she went. Only with a struggle were we able to get the bird away from her. Again, when the alarm stopped she became her normal self. We have never found a good explanation for her behavior. Perhaps it was fear that obsessed her with self preservation and self defense and created a senseless rage. Be that as it may, the other dogs never displayed any unusual excitement.

Every day we had four or five, sometimes more, air raid alarms. But I still had to get dog food if we were going to keep things going. Several times my life was in great danger. My number just wasn't up yet. Over and over my concern for the living creatures I was responsible for allowed me to overcome the difficulties. And my family was also confident I would never abandon them or the dogs.

Was This The End Of Everything?

At no time in my life had the future ever seemed so totally hopeless as then. I would have had little worry if I had been alone, but there were other people around me and my dogs. My greatest worry was for my husband. Yet he never showed pain and would grow angry if we became down-hearted and hung our heads. From all sides, foreign soldiers now began to appear. We watched them with great concern. Who would be coming as our conquerors—Americans or Russians?

That week my thoughts went again and again to my dogs. I felt strongly that I could save all of my four-legged friends if we could survive for just a few weeks more.

Meanwhile the German authorities were telling us to set aside a reserve of supplies. I had stored up several hundred pounds of flour, along with corn and barley. But I needed food for the dogs! To get that I had to cross bridges that had already been mined. Alarms warning of the approaching enemy now sounded everywhere. But we still reached our goal, picked up five-hundred pounds of dried meat and managed to get back home. I knew then I could take care of the dogs for another two months.

We heard artillery day and night. The first American units came to us from the direction of Passau. Tanks and heavy artillery moved up the steep hillside. When I saw the wild-looking soldiers with their loaded weapons, somehow the tragedy of the moment escaped me. It was a fantastic sight, and I deeply regretted that I had hidden my cameras in the dogs' kennel.

The wire fence around our property had been like a wall against the hostile outside world. Behind that fence sat my six adult Boxers. They seemed interested in what was happening, but with a rather calm superiority. No one ever tried to enter our compound without permission. When a squad of soldiers, commanded by a Pole, arrived to search our grounds, they were quite visibly nervous. The pistols in their hands shook, as six black Boxer noses inspected them. Our Ukrainian refugee warned that the dogs had been trained to attack anyone who fired a weapon and would rip apart anyone who injured us. The Pole seemed very uncomfortable. He was so impressed by the dogs that he never even noticed the bottle of schnapps on the table nor the usual nationalistic pictures that almost all homes had on the walls. In the excitement we had forgotten to put those things away. One of the Americans, however, took an interest in the dogs and told us that Boxers were the most popular dogs in America.

So Boxers became the means for the first understanding between us and the foreign soldiers. It was interesting how the different nationalities seemed to react to dogs. We never had much contact with the French and British, but they were very reserved toward the animals. Our contact with Americans came easily and quickly. During the whole occupation time, we never had any reason to complain about the American soldiers. Our dogs quickly

became acquainted with the foreigners and were friendly to them. It was different with those soldiers from the eastern countries. The Russians seemed to fear Boxers worse than the plague.

One day, five Russian soldiers came to the farm and demanded food and drink. At that time we never denied anyone bread if we had it. Although our supplies had run out and we had to purchase our bread, I still cut slices from the loaf and gave it to them. The leader then demanded more. I pointed out that there were eight people in the house, and we had to live too. But he still made his demand. His rudeness upset me. On the spur of the moment, I said to him I would show him just how much more bread he could have! I opened the door to the kitchen, where my Boxers were waiting and shouted, "Watch out! Go get them!"

Out they came! The Russians realized what was happening and ran off as fast as possible. I watched them for a long time, as they crossed over the hill and up another. Not a one turned around. The dogs had not followed them. They were peacefully sitting in the house again.

Good-bye Forever

One day I had a terrible fright. An elegant car drove up and an American climbed out. He asked if I were Frau Stockmann. When I replied yes, he told me he had some bad news to deliver. Horrified, I stared at him. Only one thought was in my mind: it's about my husband! But the American then informed me that Champion Utz vom Dom had died. I could only think "Thank God!"

Utz had been sold as a puppy and later he ended up in America. I was never aware that he had been as important to American Boxers as Lustig.

Soon I received a request from America to write an article about the condition of German Boxer breeding in 1945. I was happy to do that.

Sigurd—who had gone to America—only had one son remaining in Germany, World Sieger Fachinger von Neu-Drosedow. He had nice offspring, but no Siegers among them. The brindle grandson of Sigurd, Dorian von Marienhof, left no descendants in Germany. But in America, Dorian ranked even with Lustig. He and Lustig, along with Lustig's younger brother Utz vom Dom, are to be found in all pedigrees of today's American Boxers.

The brindle Sieger, Danilo vom Koenigsee remained in Germany. His sons were Sieger Brutus von der Hochburg and the Zonal [Western occupation zones] Sieger Axel von Gruenwaldpark and Arno von Grafensprung—whose son Heiner von Zwergeck became the Vienna Sieger and a Zonal Sieger. Heiner, after some unpleasant detours, eventually became mine. Not only was he good looking and good natured, he was a very prepotent sire. You can still see his noble and handsome head among his descendants. Heiner was the modern Boxer that most reminded me of Rolf von Vogelsberg. Although the Americans offered me $2,000 for him, he remained with me. Instead of him, I was able to arrange for Sieger Carlo von der Wolfsschlucht to go to the USA.

In May, 1945, a wave of arrests by the occupation authorities swept over Germany. My husband was one of those arrested. None of the local population had made any charges against him. Even when my son returned from his prisoner-of-war captivity in August, 1945, we were still unable to learn where my husband was being held.

Finally, I was told that my husband was well and I ought not to fear that our farm would be seized. At least the existence of my dogs was assured.

But my hardships were not over. I had great difficulties with the puppies. Only a few survived; despite my efforts, most of them died. In addition, my daughter became ill with a heart disease. For many years she had been my best comrade and helper. The doctors seemed puzzled, and there was no medicine anywhere. Finally, I succeeded in trading a young Boxer for six weeks of treatment and rest for my daughter under the supervision of a doctor in Chiemsee. And that returned her to good health. Once again, a great benefit came to our lives because of my dogs.

In September, after four months in an internment camp, my husband unexpectedly returned home. He was very thin. The internment had been bad. Would the sun never shine again? My dogs seemed to think it would. They presented me with three nice litters, and most of the puppies lived. But the joy did not last long. Five weeks later my husband was again taken, as another wave of arrests swept the country. All I could arrange was that my daughter would be able to drive her sick father to the camp.

This time it was farewell forever. Nine months later he died from an operation in the prison camp's hospital. We had been somewhat consoled by the fact that we knew where he was, that we could send him food and other things that he needed, and that we were able to keep informed about his condition.

At the time, Finni vom Dom was the darling of our home. Three days after my husband died, I realized that something was not right with her. I found her lying listlessly in her bed. Apparently, it was a heart problem. Finni had already caused us worry twice before because of that. What could I do? No veterinarians were available. All I could do was make her a nice comfortable bed and lay her upon it.

She soon fell asleep, even snoring loudly. But by the end of the day Finni was dead. We were all so sad. Then someone remembered Finni had always been the favorite of Philipp Stockmann. Perhaps he had now called her to his side. Who knows what lies behind that black curtain? When we buried Finni, it almost seemed as though we were having a funeral for a human being. There might have been a deeper meaning to that: not a one of us knew where or when our husband and father had been buried.

Several weeks later we received his personal items,

Philipp Stockmann at the 1934 show in Frankfurt

Mrs. Stockmann's granddaughter is introduced to the other residents

those that he had taken to the prison camp. Among them were several copies of *Boxer Blätter*. Under the lapel of his coat we found a Pin of Honor from the National German Dog Association, as well as one from the German Boxer Club. Until his last breath, he had remained tied to his dogs and the sport of dogs.

The First Postwar Years

Once the Americans arrived it became quiet. No more planes, no alarms, no more thunder from the cannons. But the country looked destroyed. Meadows and fields had been churned up by tanks and artillery trucks. Most of the harvest seemed destroyed, and livestock had often been driven out of the barns. Wildlife in the forests had been killed off. One day I had a terrible fright. Up the hill, I could see what looked like a dead Boxer hanging on the fence. I almost didn't have the courage to go up there, but I did so with a heavy heart. When I reached the fence, however, I realized it was not a Boxer but instead a freshly shot deer.

Beside the roads, we now saw piles of bicycles that had collided with tanks. Heaps of cars, motorcycles, typewriters, radios were piled up in gravel pits. It looked like the end of the world.

But you cannot defeat Mother Nature. And spring did come again! When I ventured out with my horse, I was hardly able to comprehend how the grass and flowers that came out every year now seemed to sprout eagerly in the ripped up meadows. It almost seemed as though the farmers were ashamed that they had given up, but the soil had not. With shovels and plows, they closed even the deepest wounds in the meadows and fields, which soon healed and were forgotten. Our requisitioned livestock and food required compensation, but what good was paper money to us? Most of that ended up with grass growing over it too.

Gradually, the rubble began to disappear or was reused for new construction. And gradually we began to see possibilities for a future. In May, I had bred my beautiful brindle Berchta. My husband was still home then and did not expect much from the breeding. But I called upon my sixth sense, and it told me now was the right time! And my decision proved right.

Many occupation soldiers came to our place and asked to buy a Boxer puppy. I could hardly meet the demand. Often they were young men who were homesick. They would tell me they had no one to talk with except the dogs. For hours they sat in the kennel and played with the animals. The war seemed forgotten!

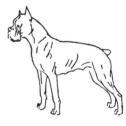

There were also officers who came and wanted nice dogs for breeding and showing. Most of them were friendly and brought groceries or other useful items. It was just amazing what we could get for a dog. I gave a brindle bitch to a young refugee I had taken in and who had worked very hard with us. This young bitch became a beautiful animal. The young man then gave the dog to an American soldier, who had in turn helped bring the refugee's parents out of Upper Silesia and even found an apartment for them, which was supposed to be impossible then.

But the bitch did not work out for the American. She failed as a breeder and seemed only happy when in my kennel. She jumped over a nine-foot fence in Berchtesgaden and tried to flee to us. After three days, they caught her in a village just north of us, and took her back. Later, when the American married a German girl and returned to the US, I ended up taking back Berchta. She stayed with me then to the end of her life.

For my son, I managed to trade dogs for an anvil and a lathe. From that he rigged up a temporary forge. He took the motor from a vacuum cleaner to make the bellows.

But in my kennel my bad luck with the puppies seemed to continue. The only way I kept any breeding program

alive was through the pick-of-the-litters from Heiner's stud service. They actually saved us during those difficult times.

And then there was Anka von Hofbauer. I had even bred her grandmother. For two years, the grandmother's whereabouts were unknown, after escaping from her owner. Then she was bred to one of my dogs. From that litter came Sanni, Anka's mother. An unfortunate dog, Sanni was passed from hand to hand, always exploited, mishandled, starved, and repeatedly offered for sale. Her last owner received a good hard piece of my mind when he asked about breeding her. But he was more stubborn than I, so eventually we made an agreement.

I allowed her to be bred in exchange for a puppy and a promise never again to put her in another home, even if the only other choice were to shoot her. My good intentions had their effect. Sanni never had to leave her home again, nor was she killed. She lived for many more years as the darling of the house, and her daughter Anka became my constant companion on long and dangerous journeys for almost fourteen years. Anka became the foundation of my present Boxers. Her place in the pedigrees of our Boxers will never disappear.

Only once did Anka cause me worry, and that was not really her fault. It happened during the currency exchange in 1948. Our worthless Hitler currency was replaced by the new D-mark, and every person in Germany received seventy-five of the new marks in cash as a start. For 95% of the Germans, that was the only money they had. As we often say, "In 1948, we all started out even." At the time, Anka was in season.

Without a second thought, I gave up my seventy-five mark payment, as well as my daughter's. We used the money to pay for Sieger Harry von der Storchenburg's stud fee. It was a great sacrifice for a risky proposition. It was our only money. But when has there been a sacrifice too great for my dogs?

Three days after the breeding, two of my other bitches

American professional handler and later dog judge, Larry Downey, returned from WWII with three Boxers from the Stockmann kennel: (l. to r.) Zack vom Dom, Sonni vom Dom, and Carlo von der Wolfsschlucht

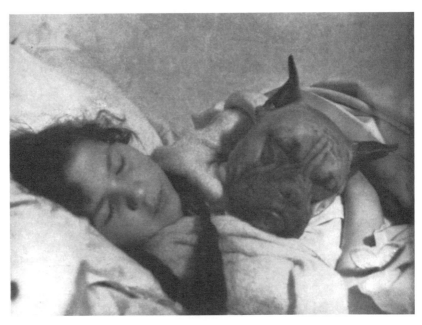

A favorite place for any Boxer

jumped her at night, bit into her rear legs—where she could not defend herself—and ripped her so badly her survival was in doubt. But Anka's strong constitution and my tender care saved her. Nine weeks later she was back to normal. She could both walk and jump. Even while she was ill, I still took her along. We would carry her to the wagon and lay her on a soft bed. Otherwise her heart would have broken.

Anka was the only bitch whose puppies survived, while all of the others perished. She gave me ten litters; she was always calm and modest. Never did she push the others aside at the food bowl. When they finished, she would walk up and calmly fill her stomach. The best chunks were gone by then, but she didn't care about that. Through it all, she remained in excellent physical condition. Her daughter Sybill, who resembled her mother very much, and both of her granddaughters, Fargott and Berchta, were the iron of my war-weary kennel.

To America As A Boxer Judge

Four years had passed since the war ended. Many things changed, and it looked as though life might once again follow a predictable path.

One day I had a visit from an American lady. It was Mrs. Shouse from Washington D.C. The visit was not an every day occurrence. She was polite and nice, but we had difficulty understanding each other. When she left, I assumed I had offended her. She had wished to buy a puppy—to take back in the airplane—and also one of my Boxer carvings. I sold her neither. The weather was miserable. Rain came down in streams, and I never had a chance to parade the dogs properly for her. For those reasons I had a bad feeling when the lady left.

Thus I was very surprised when shortly thereafter I received a friendly letter and some coffee from her. She asked me if I would be willing to accept a judging assignment at the Potomac Boxer Club's show—one of the country's largest Boxer shows. She was the president of the club. Besides that, she apologized deeply for offering me ten marks for my carving. German currency was not familiar to her, and she had thought that ten marks were equal to one hundred dollars.

Of course I accepted. But my innermost feeling was that the whole plan to have me judge in the USA was a fantasy of my beautiful visitor's mind. I had no idea that her husband was among the most influential of American diplomats.

Shortly thereafter, I received concrete instructions on everything that had to be done to get a passport and visa. Back and forth, from one authority to another I went, until it seemed as though it would never end. Finally, just as I was ready to write a withdrawal from the assignment because I did not know any American to ask for a reference—I learned that Mr. Shouse had already given the American authorities such a document. Thus it happened! At a time when almost no private German citizens could have done it, I flew to a new and unknown world.

The trip was no easy thing. My knowledge of English was close to nothing. Someone pressed a check for twenty dollars into my hand, but I had no idea where to cash it or how to find out. All through the trip I tried to concentrate on thinking about the Boxers I would be judging. Secretly, I kept asking myself what I would do with the dogs if none impressed me!

The flight was a great experience for me. For years I had lived withdrawn into the cave of my worries.

After I took my comfortable seat, the doors closed and the motors started. Suddenly a strange feeling swept over me: A part of my life was now ending and this was a new beginning. As the machine began to move slowly, and the motors began to thunder, there was a moment of nervousness. Then with great acceleration we rose from the ground. Since then I have flown many times, but it is always an exciting moment when I realize, "We're flying!"

We made several landings before we reached London in the early evening. I transferred into a larger plane for the fourteen-hour flight over the Atlantic. Now I was on my own. The only other German on the original flight—an elderly lady—never transferred. All of the running around the last few days had made me tired, so I fell asleep. Once, when the plane hit a rough spot, I awoke. But everything was fine and I went back to sleep. It seemed as though the night would never end. Later I learned that flying west extended the hours until sunrise.

Finally we landed in New York. The customs officials certainly did not make a good impression on me. They seemed so suspicious and kept asking me questions that I could not understand. After examining my identification papers and taking pictures of me from all sides, they put me in another plane for the flight to Washington DC. I wanted to see something of America, but we flew so high that the ground was hidden under clouds. After about four hours, we arrived. Our plane followed a large river, circled over a sea of houses, crossed a wide arm of the river and finally came to earth.

The American Boxer club where I would be judging was named after the Potomac river. We landed beside the river. There was a stiff breeze to greet us. On the bank of the river were flying the flags of all nations—except Germany!

Usually when I arrive somewhere to judge, there is a grand reception. I was looking forward to that in America, because Americans are well-known for their hospitality and celebrations. But not a soul was in sight. Now what? I knew no English, had a check but no cash. In contrast to New York, these airport halls were bright and friendly, large and clean. It was so exasperating! I lost my temper and swore loudly in good Bavarian dialect. And it worked! A friendly young man came up to me and asked in German if he could be of assistance.

With his help, I soon got straightened out. A taxi took me to Mr. Shouse, a very distinguished older gentleman and American diplomat who had formerly served in Austria. He spoke flawless German and introduced himself. I had finally reached the first station of my America trip!

Then something happened that I never would have expected in the dog world. A swarm of reporters and press photographers fell upon me. These people had been expecting me at the airport some five hours before we landed. I had no idea there was a flight delay. All sense of time had been lost.

The wide streets of Washington were full of cars. Luxury automobiles such as we hardly knew! Every fourth person in Washington owned a car. I noticed immediately that the American women loved bright colors. The African-American ladies had wonderful taste in clothes.

There were very few dogs around, even though Washington had large beautiful green areas. But where would a dog live in those gigantic stone structures with their countless floors? And the narrow sidewalks next to the busy streets—hardly a place for dogs.

This question was answered for me the next day. Mrs. Shouse invited me to visit their farm, Wolf Trap. It was a refreshing trip. How glorious it was to drive through the American countryside in that elegant car! All cares and worries just floated away. Two days earlier I had been in Germany. It was mid-April and the weather at home was still nasty. Our meadows and fields had hardly started to green. But in Virginia the green grass was already up, trees bloomed and Wolf Trap was wonderful! I certainly had no objections to remaining here for three days, while I acclimated myself and prepared for my judging assignment.

Now I saw my first Boxer in America. Mrs. Shouse had a very nice brindle bitch. We took her along that afternoon when we went to a television station, where I was interviewed. Then over to the Voice of America, where we recorded an interview for broadcasting to Germany. It was a relief to get back to Wolf Trap. I was exhausted, and it seemed as though this were all a dream.

The next day neighbors and visitors—some from over six hundred miles away—came to meet the foreign celebrity. Almost none spoke German, which made it difficult for me. The dreamlike state that I was in seemed to be deepening, and as I lay in bed that night it suddenly became clear that I was sick. It was a most difficult situation. Should I withdraw? I really did not wish to do that. Then I felt a pain in my arm, and I knew what was wrong. Before I left I had to have a smallpox vaccination to meet American customs regulations. I was having a reaction to that vaccination. An American doctor helped me, and everything quickly cleared up.

Mrs. Shouse gave me a beautiful, formal black gown. I was taken to a hair dresser. And Mr. Shouse presented me with a glorious corsage. With all that attention, even a corpse would have looked good. Then I was taken to the arena. Despite my hostess' urging, I declined the typical paint job most American women put on their faces. Even when somebody told me going without make-up would be as offensive as going naked in public—I held my ground.

An American Boxer Show

The entry for the Potomac Boxer Club's specialty was 140, of which 70 dogs were assigned to me. I was also to judge the best of breed competition, selecting the very best dog and bitch.

That was a big job! All dogs were unknown to me, and every dog had to be gaited and its mouth examined. In Germany the dog stands free while leashed. And the dogs are trained early to pose themselves that way. That means they are to stand calmly in the most favorable position for judging. The whole dog must be lively and alert. The neck must be nicely arched, the head held high and the ears upright. Legs should be in line with each other, with tight toes and closed paws. The elbows must be in. The whole back should be strong and straight, with a rise at the withers. In the back quarters, the dog should be somewhat stretched out and showing its rear angulation. The tail should be carried upright.

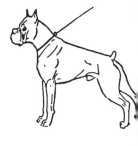

Some dogs have that born in them, and others can never learn it. To be able to show their dogs that way, our owners use almost any means, and sometimes that leads to abuses.

In contrast to our shows, which are almost always outdoors, most of the judging in England and America is done inside closed buildings. Barking in the ring can have a very bad effect, and dog fighting is strictly forbidden. Because the dogs must still be presented, the Americans and British use other methods to help the judging. While still puppies, the dogs are trained to "stack." The head is held up high by the collar, back and legs are put into position by the handler, and the dog must remain in that pose. Lastly, the tail is lifted high and held there by the handler's finger.

Those who are familiar with this type of showing are tempted to point out its advantages over our system. Certainly, a skilled handler is able to show the best sides of the dog and display characteristics to the judge that would otherwise be impossible.

My Best of Breed choice was a red-fawn dog named Master Tutt. He belonged to a charming elderly couple. Both sat hidden in the bleachers surrounding the ring and cried like two children when their dog won. For Best of Opposite Sex I chose a brindle bitch named Hot Toddy. Both Boxers were unknown to me. Americans judges are stricter in making these selections than we are.

Hot Toddy belonged to the Wagner family. They were old friends of my husband, and had invited me to visit them for a few weeks after my judging duty. Thanks primarily to them, I was able to see much of America and its Boxer breeding. I spent some unforgettable wonderful days with them.

Mazelaine kennels—then located in Milwaukee,

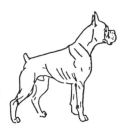

Wisconsin, near Lake Michigan—the most famous Boxer kennel in the USA, belongs to the Wagners. Its line rests on the great pioneers of my breeding: Sigurd and his grandsons, Dorian vom Marienhof and Utz vom Dom. The Wagners had already bred many champions. It is much easier to get a title in the USA than in Germany, because they have so many more shows. Points are awarded to the winning dog and bitch, ranging from one to five points according to the number of competing animals. When the dog gets fifteen points it becomes a champion.

In contrast, we can only get a Sieger title at the annual National Sieger show. Whether one can compete at that show depends largely on one's financial abilities. It costs money.

I was pleased to see how the general population in American seemed to enjoy dog shows much more than in Germany. The greatest all-breed show in America is that of the Westminster Kennel Club in New York. For its value to the sport of dogs, I would say it compares to our national Sieger show.

While I was there I saw a large picture of a brindle Boxer hanging in many stores. It was Zazarack Brandy of Mazelaine, winner of the Westminster show. This animal was the star of my friends' kennel. Over sixty times he had won Best in Show. To win that, a dog has to be exhibited several times at one show. First, it must win Best of Breed. After that the breed winner competes against the other dogs in their group. Just as with us, there are groups for hunting dogs, working dogs, toy dogs, racing dogs, and so on. One dog from each group is then selected Best in Group. Finally, the group winners compete against each other for Best in Show.

As we traveled across America, Mazie Wagner told me she had not seen her dogs for weeks. She did not even know if this or that dog were at home or on the road being shown. The handlers take care of that. In America, handlers—which we call *Führer*—are responsible for the dog's show life and earn quite well doing it. One handler would usually carry dogs for several kennels. It is the handler's responsibility to decide which dogs will be shown where. Of course, no handler would show dogs of the same breed for more than one kennel. That would mean he was competing against himself. Every Best in Show victory—such as those with Zazarack Brandy—earned the handler about $500. He not only kept the cash awards but also received a gratuity from the dog's owner. It is not rare for a dog to be with a handler on the road for several months at a time.

Usually the handler has a regular beauty shop along, which is used to bring the dog to its utmost beauty. Up to that time, I had never seen a dog in Germany so well groomed as was typical in America. My husband had already told me about that. He said that American show dogs were so well groomed it seemed as though not a single hair were out of place.

The American Boxer Kennels

Of course, only the rich can compete under such circumstances. To be successful one needed more than a handler. Even in the large kennels, the dogs had to be trained and cared for. The large cities were difficult places to own a dog, much less to be a breeder, thus the wealthy breeders had their kennels outside the cities, in the rural areas. Often a kennel is up to sixty miles away from the owner's residence. The kennels are run by a manager. In Germany we would call him the *Zwingermeister*. Usually the manager's whole family was involved in the kennel operation, because sixty to eighty dogs are a lot of work. And just as in Germany, whelping and the care of puppies were entrusted mainly to women.

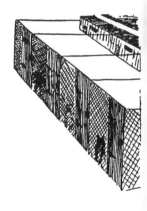

Most of the American kennels are air conditioned. A kitchen and a sick room are also in the building. Straw was not normally used for bedding; instead old newspapers were shredded. There were plenty of those available, and when dirty they were simply burned.

In the kennel, every dog had its own box with a place to lie. Should the dog wish to move around, there is a long, narrow run attached for that purpose. The dogs have it quite good, but probably every one of them would change places with our dogs. In Germany, a Boxer is first of all a friend of the people whose lives and home he shares. He goes with them in the car. I seldom saw a dog in a car in America, even though Americans make long trips and are always afraid of gangsters. When my hostess went to dog shows, she wore diamonds. I knew of her fears, so I recommended that she take a dog along. But the suggestion made no impression. A dog would be a nuisance at parties, and what could one do with the dog in the city? Thus the Boxers in America are almost all breeding animals. Only here and there did I see a manager's favorite freely roaming the grounds of a kennel.

I was pleased to see that every kennel had some veteran dogs being cared for. It was remarkable, but I saw many thirteen or more years old, a very long life for a Boxer.

Near Pittsburgh I visited a kennel high up on a mountain. Two wide streets led up to it, while down below there were large orchards. Water had to be pumped up the mountain from cisterns over six-hundred feet below. In general, these kennels looked alike. They were long wooden buildings, outfitted with all the luxuries you could think of. In numerous glass cabinets in the reception room, the kennel's silver trophies stood gleaming. When one remembers that every show dog visits from one hundred to three hundred shows, it's easy to understand what a great number of trophies would be won by a major kennel over the years.

I was not too impressed by the dogs in the Pittsburgh kennel. But some of the best were away at shows. Of course, dog shows in America do not take place only on holidays. They could occur on any given day of the week. For that reason there are more shows in a year than there are days.

In my journal I find the following comment: "Women

here are ageless. It's difficult to tell if you are speaking with the daughter, mother or grandmother. They seem to be alike. Is that just because of make-up?"

Mrs. Goff [Puckety Boxers] was different. I never met anyone in America who did not know and admire her. Small and dainty, like a young girl, she was already a grandmother. Her hair was fire-red, and a large smile lit up her face. She was wearing bright green clothes. Besides her Boxer kennel, she owned race horses. She was also a dog judge. We stopped by to visit her.

In the large garden, she had fenced in an area on the lawn and put benches around it. This was where we were to have a private show. Numerous Boxer owners had been invited. What a wonderful chance for the Americans to have a little party! Off to the side there stood a large table loaded with varieties of delicious food. You could just walk over and help yourself to whatever you liked. This type of hospitality is apparently the norm in America. Besides freeing the host of the need for servants, the guests were never disturbed by the serving of dishes.

Of course, I was to do the judging for this little show. Some thirty dogs were brought to me. For the most part they were nice, promising Boxers, but most were over-weight. That's understandable with the lack of exercise. Most of the time they only get out of the kennel to be trained to "stack." Once again I learned how a poor front quarter could be completely hidden with this technique.

The best of the lot was a big golden brindle dog, who would have had no competition in Germany. But here he was not even shown because he was not flashy, a necessary requirement for a Boxer to be competitive in America.

I had a very hard time making myself understood. Not only because of language problems, but because we had different opinions on what made a fine Boxer. A young German war bride tried to interpret for me, but that did not work either. Then I stumbled on the idea of making my points by drawing pictures. I asked for paper and pencil and began drawing what I had wanted to say. With

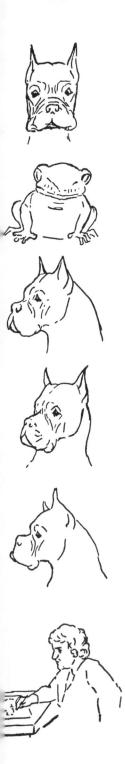

a few lines I sketched the head of an American Boxer from the front with its very wide muzzle. These dogs have no expression because they have a frog's mouth. Quickly I drew a frog's head next to the Boxer head. Then came a picture of a skull. The lower jaw was undershot but not turned upwards. As a result, the dog had no chin and lacked that Boxer expression.

More drawings followed, and then even more. Finally we understood each other. As fast as I could draw them, the sketches were snatched up, until I finally became tired and had to stop.

As a rule, most Americans go to bed about 10 PM. That's tied to a firm resolution to get up early. Most of the time it meant nothing. But I was used to some six or seven hours of sleep, which gave me extra time during the day to paint Boxer heads. Paper and paints were available in a quality that I had not seen for many years. These paintings became great hits. Thus it was possible for me to earn some pocket money in the three or four hours before lunch. Most of it I sent home to ease things a bit for my loved ones.

In my journal I wrote, "My gnarled hands are beginning to look quite decent. What you can do with ten days of care!" But the abundance of impressions from life in an American city became almost oppressive. Everyone rushing, neon signs, traffic noise—it all meshed together like a symphony. The one constant element were the dogs. They kept me on firm ground.

In Cincinnati we visited a show where there was a very nice brindle bitch being shown with six others. All together they looked like a painting. The dogs were much less impressive—too light, too elegant and over-refined.

Before we reached the Wagners' kennel, we drove to Lockport, Illinois. That was the home of Tulgey Wood Boxers, where Lustig had lived and was buried. At one time, it was supposed to be the most beautiful kennel in America. It is located within a large deer park and consists of a number of buildings with long runs for the dogs

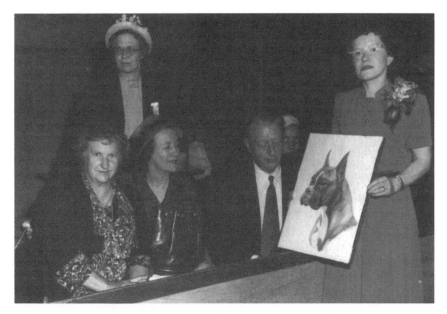

Mrs. Stockmann (left) painted many Boxer pictures while on her 1949 visit to America. Holding this one is judge Evelyn Goff; seated next to Mrs. Stockmann are Mazie and John Wagner, Alice Rosenthal is in back.

One of Friederun Stockmann's Boxer carvings

connected to them. Near the entrance to the grounds, we visited Lustig's grave.

The original American owner of Lustig no longer lives. He abandoned Boxer breeding even when Lustig was still alive. After that he turned to breeding and owning apes, and later he went over to growing rare types of orchids. He was one of those American multimillionaires who have so much money they don't know what to do with it. Eventually the kennel and its contents were taken over by the manager. Mr. Rogers knew Boxers, but he was not a Boxer breeder. Certainly Lustig was in fine hands with him. For many years, Mr. Rogers was also the editor of the magazine *Boxer Briefs*.

Mazie Wagner purchased the kennel later for her breeding. She constructed a cemetery for the great ones of the Boxer breed. The remains of Dorian, Utz and Brandy were placed next to those of Lustig. It was an extraordinary deed for an American to do.

American Boxers For Germany

As a surprise for me, the Wagners planned a trip to California. I would judge in Los Angeles. Mazie Wagner told me, "America is a paradise on earth, but California is a land out of this world. God personally created it."

But before we left for there, I finally was able to see the Wagners' kennel and dogs. And I was lucky because Brandy happened to be there between shows. Just as I had expected, Brandy was a truly superior Boxer. There were other excellent dogs in the kennel too. No doubt about it, this was by far the best representation of Boxers that I had ever seen anywhere. A beautiful villa was a part of the kennel. Otherwise the layout was the typical pattern.

Mazie Wagner was not really satisfied. In her view, there were too many repairs needed. So she wished to sell the kennel. She felt the climate around Chicago was too harsh. The winter is quite difficult. She believed California would be

the perfect place for dog breeding. America is so large it offers thousands of possibilities.

Some years later they did actually give up the Milwaukee kennel. The Wagners bought a farm in Texas and erected a new kennel. Although the Texas climate was better, their breeding did not flourish. For some unknown reason, the bitches had trouble carrying to full term. Even the best stud dogs did not seem to help. Then a recently-purchased stud dog died. Finally, after several years of trouble, they sold the Texas farm and purchased the kennel at Tulgey Wood.

I had thought the Lockport kennel of Tulgey Wood was glorious. It was my dream to have something like it in Germany.

During my visit we often talked about the similarities and differences between American and German Boxers. Which are better? It was a question I was asked over and over. And I must confess that the Boxers I saw at the Sieger show in Cologne just before my trip had indeed reflected a deterioration in quality, probably as a result of the war. We had no dominant Boxer in Germany at that time. For that reason, I expressed the desire to the Wagners to take back a promising young dog.

My hosts promised me a Brandy son. In a batch of fourteen-day-old puppies, I searched for my little guy. And once again I proved my skill at finding a quality Boxer. Two years later, Czardas of Mazelaine became the national Sieger of Germany.

We flew to California. I would have liked to travel in the car or with a train, but who has time in America to pass up the fastest transportation? Rush is the order of the day, and the more they rush the less time they have.

Los Angeles is the third-largest city in America. It is also the largest city in the world by the area that it covers. Mazie Wagner told me that the people there are very nice, and the fanciers are among the most generous in the world. The show grounds were actually at our hotel in Santa Monica. On the hotel's large lawn an exhibition

ring would be set up. The lawn was so large there was room for other activities too. Magnificent palm trees provided shaded areas; even the streets were lined with palm trees. This large park-like area was surrounded by the hotel's buildings. One whole wall of my room was a window. If I had felt like it, I probably could have judged the whole show while lying on my bed and looking out the window.

The Wagners had a similar room. They also rented a special reception room, which proved very useful because there were numerous friends—primarily Boxer breeders—who came by. As in Germany, the American Boxer breeders have close friendships. Just like a true family, the breeders have their friendships and their differences. And like in a family, they come together again and again; they have their dogs in common. Of course, it's more cheerful in America than in Germany, but sometimes there is greater anger too. Perhaps the reason is that people there seem to live easier lives, almost without worries.

As a celebrity, I was passed around like a work of art, and all kinds of honors and compliments were heaped on me. I also met some interesting dog people. Near Hollywood I talked to a former German naval officer who trained dogs for the multi-millionaires and also had a boarding kennel. He and his wife and two adult daughters, along with five helpers, ran the business. They earned very well.

Another fancier was a physician, Dr. Watson. I liked him very much because he was interesting and—above all—he could speak German. Long ago he had bought a Boxer from my kennel: Ingo von Heger.

The second Boxer-breeding doctor that I met in America was Dr. Harris. His kennel was only second to the Wagners' in size and had been the most successful Boxer kennel in America for several years. He extended a warm invitation to me to visit his layout. At the time I had no idea what an important role "Sirrah Crest" would play later in my life and my breeding.

Friederun Stockman at a puppy match in California in 1949. She chose this 13-week-old puppy, Sirrah Crest's Bang Away, as the best of ninety competitors. She called him "Little Lustig."

Penelope Harris, daughter of the owners of Sirrah Crest Boxers, Dr. and Mrs. Harris, poses with the two dogs given to Mrs. Stockmann by Dr. Harris in 1949. On the left is Abra Dabra, on the right is Goody Goody

The small house which Dr. Watson owned was right beside the ocean. Day and night the waves lightly bathed the edge of the wide sandy shore. The water was blue and warm. If you wished, you could swim anytime or within half an hour be on the mountainside skiing. At the foot of the mountains were groves of ripe oranges. The mild climate of California turned it into the orchard of America. Sometimes a glimpse of a field of oil well towers reminded one of the industrial reality of our times.

At the Boxer show there were a large number of dogs. Dr. Harris was owner of the best animals. Two bitches impressed me very much; one was an adult fawn and the other a brindle just six months old. Their breeder was in a very good mood and offered me a dark brindle bitch as a gift to take back to Germany for my kennel. Of course, I was overjoyed at the generous offer. We agreed on a day when I would come to visit the Sirrah Crest kennel.

But before that, I had to judge a puppy match. Ninety dogs from six weeks to twelve months old were entered. This type of event is completely unknown in Germany.

The puppy match began at 9 PM. If all went right it would be finished by midnight. In those three hours I would judge ninety dogs—not an easy piece of work. According to American custom, the youngest came first. Dogs and bitches were separated. I seldom amaze people when I judge adult dogs, but when it comes to judging puppies I take a back seat to no one. I've raised hundreds of the little guys. Most of them I watched very closely from birth on, just to observe how they developed. By watching how faults could develop, I became very good at predicting which would be the best of the litter.

Among the males, a little fellow immediately caught my eye, a fawn with white markings and white socks. That's Lustig, I thought. But a closer look showed he was not quite the same. Lustig was more powerful, his head more sharply chiseled. Yet the grand pose and the long graceful neck brought back memories of this puppy's great ancestor. Of all the Boxers I had seen up to then, that puppy looked the most like Lustig. And he was only ten weeks old. He took his class with no trouble.

In the last class of bitches, I saw the six-month-old brindle winner at Santa Monica. She took second place behind a very elegant fawn. It was a very difficult decision—a mature bitch against an immature bitch—both were nice and I realized that another year could easily reverse their positions.

Finally it was over. All of the classes had been judged, now I had to decide which was the best of all the class winners. Among the dogs, the little fellow with the white markings stood above the others. I called him "Little Lustig." The fawn bitch won over those of her sex.

Last came the choice for Best in Match. Little Lustig took the honors.

The next day I visited Sirrah Crest. Dr. Harris and his family warmly greeted me. They had a wonderful kennel; some sixty dogs lived there. The Harris's gave me free rein to seek out a bitch. I didn't wish to appear greedy, but both Dr. Harris and the Wagners urged me to take the best one I could find. My choice was Goody-Goody, an excellent, beautiful brindle.

To make my good fortune complete, Dr. Harris urged me to take back a male also. Once again, I learned the truth of the old saying that he who has the choice also has the agony of it. It seemed easier to me to have judged a hundred dogs than to choose one for myself out of about sixty. If I had been able, I would have taken several days to choose. It was some help when I decided not to pick an old one or a real young one. Thus I chose a eighteen-month-old male. A nice golden brindle color and a fine head were his special features. I believed that he would fit in well with our German breeding.

Dr. Harris immediately declared that he would pay all costs for transporting them to Germany. It was necessary, however, for me to find an American to receive them. At that time—and for several years thereafter—Germans were not allowed to import animals from foreign countries. Mrs.

Harris proudly told me that these two Boxers would bring Lustig's blood back to his homeland. And I had to admit, his blood line had been well cared for since he left Germany.

The Americans honored me with three dogs. I also met many fine American friends of the Boxer. What more could I possibly want? I had reached the high point of my America trip in California.

"Little Lustig" did indeed make his way in the Boxer world. He was named Sirrah Crest's Bang Away, and brought great honor to his name. He became one of the greatest Boxer champions in America, winning over one hundred Best in Show awards, a record for all breeds.

We visited still another large show on Long Island, where I also saw an excellent kennel. The vegetation and landscape there reminded me of my Latvian homeland. Of course, in America everything was much richer. I saw wonderful horses and very nice dogs. I went from one party to another. But despite the extravagant living, I actually lost 22 pounds during my six-week trip.

In Chicago, the Wagners and I bid farewell. I spent a few more days in New York visiting a German family, and while I was there I met an old son of Lustig and a very nice brindle puppy, and I saw another fine kennel with excellent dogs.

All of the Americans that I met were very friendly and warm hearted. And if I were able to give any recognition to them and their breeding, they were always most grateful.

As I boarded the airplane that was to take me to England, the steward handed me a carton full of beautiful flowers. Bouquets like that in the USA are somehow treated so they do not wilt for a long time. I laid them in my lap; all through the flight they served to remind me of the most beautiful weeks of my life.

Mrs. Stockmann judging in Great Britain in 1949

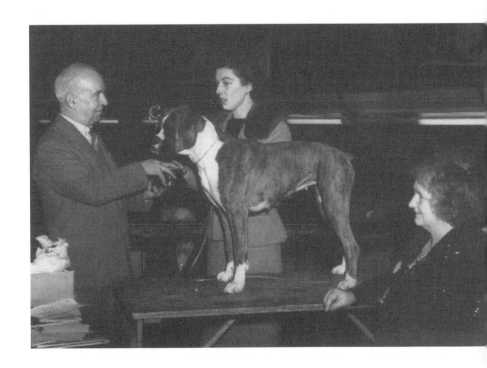

A Boxer Judge In England

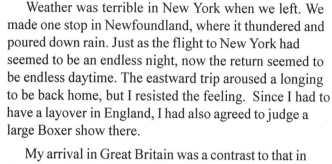

Weather was terrible in New York when we left. We made one stop in Newfoundland, where it thundered and poured down rain. Just as the flight to New York had seemed to be an endless night, now the return seemed to be endless daytime. The eastward trip aroused a longing to be back home, but I resisted the feeling. Since I had to have a layover in England, I had also agreed to judge a large Boxer show there.

My arrival in Great Britain was a contrast to that in America. A friendly, German-speaking translator met me. I had worried a bit that it could be difficult for me if I were not picked up. Laethley Grange is in northern England. How could I get there without help? But my fears were unfounded. The interpreter brought me to a short friendly gentleman who spoke excellent German. He was one of England's most successful Boxer breeders, and we had long corresponded with each other. Mr. Dawson had been concerned about my arrival. Just the day before, a similar flight had had a twenty-four hour delay from bad weather.

Together with Mrs. Dawson, who had also wished to greet me on arrival, we drove by car to the Dawsons' home. Of course, I needed some time to adjust to the rapid change of circumstances.

Clearly, there were great differences then between Great Britain and America. There were many visible reminders that the British had also suffered during the war. Mr. Dawson's kennel was called Stainburndorf. He had received several dogs from me, the last one before the war was Lustig's son, Zünftig vom Dom. Many of his descendants still survived, and I saw almost all of them. Since finding dog food during the war became much more difficult in England than for us, many owners had to give up their darlings. Even Mr. Dawson found himself in that situation and almost closed down his kennel.

For that reason, Zünftig was sold at a Red Cross

benefit and went to the United States. But he always had a special place in Mr. Dawson's heart. Although it had been almost a decade since then, his former English owner still said, "For every person there is one special dog. Mine was Zünftig."

After the war ended, Mr. Dawson bought a nice red-fawn son of Heiner from me. But he had no luck with him. Loisl vom Dom died while still in quarantine. I promised Mr. Dawson I would repay his wonderful hospitality with another puppy. One year later I was able to send him a fawn male from a breeding between the American bitch and Heiner. Known as Froehlich vom Dom, that Boxer's fame extended well beyond England.

Boxer Breeding In Great Britain

The show had 110 Boxers. All were to be judged by me. It was the first time I had judged uncropped dogs. For the most part, the entries were not very good, mainly not good type. I had a nagging suspicion that some Bull Mastiffs were back there someplace. For instance, one Englishwoman believed her nice little male Boxer was absolutely correct, thereby completely overlooking the fact that he was not even up to a bitch's minimum height.

The Boxer is a German breed, and for that reason I judged by the German standard. America had already noticeably moved away from that standard. Many of their dogs' heads did not have good balance, missing above all a chin. Americans are afraid their dogs will drool. For that reason, they have bred a too shallow muzzle. Of course, the underbite has no connection to drooling. And then there is another American feature, in addition to the fear of drooling. They want their dogs to have flashy markings in a quantity unrecognized by us. Americans claimed that we Germans have not held to the old standard. But that view can easily be contradicted. A comparison with the old pioneer dogs shows clearly that today's German Boxers

are much more like the old standard than are the American dogs.

Since then, years have passed. Both German and British Boxers have greatly recovered in that time. The American breeding, however, has remained the same. But we have to remember, American breeding did not suffer because of the war. In any case, both British and American Boxers will remain serious competitors for German fanciers.

Great Britain is the home of the uncropped Boxer. Cropping is illegal there. If we could bring ourselves to abstain from cropping our dogs, it would greatly revive our export business. The United Kingdom has always been an export land, and they export Boxers also. Most of those countries where British Boxers are imported have adopted the uncropped custom. That makes it impossible for American and German breeders to sell dogs in those areas.

The British also protect themselves against imports by using the quarantine. I looked at a few of those depots, which usually are directed by veterinarians. The dogs had runs that were surrounded by planking. For six months the dog must remain there, although they may be visited by their owners. Expenses for the quarantine are high, and for that reason many dog lovers must avoid importing a dog.

Mr. Dawson was an original: a shrewd businessman, well educated, musically talented, expert on horses and also a rider, and besides all of that a Boxer breeder. Despite his activities, he always found time for his dogs and often walked five or six together at one time. Their obedience, of course, was not always the best. On my last day, when he had collected all my necessary papers, he came cheerfully leading his dogs to me in the garden and said, "It's all in order now, Mrs. Stockmann! Here are your papers, and this time you will fly with a small plane from here to London. That will be faster. Here are the tickets to London, then from there to Amsterdam and on to Hamburg.

Your passport and visa are also here. Now be careful not to lose anything!"

Right then the dogs jumped up on me and I noticed that some of them had pieces of paper in their mouths. Horrified, I begged Mr. Dawson to check what the dogs were carrying. But of course that was not easy! First there was a lot of shouting, "Come dogs, come!"

He had no success that way. Just as it seemed totally hopeless, he decided to speak to them in their own language and actually barked. It worked! With my help, he managed to get the papers away from the dogs' mouth, and they did indeed turn out to be my tickets and visa. Since each dog had a piece of paper, everything was a little beat up. If they had decided to fight a bit, the damages probably would have been worse.

The American Boxers In Germany

After a warm reception by Boxer fanciers in Hamburg, I once again arrived back home, but I did not find things as I imagined they would be. My older dogs were thin. One was even sick. The puppies were also a disappointment. Those that had survived showed no special quality. Like a beautiful dream, my past weeks now lay behind me. As before, everyday life demanded my full efforts.

Yet something remained for me that would prove to be even more valuable than the three dogs I expected from America. When I left California, Dr. Watson and Dr. Harris supplied me with penicillin and sulfonamide. Fantastic prices were being paid for penicillin in Germany, if it even was available. The proper dosage and use of these drugs was unknown to me, but I found instructions in an American newspaper. Through those drugs, I was able to cure a nine-year-old nightmare that had embittered my life.

Meanwhile, I welcomed the two California Boxers. Abra Dabra of Sirrah Crest was the dog, and Goody

Goody the bitch. An American friend had picked them up for me, and my Munich friends registered them in the books of the German Boxer Club. Everyone loved Goody Goody, although we now noticed how small she was, even though exceptionally pretty.

It was a bit different with the dog. Abra Dabra was very thin. His eyes had an infection, and in a few days they became so bloodshot that he was almost blind for two weeks. His adjustment to the new surroundings took a long time. Now it became clear to us what the effect of kennel-rearing, the usual American practice, had upon the dogs. These animals only seemed happy when they were behind bars. When released from the kennel, they ran around like wild animals. If a pile of gravel were in the way, they would run into it head first. A wire just a foot off the ground seemed to them a complete barricade. They neither knew how to jump over nor to crawl under.

Our plan was to train Abra quickly, show him, and use him in our breeding. But in the kennel he had no common sense at all. At first he feared everyone. An American in uniform, or someone in a white mechanic's coat, would throw him into a panic. It was still the same even after he had been so well trained that he could do Schutzhund work without a flaw. The dog had tremendous protective in-stincts. When strangers came to look at my kennel, he could be dangerous if anyone neared his harem. I always took him with me. His greatest joy was to ride in the car. Once at night a stranger jerked open the car's door, and Abra—who was in the back—let out such a ferocious roar that the guy immediately slammed the door shut. It all happened so quickly—I was more shaken by Abra's response than by the boldness of the intruder. Even Abra's son, Primus, who was also in the car—never really woke up before it was all over.

When he became older, Abra's protective urges became his curse. No one dared to do anything to another dog around him. True, most dogs jump at the chance to help punish the other animal, but Abra would attack the person doing the punishing. He attacked my daughter as she tried to separate two fighting bitches, hurting her badly. There was of course one exception, and that was me. He never threatened me, and would come to me at the softest call. Thus I had a difficult problem. Relatives and friends demanded that Abra be destroyed. But I knew how devoted and faithful he was to me. It just was not possible to reject that faith.

Then my little granddaughter solved the problem. She pointed out that the death penalty had been outlawed in Germany, but his dangerous behavior certainly deserved a life sentence in prison. And so, Abra went into the kennel for the rest of his life. I did everything I could to make his stay as pleasant as possible. When I took out the car, he was even allowed to go along.

One year later, we realized that Abra was very ill. Then he suffered dizziness and lost his sense of balance. We freed him from his pain, which freed us also from watching him suffer. Abra will always be a part of our kennel's history. Goody-Goody was younger and she adjusted more rapidly than Abra. Unfortunately, all of her offspring remained small like her. Her nicest son was Froehlich, who went to Mr. Dawson in England, as mentioned earlier.

The third one of the three Americans was Mazelaine's Czardas. He was youngest of the trio. Adjusting to the new circumstances was not difficult for him. Of the two males, he was not only the nicer but also the luckier. He won the Sieger title in Munich. Some people complained that he was over-refined and was more like a bitch in type, but Czardas was actually a typical American Boxer.

There were people who predicted that my breeding program would suffer and even lose type because of these American Boxers, especially in regard to Abra's weak chin. Such comments only made me laugh. And not a one of those prophecies has come true either. Abra—who almost did not get a breeding permit—proved himself to be a sire of dominant, intelligent working dogs. His son, Primus, both in terms of beauty and performance is still among the best.

Move To America?

My wonderful American dream soon faded away. The worries of everyday life surrounded me once again. Our refugees who had once lived with us now had their own homes and existence. It became more and more difficult to find workers, and they were becoming more expensive. Only with great effort were we able to restore a semblance of order to our farm. Was my daughter going to have to do such hard physical labor all her life as I have? Just who first mentioned that we might be better off to sell Reich-Schmitt farm, I no longer remember. Every day we watched as more thistles and weeds took over our land. We had to make some kind of a decision!

Once again, we watched as a big car made its way up the hillside to us. An elegantly-dressed, middle-aged gentleman stepped out and asked if he could speak to me. I led him into our Boxer room. It was the same room where we had negotiated with many foreigners, both before and after the war. The gentleman was an American who had been interested in the vom Dom line for many years. Apparently he had read about me and admired my success in breeding. As with many rich Americans, he had carried out a breeding program, but he had also learned that success takes more than money. His great ambition was not only to breed the best Boxers in America, but in the whole world!

According to what the American said, he could do whatever was financially necessary to produce great Boxers. But he needed people he could have full confidence in, and whose breeding knowledge and experience would lead to that success. Lastly, he stated that he needed a person of such excellent reputation that all others stood in her shadow. Only I, in his view, would fit that description.

He made me the following offer. My daughter and I would move to America, where I would take over the operation of his kennel. We would receive a very good salary, along with all of the amenities of American life: a small house, a car, telephone, etc. It would be all spelled out in a five-year contract. He encouraged me to ask the German consul for information on him. There was only one condition: I must keep it confidential until all was agreed and the time was best.

The offer stunned me. Although I certainly did not agree with everything the man had said, I still understood very well what he meant. Wasn't this a gift from God for me? But then came the doubts. What would happen to our farm and my dogs?

But he had an answer for that too. I could either lease or sell the farm, and my three favorite dogs could be brought along to America.

Why didn't I take the offer right away? No—things just don't go that fast. I had to talk to my children first. So I asked for two weeks to consider the proposal. He agreed to that, as well as a six-week period to liquidate our affairs if I accepted. With that general agreement, he said his good-bye. Was it not a gift? Worry free years, as I had for eight weeks in America and Great Britain? There would never be such an opportunity again in my life, I knew. My daughter and I now began to discuss the implications of the plan. Farming was not going to last for long on our small acre-age. True, we knew every tree and blade of grass, but we also knew how much sweat and worry were attached to every little hill. Sooner or later we would have to give it up.

For our cows and chickens, the change would mean nothing. But then there were my two little faithful ponies. In rain and snow, they had taken me back and forth to haul dog food twice a week, thirty-five miles over bad roads. During the days of great hunger I had only been able to throw some straw in their pens. With such thoughts, my heart began to crack and weaken.

And what about the dogs? The most promising young ones could easily be sold. But what would happen to the

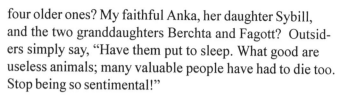

four older ones? My faithful Anka, her daughter Sybill, and the two granddaughters Berchta and Fagott? Outsiders simply say, "Have them put to sleep. What good are useless animals; many valuable people have had to die too. Stop being so sentimental!"

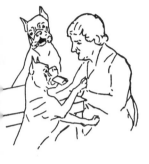

We never said much about these problems to each other, but our thoughts were always there. When I stood by the stove in the morning to make the fire, Anka would bring me one piece of wood after the other. She twisted and turned herself in joy as she helped, all because she could give me something. Her jowls pulled upward and her face was a big smile—despite her ten years she had very little gray.

When we ate breakfast, Fagott, Anka's granddaughter, would hop up on the bench next to me. If I finished eating and forgot about her, she began to talk. We would joke that she was telling me about Little Red Ridinghood and the wolf. Her mouth would open and close, the flews went back and forth as she growled and hummed in her Boxer way. It was so funny.

If Fagott had been a human being, we would have considered her mildly retarded. That was my fault, although purely accidental. A veterinarian had given me some medicine for her that contained a nerve poison. He knew that, but how was I supposed to? Anyway, I gave it to Fagott and it did not work right. For the rest of her life she had reactions from that. As a result, I felt guilty about this big beautiful animal. Twice I saved her with extraordinary care from an early death. She repaid me with total devotion.

And then there was my little granddaughter. When we told her we would have to give away many of the dogs, she quickly ran over to Anka's second granddaughter, threw her arms the dog's neck and begged, "Don't give away my Berchta!"

We knew that Berchta could only be happy with us. There was also the fourth older dog, Sybill, Anka's beautiful big daughter. As calm and modest as her mother,

The four "old ladies" of vom Dom kennel with the Stockmann granddaughter: (l. to r.) Anka von Hofbauer, Berchta vom Dom, Sybyll vom Dom, Faggott vom Dom

Wiking vom Dom, the image of his great great great great grandfather, Lustig vom Dom

Abra Dabra of Sirrah Crest

Rival vom Dom

Sybill also had those wonderful, expressive dark eyes. Those eyes shone with an endless trust in us. And we were supposed to destroy them all? For only a worry-free life of comfort, which might easily not work out?

Do humans actually hold such a right over animals—whose very existence is a human responsibility—that their lives can simply be ended? Since we brought those animals into existence, aren't we then pledged to care for them the rest of their lives?

Not a one of those four dogs would have ever left me. And if I had driven them out, they still would have secretly sneaked back—simply because they loved me. Should I not get on my knees in front of them all to show my shame? I broke faith many years ago with my first Boxer. Since then I have never been able to overcome that completely. Did I not swear to myself then that I would never do it again?

Indecision is something I have never liked. So it was good that the American wrote, urging me to make a decision soon. He had been able to arrange that all formalities for me would be quickly completed. Nothing more stood in the way of our move to America. Without hesitating, I sat down at my writing desk and wrote that I would have to decline.

My children fully supported me in that decision. Only my daughter suggested that I always had far too many thoughts about all of these things and sacrificed too much, especially for the dogs. Who would ever thank me for it, she wondered. But I had not seen my choice as a sacrifice. And if it is really a matter of thanks, then my dogs give it to me over and over again. Besides, life had taught me that you can never go back to that place where you were once happy. It would never be the same as it had been then.

We decided not to breed the four older bitches any-more. Anka had already passed the permissible age by two years. Berchta's puppies seemed unable to survive. Fagott was ill again, and Sybill was already eight and had no milk.

I might have tried it once more with Sybill, but then my daughter wished to breed her to Czardas, and that was not a match to my liking. Thus, Sybill too should live on without any more offspring.

Of course, the last word was not for us to say. Abra Dabra turned out to be the black sheep of the family. He had eventually overcome the kennel stupidity of his youth, and was confident and full of foolish tricks. Most of all, he had become a great lover, quite dear to all the lady dogs. All of our bitches preferred him to the cautious, lazy Czardas. Abra was always nice, never pushy or too eager with the bitches. So it was not too surprising, when we sometimes forgot to put him right back in the kennel.

Abra had his own style with the bitches. During the day the dogs would lie peacefully beside each other. Toward night, Abra would awake, move next to his lady and whisper something in her ear. With her head cocked to the side, the chosen one listened, then arose, shook herself, and the two trotted off in the darkness. After a while, they were back at the door. They would then lie down next to each other and go to sleep. Who could think any bad thoughts about that?

But when I noticed Sybill was getting bigger and bigger, things did not seem quite right. And what do you know— she presented us with three healthy, strong Boxers. Destiny was once again kind, because our Miniature Schnauzer had a false pregnancy at the same time. So she became a wet nurse, and that little Schnauzer bitch raised those three giants quite easily.

In this litter was Primus vom Dom. Many Boxer fans have met Primus. He belonged to the top rank in both conformation and performance. Several came in second to him, but because they had stronger financial backing were able to beat him out for a Sieger title. Primus belonged to that group of dogs who could not be a Sieger but could help produce a Sieger. Up to now, his best son is Bel Ami von Wikingsblut. Bel Ami is now the best of his breed in South Africa. For us, however, Primus was the embodiment of our four older dogs' gratitude. If we had destroyed them, there would have been no Primus given to us.

The Circle Closes

Once again the years passed by. Many things have changed for us. We could not keep the farm. Instead we bought a smaller piece of property with some four acres. One way or another we struggled through and survived with our four-legged friends. Despite our best intentions, we have as many now as before.

The four old ones are long since dead. Czardas had an interesting destiny. In a last attempt to keep the farm, I sold Czardas to Mr. Dawson in Great Britain. Two of Czardas' sons remained in Germany: the brindle Sieger Quickli vom Dom, who is now in Brazil, and the fawn Visky vom Dom. For reasons unknown to me, Mr. Dawson gave Czardas to an American officer who took him back to the United States. Thus, Czardas returned to the land of his forefathers as the only American Boxer to have ever won a German National Sieger title.

I do not wish to write of my present kennel. When old friends who have known my dogs for over twenty years visit me, they stand at the fence amazed when the pack of Boxers comes storming up to them. And sometimes I hear the question, is Lustig back in my kennel? I always have to smile. No, I am not really Sleeping Beauty. No twenty-year sleep for me and my attendants. Lustig has been dead for fifteen years. The dog in my kennel that draws the question and resembles his great ancestor so much is a great, great, great, great, great grandson of his. In his pedigree for eight generations, Lustig's name appears thirty-four times. When only ten-months old, one could see that he would be carrying on the glory and tradition of his ancestor.

As I pen these last lines, I think again of all my dear comrades who have traveled with me through life's good and bad days. And when I see my young Wiking, the multi-great grandson of Lustig, standing among the pack—then I know that Lustig lives on and will continue to live on, even when I will no longer be among my four-legged comrades.

Epilog

by Friederun Stockmann

The ring closes, but it now becomes a wheel and rolls further through my life. Like pictures from a movie, the scenes of my life go through my mind: the dreams of a little girl with two long braids.

Those dreams were rooted in the ideal image of a large, tiger-striped dog with a black face. The ideal became reality and wove itself through the entire life of that little girl. It was with her in her marriage, through good and bad times.

Somehow everything that I have experienced has been entangled with my animals. My love and my life belonged to them, and if one of my dogs died—sooner or later it returned to me in one of its grandchildren. It was that way with Lustig. It was even more so that way with Champion Rolf Vogelsberg. Twenty-five years after his death, a great grandson of his—Sieger Heiner v. Zwergeck—arose with all the nobility and good features of Rolf. Even Heiner eventually had to go, and again more than twenty years later he appeared again in almost the exact form in his great grandson, Sieger Godewind vom Dom. Although he resembled his ancestor greatly, Godewind is the most complete of the two.

Godewind vom Dom came from a difficult birth. His mother required a Caesarean section. He required much care, and his life struggle worried me greatly. And then he became what he is today, the top Sieger of his whole line. Undefeated in his color, just as Champion Rolf and Sieger Heiner before him, he received the grading of "Excellent" ten times with first place rankings. He won the Sieger title at the ATIBOX show over 287 Boxers, and was judged by a seven-member judges' panel to be the "Most Beautiful Boxer in Europe."

How could I ever ask for more? Since childhood I have

carried my ideal of a dog with me. It has become such an integral part of my life that I can no longer separate the two.

A long life has allowed the fulfillment of a dream. Of course, there are higher ideals in life than a great dog, but perhaps that is not what life is all about.

All of us pursue something in life, and if we reach the desired goal, shouldn't our ambitions be satisfied? The wheel rolls on, perhaps in others' hands. Godewind's children are already on his heels.

I wish all the young breeders the kind of success I have had. I am certain they will achieve them if they love their Boxers as I have loved mine.

Prominent People

From *Der Hund* (1937)

Philipp Stockmann, Pleiskirchen near Mühldorf in Upper Bavaria, Breed Warden and editor of the Boxer Blätter, born March 15, 1877, in Kamberg (near Wiesbaden).

As a matchmaker, a Boxer brought two people together twenty-five years ago. An art student, Friederun von Miram, although a native of Riga on the Baltic, studied at that time in Munich. Boxers had been in her grandparents' home, and she purchased her first Boxer bitch in 1910. It brought her success in the show ring. Although Friederun was only twenty years old, she had already joined the [German] Boxer Club.

Godewind vom Dom, perhaps the Stockmanns' greatest Boxer

Katharina Gabi Stockmann, daughter
of Friederun Stockmann, on her 75th
birthday in 1989

Head study of Godewind
vom Dom

Philipp Stockmann also had a Boxer, and he and Friederun became engaged when they visited Riga that summer. One of the conditions required for marriage with Friederun was that the Boxer "would be completely available to her." And that is how it has remained to this day: the breeding of their Vom Dom kennel—from which there have been a dozen Siegers and Champions—is her domain.

Immediately after marriage, Philipp joined the Boxer Club in 1911, and in 1912 became the chairman of the Munich regional club—an area that included all of Bavaria, Wuerttemberg, Thüringen, Switzerland and Austria. In 1913, he became Vice-Chairman of the whole [German] Boxer Club.

After the war [World War I], their purchase of a rather distant and isolated farm led him to turn down further posts in the national organization. But the creation in 1925 of a national Breed Warden's position led him to accept that role and title. Along with his wife, he had been a participant in the *Boxer Blätter* and in 1934, became its editor.

In January 1912, he purchased for his wife the brindle Champion Rolf von Vogelsberg, followed by Champion Urschi von Hiltenberg and other fine bitches. Their primary breeding goal was first to get Rolf's head and then breed it so deeply into their bloodlines that it would be constantly inherited. Along the way they had to breed out Rolf's roached back, which was typical of the brindles then. Mrs. Stockmann achieved that, and the Boxers of the Vom Dom kennel soon became world famous for their excellent heads.

The battle against the brindle roach was very difficult. But the Stockmanns never strayed from the goal. Their guiding principle of breeding is a typey Boxer head on a correct, powerful body of good height and substance, but not lacking in nobility. Sigurd v. Dom came close to this ideal, and he is still reproducing his type. The Von Dom kennel breeds mainly from its males, but male and female types are carefully kept separate. That makes it difficult for them to exhibit in the brood classes, because their bitches and males do not fit well into a group. The differences between male and female—which is also required in general agricultural-animal breeding—are carefully maintained by Vom Dom.

Their dogs are not alike in color, because color is the last consideration of their breeding.

Along with Boxers—as we see by the monkey on Stockmann's shoulder—the Stockmann family has a collection of animals from large livestock to tiny rodents. It was one of the reasons for buying the farm, a fine place for animal breeding of all kinds.

And finally—best wishes for a happy silver wedding anniversary!

v. Otto.

Letter from Frau Stockmann to Mazie Wagner

January 31st, 1961

Dear Mazie,

Please don't be angry that I haven't written until now. Don't forget that I have become an old woman and I can't work as quickly anymore. Also there were the Christmas holidays and I had to carve wooden gifts for my livlihood. Besides, I have 30 dogs and must do all the work in caring for them with only my daughter's help.

I have so much to tell you. Every day I rejoice more and more over the gift of the two Boxers. In August I exhibited them at Augsburg, and both got First prizes and "Very Good" in their classes. They were still too young for the "Excellent" rating. I hope Scarlett will still get this rating, although Friday has a much better head. But Scarlett is a very strongly built, short-bodied female with a deep chest. Friday is more correct in shoulder and better in head, but he is very tall and I don't know whether he will get the desired weight and depth of brisket. I don't have the money to enter many shows, but Friday is fine for my breeding program.

Above all, Friday has wonderful temperament and character. Perhaps Abra, Czardas and Goody were more beautiful, but they were no better in temperament and courage. Friday has the best temperment--he is afraid of nothing, but nevertheless a dear and kind dog. At the training school he is called the "American Atom-bomb." I have gotten some very fine puppies from him. They are now 3 weeks old, and the finest puppies I have ever bred.

I am glad you are pleased that I will judge in Chicago. For the last two years I refused all invitations to judge anywhere, but I didn't dare to hope for an invitation to come again to Chicago, and to see you and Jack again. For me this is the greatest good fortune! But, don't forget that I am 70 years old, and am hoping that my physician does not forbid a voyage next Autumn. If he should do so, I hope you all will not be angry. Yet, I hope that all will be fine.

I don't know whether you still receive the "Boxer Blaetter." If you do, you read that I had my 70th birthday and the 50th anniversary of my kennel. I was honored at a big celebration in Munich. Those were great days for me! You asked about my body measurements. I regret that they have not changed much. I often think about the store in Chicago where you took me, where people can buy clothes for large men (Lane-Bryants). Here we don't have such stores, and therefore it is difficult for me to buy my clothes. If you would like to send me some clothes, choose the biggest size! I can make them shorter and tighter.

I am sending you a copy of my new Boxer book from the printers. I hope you will like it. In this book you will find yourself and some other well-known people. When I come to Chicago I shall write a dedication in your copy.

Of course, I shall tell no one about my expected trip over.

Many greetings from your every thankful

Friederun

[Note: Mrs. Stockmann did not make the trip to Chicago. This letter came from Wagner memorabilia owned by Mrs. Barbara Pieper.]

A Life with Boxers
has come to its end

With our breed the Boxer, there is one name inseparably bound:

Mrs. Friederun Stockmann

Born January 1, 1891
Died November 12, 1972

This woman, whose death touches us deeply, dedicated her life to the Boxer. It was she who opened the path for the devolpment of our breeding. Through her artistic talent she produced many drawings and carvings of unique stature. Her knowledge of the Boxer was revealed in her book, *My Life With Boxers*. She was the one who after the war used her name, and her kennel's name, to make the German Boxer once again respectable around the world.

In our materialistic times, it is difficult to imagine that there could even be such a person as she, who dedicated her very existance to her animals. Unfortunately, the young members of the Boxer Club never knew this extraordinary personality, but those who did know her will always remember her when they look at their Boxers, and for all times there will be in our Boxers' pedigrees the kennel

Vom Dom

From one of many who will think of her often

Friederun Felicitas b. Miram-Stockmann in Memoriam

The cold and unfriendly fall wind pushes rain showers over us. It is a day without joy and carries a hint of the coming winter. At the cemetery in Muehldorf on the Inn, a few people stand quietly, wrapped in winter clothing, to be with the departed one for the last time.

With the next of kin stand four friends from the Boxer world. The pastor delivers the necessary (obligatory) words, gives a short review of her life, and then comes the sound of earth landing on the boards of the coffin.

Mrs. Friederun Stockmann is no longer with us. She has departed, following the fate of all life on this earth. And yet—she still lives on! She lives on in our love for our Boxers. No one can ever take that from her. Her work, determination, sacrifice and performance remain alive now and will do so in the future, as long as there are Boxers.

Who was this unique woman? She was born on January 1, 1891, in Riga, and grew up there. In the years before World War I, she came to Munich to study at the Academy of Art. It was there she met the Boxer, fell in love with the breed and dedicated her whole life to it. In the January issue of 1911, we find her listed as a new member. Her great gifts were an instinctive breeder's vision, and enthusiastic willingness to learn about dogs, a natural sense of form and anatomical correctness, and above all an honest ability for self-criticism. With all of that went an almost excessive disregard for material goods, and only her work and love for the Boxer seemed to drive her life.

As the earliest sign of her critical abilities, we read of her decision not to breed her beloved first Boxer, Pluto. Instead, her clear vision saw the superior qualities of Rolf von Vogelsberg, whom she later purchased as the founding sire of her kennel. Success came quickly.

Just one year later in 1912, she won her first Sieger title

with Dampf vom Dom, a Rolf son, in Hamburg. From that time until well after the Second World War, she stood at the peak and forefront of Boxer breeding in the whole world. Her instinctive sixth sense, which a good breeder must have, kept her on the path of success; ambition and pride in her breeding served as motivation.

Rassel and Zwibel vom Dom led direct to Ivein, whose male pedigree goes back to Caesar von Deutenkofen, Moritz von Goldrain and Rolf Walhall to Rolf Vogelsberg.

Ivein's son Sigurd was the first Boxer to be prepotent in type. His sons and daughters dominated the top rank without challenge. Sigurd was also one of the first to go to the United States. Sigurd, with his undefeated grandson, Lustig vom Dom, and Lustig's brother Utz and another Sigurd grandson, Dorian von Marienhof—were the foundation of American breeding. Other Dom Boxers—down to Zünftig—stamped the Boxer in Great Britain.

Lustig was only used 42 times for breeding in Germany. But what great descendants he gave us: Danilo v. Königsee, Buten v. Elbufer, Carlo v. d. Wolfschlucht, Ajax and Arno v. d. Holderburg serve as a representative group for many more who could be named.

Although many years have passed, one incident still stands clearly in my mind. During a visit with her she told me of a litter she was expecting, one which I should see without fail. With all of her experience, she stated that she expected a new Rolf von Vogelsberg. Four months later I visited Mühldorf, and with pride she showed me a little elegant brindle dog: Godewind vom Dom. He did indeed look like his ancient ancestor. Even more amazing was that she had predicted it. Was it just an accident, a game played by fate?

She began with Rolf, and with Godewind she bred her masterpiece. In-between lay decades of a life for and with Boxers. How fortunate for the friends and breeders of the Boxer to have such a person among their ranks.

What was the Boxer in 1910/1911? An unbalanced dog creation with damaging mixed lineage, it still carried the results from a dead era of dog breeding—some 80-100 years earlier. She alone pulled the Boxer out of that canine darkness the fastest. Without Mrs. Stockmann that breeding would have taken generations longer.

Does she deserve our thanks for that? Yes, if you think of how few have been life-long Boxer lovers like her; yes, if one knows how the Boxer and her love for him were the main things in her life; and yes, if one knows how happy she was with her successes. But she never broke into tears when things went wrong. She always remained capable of self-criticism, was never entirely satisfied with her achievements striving always for improvement.

But she also had to experience ingratitude, hatred, and above all, jealousy. Those were probably the best expressions of how successful this unique lady really was. Envy and jealousy pursued her into her last years—mostly by people who were still in short pants as dog breeders and placed a well-cleaned kitchen ahead of their love for Boxers. Now she is gone, but she lives on in our dogs. How fortunate is the home where one of her unequaled statues and carvings stands. Through those we see the creative hand of this unique breeder.

Sadly but proudly I look at the Boxer head statue in my living room. Am I looking at Rolf, Sigurd or Lustig, or is it her last Wick? No, it is none of them.

It is a nameless Boxer that I see, one of many, of thousands and thousands across the whole world. That is how it should be and no other way! I now see the great old lady raise her finger in warning, and I feel bound not to do it—but I cannot prevent a few tears from falling. It is now snowing, and all will be soon be covered with a white blanket. Even her grave. Farewell, you fine, honest old lady.

Both obituaries were written by Otto Donner

Published in *Boxer Blätter,* by the German Boxer Club

Friederun von Miram-Stockmann at seventy-two years of age in 1963, shortly after the publication of her book .

Appendix I:

Origins Of The Dog

We share this old earth with about a million different species of animals, most of which are either indifferent or hostile to us. Only a few species have proved willing to train, and thus be of use to man. Even fewer animals have bonded with humans. They are recognized as our domesticated animals or pets.

But apart from their practical uses, some animals give us pleasure just by reason of their peculiar shape, attractive colors or interesting behavior. As humans became more civilized, the gap between them and nature grew wider and wider. Yet our affection and interest toward animals increased. Today countless homes contain beautiful aquariums stocked with brilliant tropical fish, while singing birds of all kinds live long, happy and carefree lives in the safety of their ornate cages.

The horse, man's noblest and truest friend, still claims the hearts of an ever-increasing number of fans, despite the universal popularity of the automobile.

Dogs occupy a place in human affection that is surely unique. This man-dog relationship is closer and more binding than our love for any other animal. It is not based on any notion of usefulness, but seems to stem from a sort of instinctive need which defies analysis. But it is well appreciated and understood by anyone who has ever owned a dog.

The beginning of the link between human beings and dogs dates from prehistoric times. Some fifty million years ago, a group of animals evolved, from which the beasts of prey later descended. The dog belongs to one of the oldest of the families which followed. Fossilized remains of the dog were first discovered in deposits of the old Stone Age. Although one cannot know for certain, it seems likely that the association between dogs and people started about 8000 B.C.

Among the most likely ancestors of the dog are the wolf, the jackal and the fox. Lately, however, some doubt has been expressed as to whether the fox had anything to do with the dog's evolution. This is based on the fact that the dog is essentially a pack animal, whereas the fox is solitary. Certain differences in the structure of the head of the dog and the fox also lend support to those who claim that the fox cannot have played any role in our favorite's ancestry. In addition, matings between dog and fox have never been fruitful, whereas crosses between dog and wolf or jackal can be achieved without difficulty and have produced hybrid offspring.

The first known accounts of selective dog breeding come from ancient China, Egypt and Mesopotamia. Dogs of several different types are shown in carvings and decorations made about 4000 B.C.: broad-muzzled ones as temple guards in China, long-legged greyhounds in Egypt and, about 2000 B.C., little short-legged dogs at the grave of Ben Hassan. Dogs which looked very much like our Boxers were found in old Inca graves and in South Africa and Sicily.

Dogs for a special use, and confined to a particular area, would inevitably inbreed. This helped stabilize the type. In time, the different types of dogs would have been used for different purposes, and the selective breeding of the most valued performers would gradually have influenced shape and appearance. Perhaps the first domestic dog came as a result of a wild puppy being brought back from a hunting expedition and given to the children to play with. It seems to me most unlikely that a full-grown wild dog could ever have been trained and used as a house dog. The possibilities of how it really all began are so many and various, we can hardly reconstruct them today.

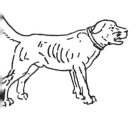

The original homeland of the Boxer may have been Tibet, where the Tibetan mastiff still exists. Chinese literature mentions hunters using these dogs as long ago as 1121 B.C., Alexander the Great is said to have brought some large mastiff-like dogs with him when returning from his travels in India. The Greeks produced the Molossus dogs, which were later given to the Romans, where they were unrivaled until the arrival of the British mastiff in the second century AD.

This mastiff was broader in muzzle and stronger than the Molossus dog, which it gradually replaced, although surely some crossbreeding between the two occurred. We can still study the general appearance and structure of the descendants of these dogs in old pictures, carvings and sculpture in art galleries and museums. In one of his works, Professor Hauck refers to a painting dating from the era 2283-2150 B.C., which shows a Dane-like dog with the head of a bulldog. There are also records of the war dogs of Nineveh existing in the seventh century and many distinct types of dogs are represented in the art of ancient Greece and Italy.

The British mastiff was certainly one of our Boxer's ancestors. The Britons kept big, very heavy dogs, both to protect their homes and livestock and for fighting purposes. These were well known before the time of the Roman occupation. These dogs were also used to hunt boars and bears and later, by the Romans, for fights in the circus arenas of Italy. In ancient law books, these dogs are referred to as *Canis percatoris* (boar hounds), *Canis qui vaccan et taurun prendit* (bulldogs) and *Canis ursoritus* (bear hounds). We know they were highly valued because

of the severe penalties imposed on anyone convicted of killing one of them.

Broad-muzzled dogs are found among the native breeds of practically every country in Europe. They were crossed with other types to produce dogs suitable for different uses. In Britain, the mastiff-cross gave rise to the large bull-baiter. The dogs known on the continent as Dogges were also created by this means. A pure type of old mastiffs still exists in the St. Bernard and in the smaller bull-baiter known as the Brabanter, in which reduction in size may have been caused by unfavorable environmental conditions.

Eventually, people came to realize that the small type of bull-baiter was more agile and therefore a better attacker than its bigger relative. As a result of breeders striving to get dogs with shorter muzzles, inequality in the length of the upper and lower jaws was encouraged and the project-ing, or undershot, jaw was stabilized. To hunt the wolf long jaws were most effective. But for boar hunting a shorter muzzle with an upturned underjaw enabled a dog to breathe while retaining a grip on its quarry with its in-curved fangs—something a dog with long, level jaws would find impossible to do.

Cropping may have started because the owners of the attack dogs found by experience that ears were easily bitten or torn and always bled a great deal. The cropped ear gave the enemy less chance to do damage.

Docking the tails of hunting and attack dogs probably originated in the same way.

The Bulldog family is still well represented in most countries by a number of different varieties, and the old mastiff survives in such breeds as the Dogue de Bor-deaux, the Bull Mastiff and the English Bulldog. Our own favorite, the Boxer, is a direct descendant of the Brabanter Bullenbeisser or smaller bull-baiter.

The German Boxer

From time immemorial, there existed in Germany a wide-mouthed dog of medium size. Though normally of quiet disposition, it was absolutely fearless when roused. Two pictures of the notorious Bavarian robber chief Hiesl (1738-1771), hang in the Munich National Museum. He is shown with his son and a large dog. This dog had a thick head, cropped ears, a docked tail, and its general appearance is strongly reminiscent of the modern Boxer.

How the name Boxer originated is not known. Perhaps its use may be taken as suggesting that the breed first came to Germany from England. On the other hand the name may have been used in allusion to the dog's technique and ability as a fighter.

The Boxer Club was founded in Munich in 1895, with the object of collecting and collating all available information regarding the origin of the breed, to draw up an official standard by which the breed should be judged and to produce and maintain a stud book. All these objectives were satisfactorily achieved, and both its standard and its stud book soon won international recognition. But in its early days the club had to weather many storms.

There was a good deal of disagreement as to what were the most desirable breed characteristics or structural features. Every Boxer owner believed that his own dog should be accepted as being the ideal type. Some were in favor of a broad, heavy skull similar to that shown by dogs crossed with the English Bulldog. Others preferred a somewhat taller, more agile dog that was neither unduly heavy in build nor too short in the leg, yet still had all the good qualities of the old-fashioned Boxer as he then existed, but with greater longevity. In those days, a Boxer was at its best when about a year old and aged very quickly. By the age of four, it usually looked very old and coarse.

At that time, too, most Boxers showed a lot of white,

many of them being either all white or piebald. The best heads were, for the most part, seen on dogs of the heavier type, and it was feared that the efforts to produce a smaller, more active dog might result in the loss of the correct breed type. For a long time many of the best puppies born were piebalds (checks) or showed heavy white markings.

At the Munich Boxer show at the beginning of this century, fifty dogs were entered. Looking back, it seems unbelievable that the great number of Boxers today have all been bred from those animals. But it shows the importance of the Boxer Stud Book started in 1904, nine years after the founding of the Boxer Club and carried on without interruption ever since.

Early Ancestors Of The Modern Boxer

The first Boxer entered in the Stud Book (No. 1) is Flocki, a son of the white Bulldog Tom, owned by Dr. Toenissen. This bulldog evidently played a leading part in laying the foundation of the Boxer breed, for many of the early entries in the stud book were his progeny. In later years, Tom came in for a good deal of criticism, but he undoubtedly possessed the correct type for that period, when nobility and length of leg were desired.

The next most important early ancestor was Meta von der Passage (No. 30), a granddaughter of Tom. Meta was white with brindle head patches. She had very heavy bone, a flat skull, heavy jowls and no chin. She proved an exceptional brood bitch, producing a remarkable number of very useful offspring. Also of importance was the fawn bitch Mirzl (44). Among the leading dogs were Flock St. Salvator, a fawn, and Wotan (46), a brindle. Flock was much nearer the elegant modern type than his contemporaries. He was a light fawn, very elegant in outline, but his head lacked the characteristic stamp.

In contrast, the brindle Wotan was heavy in build with massive bone and showed a lot of dewlap. Nevertheless,

he had the desired Boxer head. These two were later joined by Bosko Immergrun (24). From his photograph he appears to have been a pleasing fellow but his parentage is unknown. He exerted a great influence for good on the breed during its formative years.

Flock (14) and Meta (30) were the parents of the dog, Hugo von Pfalzgau (85), who was destined to become one of the foundation blocks of the breed. He had no right to the name of Pfalzgau; his name should have been Hugo von der Passage. He was bred by Josef Frey of Munich.

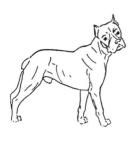

The dog Moritz von Pfalzgau (104) also came from Munich. He was a son of Wotan (46) and should have been called Moritz vom Angertor, but in those days breeders attached very little importance to kennel names.

These two dogs founded the Pfalzgau line, which in later years became famous for the quality and type found in its representatives. The first Boxer that showed true Boxer type, as we recognize it today, was produced by mating Meta and Wotan. He was the brindle Champion Giggerl (113). Even today he would have been considered a very good Boxer, with a pleasing head. Unfortunately, he had a roached back and weak hindquarters, faults that were shown by all brindles for the next ten years. Giggerl's granddaughter, Venus von Vogelsberg, became the dam of Rolf von Vogelsberg.

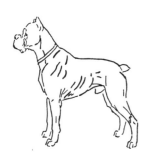

From a mating of Flock (14) and Meta (30) came Schanni von der Passage, a younger brother of Hugo. Schanni's son was Rigo vom Angertor (299). He was without doubt the most beautiful Boxer of his day, and the first of his breed to be sold for one thousand gold marks—a sensational figure at that time. In the year 1906, Rigo vom Angertor won a huge class of thirty-two dogs at the Frankfurt Show and was carried from the ring by his owner in triumph. Most of Rigo's best progeny were bitches, though he did sire some first-rate dogs.

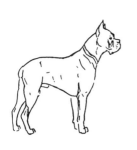

His daughters' offspring had a considerable impact on the future of the breed. One of Rigo's daughters, Dora von Vogelsberg, became the mother of the Champion Adda Walhall (3163) and of Champion Rolf Walhall (3091), a dog whose stud record overshadowed even that of his grandsire Rigo. At the age of seven, Rigo sired a litter from which three dogs became Champions. Looking through pedigrees of that time, we see that only three generations separated Boxers from their non-pedigreed ancestors. The three Champions from Rigo vom Angertor were Heinz, Golo and Rigo von der Elbe. We will read of them again later

Old Hugo von Pfalzgau, although his pedigree was known for only two generations, sired two fawn Champions, Kurt von Pfalzgau (481)—sire of Rolf von Vogelsberg—and Remus von Pfalzgau (719)—sire of Rolf's unbeaten rival, Milo von Eigelstein (1921). At that time, entries in the Stud Book had not yet totaled two thousand. At the beginning of 1960, they had reached ninety-two thousand. We have traveled a long way.

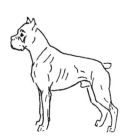

Characteristic Features Of The Boxer

More than fifty years ago a standard was drawn up which described the distinguishing points of the Boxer. It was a considerable and thankless task. Today, as then, the perfect dog has yet to be produced; the faultless dog exists only on paper.

Boxer breeders of the time had to decide the ideal breed type and its future development. Present-day Boxers are fairly uniform in type, and their faults have to be searched for. At that time, however, neither size, weight, type or color were standardized. It was therefore difficult to establish a true type acceptable to all breeders.

Horse-breeding, a far older art than dog breeding and unknown to most Boxer-breeders of the day, provided a pattern. Anatomy, the structure and relationship of all parts of the body, came first. Horses, which have been trained for centuries in all gaits and performances, provided the knowledge that only a well-balanced structure could achieve top performance. It proved also that the perfectly proportioned animal is always beautiful.

These facts indicated which features should be bred for in dogs, and general observation of nature confirmed those.

English and American breeders had instituted field trials with enthusiasm. Sporting dogs had to prove themselves in all situations and their occasional failures were obvious. German breeders adopted much from English experience.

The typical appearance of the dog must be accompanied by practical working ability. Each breed has its own special talent. For instance, the long back and short legs of the Dachshund enable it to dig deep; the long, flexible back of the Greyhound gives it great speed, and so on with other breeds.

Not all breed peculiarities are favorable; their value can often be doubtful, and sometimes they become almost a caricature. This goes for the wide front, the arched back and the short heavy head of the Bulldog. Naturally the peculiarities of all breeds cannot be usefully employed. Usefulness and beauty must always be in balance. An example of this basic attitude is provided by the Boxer, with his characteristic head, his broad muzzle and his endearing and unique expression.

General Appearance Of The Boxer

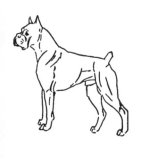

The Boxer is a medium-sized dog of great strength, but he should never appear either heavy or fat. He should combine his strength with ability and nobility. A dog should be from 57 cm (22 in.) to 63 cm (24 in.) at the withers and a bitch from 53 cm (20 in.) to 59 cm (23 in.). A dog of medium size should weigh 30 kg (66 lb) and a bitch 28 kg (59 lb). The Boxer should be a faithful companion and guard dog that can be implicitly relied upon never to fail in his job. But to enable him to carry

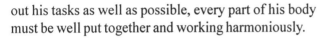

1. Ideal head. 2. Mastiff head. 3. Pinscher head. 4. Bull-dog head. 5. Loose dribbling lips. 6. Lips too short, too much undershot.

out his tasks as well as possible, every part of his body must be well put together and working harmoniously.

The Head

The head gives the Boxer its unique stamp, but head and body must be in proportion to each other, neither being too heavy or too light. In judging, the head must always be the deciding factor. However perfect the body may be, unless the head formation is correct a dog is no Boxer. The beauty of the head depends on the harmonious balance of muzzle to skull. When viewed from the front, the head should be nearly rectangular, the width of the muzzle being as equal as possible to the width of the skull. Such proportions are usually found in good puppies, but with age the head becomes broader and there is often a tendency for it to look cheeky, especially in dogs. The ears should be cropped long and set close together, and there should be only a little wrinkle between them. Correct wrinkle is necessary to give the typical Boxer expression. When these features are present, they contribute to the nobility of the general appearance.

The Muzzle

The muzzle must be short but not stunted, and well developed in all dimensions, but neither pointed nor

narrow. The formation of the muzzle is governed by the shape of the jaws, the placement of the teeth and the nature of the lips. The lower jaw is longer; hence the Boxer is undershot. The muzzle starts broad at the top and runs forward without narrowing. The canine teeth or fangs should be as wide apart as possible and the incisors, which generally number six, but sometimes seven or eight in the upper jaw, should be set in a straight row. The bite must be strong and gripping, the teeth being as even as possible.

The lips complete the shape of the muzzle. The top lip must be thick and well padded, filling out the hollow caused by the lower jaw being undershot. In this way the muzzle should appear blunt, broad and square. The upturned portion of the under jaw is termed the chin. The lower edge of the upper lip should rest on the edge of the lower lip. Although not protruding so much as in the Bulldog, the chin must be clearly defined both from the side and from the front. This imparts the true Boxer expression. A too prominent lower jaw makes the expression unduly pugnacious or sour and also interferes with gripping and feeding. On no account should either the teeth or the tongue be visible when the mouth is closed.

The nostrils should not be like those of the Bulldog, divided and upturned. They must not turn down. The tip of the muzzle must be higher than its root.

The skull must be rounded but not excessively, and neither flat nor too wide. The forehead is sharply divided from the skull to form a "stop."

Because of the powerful bite, the cheeks are strongly developed, but they must not protrude beyond the line of the skull. The soulful dark eyes must neither protrude nor be slit-like. The light eye, like that of a bird of prey, is a disqualification. Dark eyes indicate intelligence and energy but the eyes must not be threatening or piercing. The eye rims must be dark in color. The nose is broad with wide nostrils and slightly turned up. It must always be black.

Faults: lack of type and nobility; somber face; badly developed teeth, either from disease or malformation; Pinscher or Bulldog head; badly cropped ears; dribbling;

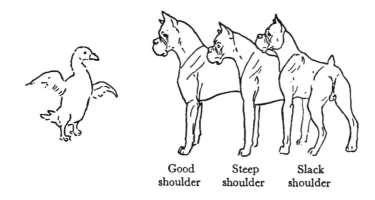

| Good shoulder | Steep shoulder | Slack shoulder |

obvious hew; projecting teeth and/or tongue; wild, light eyes; too short or too long in the jaw.

The Neck

The neck contributes much to the Boxer's appearance of elegance and nobility. It should be strong but not too short and not too thick. It must be muscular with a distinctly marked nape and an elegant arch down to the back, and must be held high. Faults include too much loose skin (dewlap) and anything that makes the neck appear short or heavy.

The Frame

The frame should be square. The height of the dog is measured from the ground to the top of the withers; the length of the body from the front of the chest to the seat bones *(ischium)*. Both distances should be practically equal. As a rule the bitches are slightly longer than the males.

Chest And Forelegs

The chest should be deep, reaching down to the elbows. The depth of the chest is generally exactly half the height of the dog. The ribs should be well arched, but not barrel-shaped, and extend well back. The loins should be short, close, taut and slightly tucked up. The underline

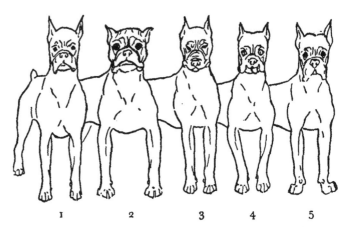

1. Ideal head. 2. Broad 'cheeky' head, front too wide. 3. A typical head, narrow chest. 4. Light eyes, too much undershot, shows tongue, ricketty forelegs. 5. Eyes too big, French stance.

of the abdomen should run in a graceful curve to the rear. The shoulders should be long and sloping, well knit, close lying and not excessively covered with muscle. The upper arm should be long and set at right angles to the shoulder-blade. The forelegs must be straight, parallel and vertical. Since they support the whole body, they must be firm and well boned. The elbows should not be too tight to the body, but must not stand out or be loose, and the pastern or ankle should be short and slope only slightly from the perpendicular. The feet should be small and arched like those of a cat, the toes being close together with hard pads, Major faults include: front too broad and low or too narrow in chest; loose shoulders; chest hanging slackly between the shoulders; hare feet or splay toes; hollow flanks, hanging underline; bowed forelegs and out-turned feet and toes.

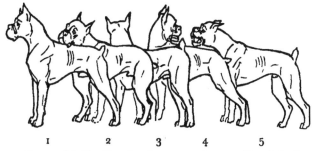

1. Boxer with ideal head and construction.   2. Roach back.
3. Straight stifles.   4. Low tail set.   Too lean in flank.

The Back

The back ties together the front and the hindquarters.
The withers should be clearly defined.

The whole back should be short, straight, broad and
strongly muscled. Grave faults include a roach back, a
sway or dipping back, a narrow back, long, narrow, sunken
loins and weakness at the union with the croup.

The Hind Quarters

The quarters should be strongly muscled, for they

Bowed legs   Correct stance   Cow hocks

provide the driving force that gives the body its forward impetus. Their anatomy is suited to this task. The muscles should be iron hard and be seen rippling beneath the skin. The thigh should be broad and curved, not flat and narrow; the second thigh being strongly developed and well muscled. Both the upper and lower thighs should be long. The croup should be slightly sloped, slightly rounded and broad. The tail must be set high rather than low, be docked and carried high. The pelvis, especially in bitches, should be long and broad. The hip and knee joints should be strongly angulated. When the dog is standing the knee (stifle) should reach so far forward that it would touch a vertical line drawn from the point of the hip to the ground. The angle at the hock should be about 140 degrees; that part of the foot below the hock joint making an angle of from 95 to 100 degrees with the ground. Viewed from behind the hind legs should be straight and neither bowed nor cow-hocked. The hind feet should be somewhat longer than the forefeet and be strongly padded. The main faults are: croup falling away or too much arched, low set tail, steep or too little angulation of hind quarters, hollow thighs, cow hocks, bow legs, narrow heel, hind dew claws, weak hocks, tottering or waddling gait, open feet, hind quarters set either too far under the body or extended too far behind.

The Color

The color of a Boxer is either fawn or brindle. Fawn comes in many different shades, from deer red to very light fawn. The light yellowish fawn is not much liked and is therefore not seen very often nowadays. The intermediate colors such as gold or red fawn are the most popular. In the old days, the very deep brown red was not a permissible shade and even today finds little favor in comparison with the red fawn. In solid-colored dogs, a black mask is essential and adds considerably to the animal's appearance. The mask must be confined to the muzzle and not reach above the eyes, otherwise it gives the face a sombre expression.

Brindles have black stripes on a red-gold or fawn ground. The colors must be clearly defined. In the brindle color group there are many variations, the darkest of which look almost black. But there are no truly black Boxers today, as this color is now extinct in the breed. The background color of a brindle should be as colorful as possible.

White markings are permissible but must not exceed one third of the total coat area. Formerly only solid-colored Boxers were esteemed, but public demand for white-marked dogs was so great that they were officially recognized as being just as correct in color as the more solid-colored dogs. In England and America, one hardly ever sees a Boxer without white markings, since in these countries a plain-colored dog has practically no chance of winning high honors.

All-white Boxers are not eligible for entry in the Stud Book, neither are all-black ones. Mismarkings, like a half white face or uneven leggings, are also disliked.

The Character

In the Boxer, character is of the greatest importance. Loyalty and faithfulness to his owner and household are inbred traits, and he is renowned for his unfailing vigilance and dauntless courage. These make him unsurpassed as a guard and protector. Within the family he is docile and reliable, a great friend to children, quiet and trustworthy, even with strangers. He is joyful and restrained in play with his friends, but can be terrible when roused to anger.

The training of a Boxer calls for a firm but loving hand. Although determined and completely fearless towards his enemies—even heavy blows will never deter him—with his master he is often as gentle and sensitive as a child.

One should never forget that the Boxer is descended from fighting dogs. He can be completely spoiled by bad handling or inconsiderate treatment.

His natural dignity and grave, somewhat formidable, appearance are usually enough to ensure that both he and his master are received with respect wherever they go. The Boxer is generally recognized as being one of the best of all guard dogs. He is also highly esteemed as a house and family companion. His quiet nature, medium size, short, clean coat and general hardiness are all very much in his favor, and he has held a high position in the affection of dog-lovers for over half a century. In that time, fashions in dogs have undergone many changes, many breeds have come and gone, but the Boxer's circle of devotees has remained true to its favorite, and he is still adding steadily to the number of his admirers.

The Boxer is the soul of fidelity, bravery and honesty. The worst faults of character a Boxer can show are viciousness, treachery, unreliability, lack of temperament and cowardice.

Appendix II:
Miscellaneous Essays
by Friederun Stockmann

Note: These essays, some published in German when written and others collected from unpublished manuscripts, appeared first in the third German edition of Ein Leben mit Boxern *[My Life With Boxers]. Ingeborg Gollwitzer, the publisher, collected and edited the material. Whenever possible, the translator has listed an approximate date beside the title for the composition of the essay. Most of the essays carried internal clues as to when they were written.*

[CDG]

The Dog Pack And Its Leader   [ca. 1936]

Our pack leader [German: *Führer*] for many years was Ivein, and his death left a void. Some may read that sentence and think that the dogs of the vom Dom kennel have accepted the present fashion and gone over to the Führer principle.

If so, then that person is wrong. The instinct among animals to form herds, flocks and packs—always led by an alpha animal—is primitive and ancient. In our Boxers lie the instincts of the wolf to live and struggle for survival together in a pack. We must understand that or we do not understand the true nature of dogs. Of course, most dogs are not in packs but alone, and the owners might not see the pack instinct in operation.

There are solitary animals in nature—the so-called "loners"—who have lost contact with their pack and must seize every chance to secure their survival. It's often the same way with the pet dog. They follow their instincts by attaching themselves completely to human beings in what is a environment foreign to their nature. No longer is the pack one of dogs but is now made up of human beings. The dog's social and protective drives now focus on people, and worry about food disappears. Every strange dog of equal or greater size becomes an enemy, unless the owner is very careful.

When I was a young beginner in dog breeding, my plan was to allow the dogs to live openly together, and the other breeders ridiculed me. They told me the most frightful stories. And, indeed, my first attempts with two newly-purchased older dogs were not too successful. I also read Fridjof Nansen's *Night and Ice*, and it made a deep impression on me and gave me many second thoughts. Nansen wrote:

> *Once released, the dogs immediately began to fight among themselves, and some of the poor creatures hobbled away from the battlefield, bitter and beaten. This morning we received the bad news that Hiob was dead; he had been ripped apart by the others. They found his body quite a distance from the ship. Suggen was guarding the body, and would not allow any other dog to come near it.*

> *These dogs are a bunch of scoundrels that fight every day. Barabass has almost lost his mind from fear. We keep him on board now and do not dare to put him out on the ice. He knows that the other monsters will attack him. There's not a shred of nobility or chivalry in the mutts. If there is a fight, all of the others join in attacking the underdog. Perhaps it is a law of nature that the stronger and not the weaker be protected. Have we human beings perhaps tried to reverse nature when we always try to protect the weaker and help them survive? This time it was Ulabrand, that old brown toothless fellow. Hiob and Moses met their fates earlier.*

> *(29 November): Another dog was bitten to death today. Fix, a pretty and powerful*

animal was discovered dead and stiff.
Suggen did his usual duty and guarded the
body.

After that depressing picture, I read Amundson, who had much better experiences. He kept his northern sled dogs in large packs. When there were incidents, the assumption was that the fault lay in the arrangement of the dogs, as usually happens when man blindly tries to force his will against nature's laws.

We can learn much from that short excerpt from Nansen. First of all, there is no doubt that Suggen—the protector of the dead—was the moral leader of the pack. Second, the submissive ones were mostly the old and weak and cowardly in the group. Third, dogs always stand together against the enemy. And the inferior is treated like an enemy; it must submit because otherwise all the others together will attack him. If it were any other way, there would be constant fighting and great losses. The pack always works together, which is necessary for survival but gruesome when they destroy other pack members simply because they will not accept the pack rules.

Nansen's report also demonstrates that you cannot assemble a pack out of solitary animals that do not know each other. You must build up a pack systematically and carefully. The best way is for the dogs to grow up in the pack. A natural hierarchy develops around a strong, intelligent male dog; the others—whether dogs or bitches—will assemble around him. Finally, there are the puppies who have now outgrown that stage when their mother supplied all their needs.

The sire quite naturally protects his bitch against enemies and intruders. Even a dog that is not usually a scrapper can become one easily when a bitch is brought to him. But there are many dogs that try to keep the peace in their packs. When two bitches begin to fight, the male alpha separates them immediately. Whether they are in heat or try to bite back, the alpha never seems to injure them.

Many times I have noticed that the peace of the pack is upset by a nervous, fearful animal. If a dog has been re-moved from the pack for awhile, it is common for the others to surround it when it returns. A courageous dog is not afraid and runs right to the pack. But the coward is afraid, his hackles go up and the tail down; perhaps he snarls or even bites. That is often the beginning of a fight.

It is different with the notorious troublemaker. If the pack leader does not put him in line or he doesn't voluntarily restrain himself, then he is best removed from the pack altogether. Often those dogs that are most likely to fight strange dogs will be the most tolerant fellows in the pack. The other side of the coin is like the one troublemaker I had in my kennel who was a cowardly, weak animal among unknown dogs.

Strange animals, however, can be brought into a closed pack. But if it is a bitch, she should not be the nervous, quarrelsome type. And if it is a male, then it's best that he is not too old. I usually lock up the new animal for three or four days, if possible with youngsters or a completely reliable bitch. Best place is a kennel area that is open and visible to the other pack members. Very quickly the new-comer takes on the scent of the family. And if the stranger is not belligerent because it will not accept the pack order, then the other dogs will usually accept it peacefully into the pack.

Proper training at the right time can be very important for puppies and young dogs. It can definitely help suppress the fighting instincts. I will not tolerate any biting among the little puppies, nor too wild rough housing among the bigger pups. Food-envy and jealousy can easily be eliminated if one just fights against them from the puppies' earliest days on. Likewise, fighting over sexual attractions and also hunger can be totally suppressed, if the kennel owner is conscien-tious about it.

One example of how an emotional struggle for a common goal can be peaceful—even comradely—is something I see every day. In our fields, there are moles and mice, and digging them out of their hills and runways is one of life's greatest victories for the dogs. When the day is hot and the ground hard, it is hard work. Three to five dogs work on one hole; when one tires another takes over. But when they find the mouse, then the Alpha takes over. The booty belongs to him. If the mouse hops out of a different hole and is caught by a different dog, then all hell breaks loose. Unless the winner can swallow the mouse quickly (which seldom happens because they are too big), then the unhappy winner will have to surrender the rodent to the pack leader.

My description of a typical pack leader is based on Ivein. He was a fanatical mouse catcher when young. Later, he only watched until the others had dug to the point that the mouse was ripe for catching. Then he stepped in. Only after he had become older, did he sometimes turn the mouse over to Dudel. But no one else.

Outside our premises, Ivein could be a ferocious fighter. No strange dog ever came up to Ivein without carrying scars for it the rest of his life. Two incidents demonstrate his regular performance in such matters.

Ivein always accompanied me when I went out with the horses and wagon. If I approached a place with a big dog, I would always put Ivein on a leash. He then trotted along with his head under the axle between the rear wheels. He was so used to that position that he often trotted there for miles, even when not leashed. One day I approached a spot where there was a big mutt who attacked all dogs that passed. I leashed Ivein so close to the axle he hardly had any free line. Suddenly this farm dog, four inches taller than Ivein, attacked Ivein. I felt so sorry for my dog, because he was unable to maneuver against this apparently superior hound.

Under the wagon, the battle was in full swing. I heard a terrible howl and loud growling, but could not do anything. Finally, I succeeded in freeing the leash and pulling out from under the wagon everything attached to the other end.

Ivein came out first; he was the one doing all the growling. Clamped in Ivein's jaws, hung the big mutt! I was only able to get those jaws open by prying them with a linchpin between the back teeth. The other dog then fled, probably as he had never fled before in his whole life. Just how Ivein managed to get such a grip when he had so little room under a moving wagon is still a mystery to me.

Another time later, Ivein accompanied me—this time he had a muzzle on—running free next to the wagon. A tavern owner in the next town had a very aggressive dog, famous for his fighting and much larger than Ivein. This dog had not only attacked many dogs, but had even bitten people, including children.

As we came around a blind corner, suddenly this mutt appeared. Ivein did not hesitate for a second: he leaped on the other dog and knocked it down. Because of the muzzle, Ivein could not bite. So he boxed with his nose! Each time the other dog tried to get up, Ivein would skillfully flip him over. In one place where the road ran next to a steep embankment, Ivein shoved his opponent over the edge. The dog hardly landed at the bottom before Ivein was there standing over him. When Ivein jumped back for a moment to try to get the muzzle off, the mutt took off at high speed. Ivein never came out of a fight with even the slightest injury.

Still, in the kennel with his pack members, Ivein was very patient, although he never expressed strong affection. When the young males reached a certain stage, at some point Ivein would give them a quick lesson as to who the boss was. That only happened one time to a youngster, but I had the impression all Ivein wanted to say was, "I am the master." After that he never touched the dog again, as long as it minded its own business.

Sigurd was visibly devoted to his father. He was better humored than Ivein, but when angry he could be more dangerous. But he did not seek to dominate. After a little skirmish, he would go his own way and amuse himself by chewing on a bone or finding a toy.

Ivein really enjoyed playing with his pack. He would stand in the center of them, legs apart, mouth slightly opened. The others surrounded him, barking, leaping at him, attacking him. Ivein just warded them off with his head, pushing the attacker to the side but never injuring any of them. He was the picture of confidence, strength and calm superiority.

When Zorn became about a year old, he began to get sassy. One day Ivein grabbed him by the back of the neck, for no apparent reason and completely unexpected for me. He shook him so hard I became frightened. But to my amazement, Zorn did not have any injuries. Usually, in his fighting Ivein would do serious biting. Zorn never forgot the lesson. He had no respect for his father Sigurd, but Zorn always paid homage to Ivein.

Some time ago, the adolescent males started a brawl over a new bitch, and eventually Zorn and Ivein became involved. Ivein was only a shadow of his former self, Zorn was at his peak with his three years. Who knows how that would have ended up if I had not intervened! This time Ivein might still have won, just because he was such an experienced brawler with great technique—an old but tricky fighter. Zorn still kept his respect for Ivein. But there certainly would have eventually been another fight between the two, and it would have gone to the younger dog with the same probable result as Nansen described. The younger dog, when once aware of his strength, would have taken over the pack's leadership. But we were spared the battle for domination between them. The elderly Ivein had to be painlessly released from his suffering, which had been torturing him for his last weeks.

Who would now be Ivein's successor? Had Sigurd been there, then probably he and Zorn would have fought for the role. Today, Zorn is the unchallenged ruler. Only Zorn's son, Lustig, stands as a possible future rival, and which of those two rules will probably be settled at their next argument.

A bitch's whelping area is something that all members of the pack respect. My bitches always whelp in the same room where the whole family gathers most often, where the dogs all come and go as they please. All of the dogs are here in the evening and through the night. The litter box is somewhat separated, because it has a blanket-roof over it. But once the dam begins to whelp, all other dogs move away from the area. Most likely the odor causes that. If a curious young dog starts to approach, it only takes a low growl from the dam and the intruder quickly retreats.

Having two bitches with puppies in the same room can be dangerous. It is only too easy for one or the other to feel jealous or else overprotective, and a fight can soon erupt. I believe it is better not to separate a mother from her pups for a very long period. It is possible that the other dogs—if the mother is absent for a long time—will regard the puppies as strangers and attack them.

Only Ivein was allowed to inspect all newborn puppies without the dam growling at him. Ivein had a peculiar habit along these lines: he loved to eat the trimmed-off portions of the puppies' ears and tails. Otherwise he was a very fussy eater. And he would not touch any pieces from puppies that were brought to me by others.

As I said, not every dog can be kept in a pack without trouble, if you wish to avoid any great dangers. Especially those lacking confidence and the cowardly should be separated, but also the overly-aggressive dogs are a constant danger to their kennel mates. I once owned a bitch that would attack any dog in the kennel, after I had disciplined it. She was very dangerous at that time. Also those dogs that are too aggressive toward people can be a danger in the pack, because the other pack members might eagerly join the aggression. What happens when a dozen or so aggressive adult dogs attack a human being can be easily imagined.

Dogs with a passion for hunting and roaming should also be removed from the pack, since they could spoil them all. A dog seldom hunts alone, preferring to take along a companion. You can see beforehand exactly how they come to agreement. They sniff each other in an unusual way, then one nudges the other, and suddenly they race away. Calling and whistling for them to return is a waste of time. Sometimes it is enough just to remove the two with such an obsession, and the problem is solved.

Even if a breeder has several dogs in special situations and cannot completely give up kenneling some, there is still an advantage in keeping most of them in a pack. Of course, it takes much more time and the animals must be nearby and under control. But the big advantage is that dogs raised in a pack are not as silly as pure kennel dogs.

All the animals of the pack have a common environmental experience, a kind of family odor. It is always dangerous, when one returns after a show or some other multi-day absence, just to put a dog back in the pack. The returning animal runs to greet the pack members, but they regard him with mistrust. Often that is taken for jealousy, but it is not that. The foreign smells that the returning dog carries are the sole cause for suspicion. Understanding this is extremely important for keeping peace in the house. The best way is to separate the dog for a day. That is enough time for him to pick up the home's smells. If I have a freshly-used stud dog, I usually rub him down lightly with creolin. After that I can put him together with other adult males without worrying that some jealousy-scenes might erupt.

Of course, there are some disadvantages to allowing dogs to live in a pack, and the breeder must use the kennel to overcome them. Adult dogs raised in a pack will find it very difficult to adjust to a change in residence, much more so than the kenneled dog. This goes for a change in ownership, also. The pack dogs often seem shy and fearful in those circumstances, even though that is not their nature. One has to understand that. A dog that changes masters only has to adjust to another person, usually with about the same life-style. A kennel dog is happy just to have a little more freedom and be useful, especially when it can also interact more with a person.

But for the pack dog, a change in location is a change in its whole environment. It's no different than it would be for a wild animal that has been captured and must now live under totally different circumstances.

Only when the dog has completed its second year (an important threshold for our Boxers), does the pack dog begin to be more of an individual. A separation is easier to handle after that second year. I have often had dogs, which I have given up, return later and show that they had never forgotten my kennel. Sometimes they are homesick long after leaving. But I have never taken in a strange dog (including adults) that did not feel completely at home within one week, at the latest. In fact, after a very short time, most of them hesitate to follow their old master. That is not because of me, but because they are in a more natural situation here in the open.

Another interesting thing is that a pack dog matures much more slowly than the kenneled dog. But there remains in that animal a healthier, less corrupted core. It grows up to be a solitary dog, such as one in the city, just as an awkward farm girl can develop into a normal city woman. But it takes longer.

The pack leader must be a complete dog, one of sound health, calm confidence in himself; one that can easily handle the loners as well as the trouble makers. All of the others will gather around him, with each knowing its exact place in the pack. When I watch all of that in operation, what pleases me most is that this is something functioning without human direction. The dogs have chosen their leader; the best becomes the alpha and the others follow. Nature's ancient law is in force.

What We Should Not Forget: Thoughts About Dogs In World War I

In my long life as a dog breeder I have lived and experienced many things. Today I can look back and say that I have brought my dogs through many difficult times, through the hard war years and the sometimes even harder postwar years. Together we have starved and even swindled a bit, just to survive. Because the younger folks and the know-it-alls from that time really know nothing, I would like to discuss the hardships of those years as they pertained to the dogs. Sometimes those hardships were worse than for their owners. But it was all worth the trouble. Not only did I manage to keep my line intact; I was also able to supply the army with excellent service dogs.

When we heard about Serbia's refusal of the Austrian

ultimatum in the summer of 1914—I was at a dog show in Ulm at the time—we were actually enthusiastic about it. That is something I will never forget. We knew it probably meant war, and we did not really sense the tragedy of the moment. At the time, I had several dogs at the show, and I also wanted to buy a bitch. No one had a clue what would happen next, but if war were to come we all believed it would be short.

Just to be cautious, I did try to store up some dog food: lots of potatoes and lard. Use of lard created diarrhea, and one had to be careful to introduce it gradually into the diet. But it was good sustenance. Of course, we had our little farm, but that was not much. With the threat of war, I began to raise rabbits, chickens and even had ten goats. I also leased additional land next to us. Of course, with those preparations I was certain I would have no trouble bringing the dogs through any troubled times.

My husband was called up in September, and that made life much more difficult. After all, my training was as a sculptress and I had already made a successful start in that. When I was just eighteen, my first work was shown and at the Munich Glass Palace. A few years later, in 1913, my bronze statue of a French Bulldog had a record sale at the same place. Then in 1914, another piece of mine was accepted by Salon-Paris; and I had successfully shown and sold works in Berlin and other cities.

With the beginning of the war I lost all contact with my parents living in Riga [Latvia]. No longer could I count on their help and encouragement in either my professional or personal life. Thus I began the war with a big, newly-built house, a child less than a year old and a dozen dogs. So it became a matter of surviving, both for my family and my dogs.

Soon some of the other kennels began to shut down. The owners went into the service, often killing their dogs, but sometimes offering them to me. As much as possible, I took those dogs, and often I was able to place one of my older bitches with the owner's wife for a house pet. Two of those adopted dogs made a memorable impact. One of them killed my favorite bitch right after coming to me. The other became the foundation bitch of my breeding program right down to today.

Shortly after the war's outbreak, something happened that had a great impact on our Boxers. Right after the invasion of Belgium, a high officer in Munich received a report that German patrols were being fired upon by civilians, and the troops were not able to capture the snipers. The report went on to express a wish for some well-trained aggressive dogs to help in capturing them. Since the officer knew Boxers well, he turned to the Boxer Club and that very night six Boxers were taken by private car to Belgium. At the same time, a training program was set up to supply more dogs. My husband and I went to Munich as often as possible to help in that work.

In just a short time, some sixty Boxers from the Munich region were turned over to the army. The dogs were outfitted with good collars and long leashes, all paid for by the local Munich Boxer club. Other breed clubs from the working group also joined with us, thus beginning the use of dogs in the battlefield.

My husband, who had been called up by the reserves in September, then received a direct assignment from General Headquarters to move to the Western Front with an infantry battalion and ten Boxers that he had personally trained.

What I would like to do here is report what happened to the dogs at home and perhaps set a few things straight. First of all, it must be emphasized that it is not true that mostly surplus and unwanted dogs were turned over for military service. Actually, it was just the opposite. Dogs sent from the Munich area were some of the best working dogs available, and many were given with a heavy heart. Sometimes they were the family favorite, but sacrificed for the good of the Fatherland. In one family—a childless one— a dog was turned over that was the owner's darling. The owner told me, "I can't help the Fatherland because of my age, but this is our most faithful Boxer, and I am convinced he will serve the country well."

The dog was delivered with a nice coat tied on with pink ribbons, so it would not get chilly if it had to sleep on the ground. That Boxer became one of the best service dogs, and he never needed the coat!

Very few of these dogs returned from front service. Perhaps their deaths were not as painful for the owners as were those that died at home. One of my most valuable bitches died of a rapidly growing tumor on her head. Since almost all veterinarians were in the service, we were unable to find one, but even those vets at home would have been unlikely to spend time on a dying dog. After watching her suffer for three days, I put her away myself. It still bothers me today that I may have given up too soon. I loved my dogs dearly, but for most people a dog's life was not of great value.

Finding sustenance was difficult, both for people and dogs. In order to get potatoes for human consumption we began to slaughter and trade our pigs. There was little left over for the dogs. Every day I rode my bicycle for hours, just to get some intestines from a butcher or some watery butter-milk from a farmer. The women's club collected dried potato peelings, discarded vegetables and the remains of grain-coffee grounds. Sometimes there would be some crumbs from old bread, which I could use for chicken feed. But the chickens did not seem to care for that. They preferred searching out food from what grew on the grounds of the farm. Finally, I was able to scrounge up some barley. That produced eggs which I could barter for large amounts of dry food for my dogs.

One incident in passing: once when my hens seemed to suddenly slow down with their laying, I began to suspect the dogs were stealing eggs. One day I had carefully collected 20 eggs, put them in a basket on top of a box, and the eggs disappeared. There was still a wet spot in the basket when I discovered that the eggs were gone. But no dogs had been around. Then I saw one of the goats still licking its mouth. I could hardly believe that a goat was an egg thief! So I held out an egg to her as a test. Yes, she took it out of my hand, bit it and then swallowed it!

It was mainly the goats that helped me over this difficult time, because their milk did not have to be turned over to the authorities. I thought it was inconsistent that our dogs were at the battlefield doing their duty, but at home the authorities could not have cared less about those dogs that were being raised and trained for that same duty. No one cared whether the dogs even received minimum sustenance. Yet they kept demanding more and more dogs. Of course, if children and adults are not receiving enough food, then the dogs have to take second place. But they had no organization in taking care of garbage.

A typical example was a large dog food manufacturing firm whose director recommended that I feed the dogs their "prime" canned food. One can cost 1.10 marks and consisted of a lot of liquid in which two pig's ears floated. But no matter how hungry, not a single dog would eat one of those ears. No one could figure out why. It was the same with the dried food put out by that company: it looked like baked horse manure and probably tasted the same. One Boxer judge wrote, "My dogs just could not make friends with it."

At that time we had to resort to things which we would not do today. After a time to get used to it, my dogs even learned to like eating dog meat. What could you do? From the packing houses you got nothing; the horse butchers' shops had long lines waiting outside. There was hardly enough for people. I tried to feed normal food, but there just was not enough. One time I had a litter, and I placed the smallest bitch puppy. About six weeks later she came back for cropping, and I was amazed to see that she was bigger than any of her litter mates. All because she had eaten better than they.

And then came the time of severe shortages. Our dogs became sick and many died. Yet, the authorities kept demanding more dogs for the military. I put an ad in a magazine once and received a telegram from a private party saying, "I will pay twice the asking price if I can get one of your dogs."

But that's enough from those sad days. Of all the dogs we sent to the field, only my eleven-year-old champion, Rolf von Vogelsberg, came back, and died shortly thereafter in the homeland. His name still appears in our pedigrees. Still, I would have been proud if the good old battler had died doing his service in the battlefield.

In the course of the years, I have received many valuable trophies and personal awards. But the only documents I have framed are two from the army's training branch, as a representative of the Bavarian Department of Defense. They were issued to me and my husband for supplying dogs to the military.

We breeders of working dogs can be proud that we bred, raised and trained animals that served their nation in a time of great need! One of the most important duties was that of the messenger dogs. They ought to be praised by all. What a great service they performed! We will never know how many valuable human lives were saved by the wonderful work of the service dogs, but we must always be grateful to them.

Thoughts On Watchfulness And The Drive To Protect

There are so-called "dog experts" that give the sport of dogs a bad name. Usually they are like the mayflies, who are around for only one day or so. The mayflies of the dog game suffer the first defeat and start throwing sawdust in the flour. They have not grasped the fact that it is a voluntary, fair competition among folks of a similar mind. Nor do they understand that the dog game requires self-discipline, personal sacrifices, and a great amount of knowledge about dogs. The requisites for breeding, raising and training dogs are broad knowledge and a special talent. Raising and caring for young dogs is much closer to baby care than most people can imagine.

Above all, the breeder must be familiar with the laws of inheritance, the sicknesses and care of dogs, and how to give the dog training after it grows older. All of that takes time, lots of love for animals, and a good amount of energy. But the more difficult it is to reach the goal, the more desirable it is. And once bitten by the sport of dogs, it is hard not to give it your body and soul.

Today, it is apparent that breeders and trainers are in different camps, marching separately. But despite that they are not pursuing different goals. Sometimes the work, time and cost are too much for one person, so they choose either breeding or training. For breeders it is often not only impossible but also unimportant that they train their own dogs.

Regrettably, today there is a falsehood going around that only protection training is worthwhile. We always hear someone say, "Oh yes, protection training **is** something you can always use in a dog. But what good would tracking or even messenger training be?"

I have been breeding around thirty years and have trained my own dogs since 1911. Never have I had an experience where one of my Boxers had to bare his teeth to protect his master in real life. But numerous times, my dogs have used their messenger training, as well as tracking and watchdog training to my advantage.

Some time ago I noticed late at night that I had lost my purse in the woods. The next day (almost 24 hours later), I let my Boxer bitch search for it. She sniffed and searched and actually found the purse with 180 Reichmarks in it. Our dogs with messenger training regularly carry messages from the house out to whoever is working in the field. They carry food to them also.

But I do not see the primary importance in dog training in just its practical application. More important is that the breeder can develop breeding goals by learning how the dogs react to training. One soon recognizes training abilities in even puppies and very young dogs.

Take the courier dog as an example. Not every dog can do that, even with extensive training. A courier dog must have great endurance, a love for running, courage and a desire to obey. I have had Boxers that just shook with eagerness when they knew they were going to carry a message. But others did their duty because there was nothing else for them to do.

Most dog owners want to have a house dog that is a protective companion. In an essay about the different responses to the protection test, Herr Sch. presented a somewhat different view. In his opinion, about 90% failed the test. In his opinion, many dogs without training would have passed the test, while many trained for the degree did not. But he also demanded that one only breed to dogs that had achieved a Schutzhund degree.

In my view, it was not the dogs at fault for failing, but the type of examination that Herr Sch. described.

Mostly what we saw in our training was that even the most intelligent dog is still an animal, and that must be taken into account. Very often excellent dogs would fail when there was a change in location for the test, as was the case with his examinations. Certainly, we cannot be sure if that is an error or just normal dog thinking. It would be best if we tried to understand why that was—and could be no other way.

A dog defends a house or thing only when that dog believes the object is connected to his master! It is completely wrong to place a dog in a strange location all by himself, and then expect that it will immediately protect the house. Actually, there are some dogs that will do just that! But this is not necessarily a good thing. Anyway, most dogs—especially when they are very attached to their masters and homes—will not do that. Certainly, no one who understands dogs would be surprised by that or consider it a fault in them.

During the past year, surely over a hundred bitches came to us for breeding. Not a one showed a desire to protect our place, even though I personally know that most of them would have done so for their own masters and homes.

Guarding is nothing other than defending their "territorium"—in this case the home—against all intruders, even the friendly ones. No dog is interested in defending a strange place that has no ties to him. Of course, a biting dog—especially a fear-biter—often attacks everything that comes near. But that type of guarding is usually worthless because of the constant barking that goes with it.

Tests using a fake burglar should not be used. He might indeed be attacked by some dogs that are over-aggressive but perhaps not good watch dogs. Either the dog recognizes the burglar or the situation from earlier experiences, or the person arouses the dog because of some unusual appearance or action. In which case, the dog attacks mainly to protect himself, rather than a foreign house.

Testing for a dog's protective qualities should only be done where the dog is at home, without the owner being present, of course. I believe very much that character is an inherited feature, just as much as appearance. But many times we overlook the fact that character is often as polygenic as appearance. Many inherited factors make up both. And the complete dog must be a balance of these. The head alone does not make the dog, nor does aggression-impulse alone make the good Schutzhund. A good protector of the master does not necessarily make a good watchdog.

Precisely because guard instincts have been an ancient part of our Boxers' background, we must continue to give that feature our attention in breeding. Watchdogs are as a rule born. Without that instinct it is very difficult to train them for that—if one can do it at all. My old Rolf von Vogelsberg is an example. He was an excellent working dog, as he proved in Schutzhund tests and on the battlefield, but he was a complete failure as a watchdog. He could not have cared less who came into the house; the more suspicious the person, the friendlier he was! But that could change in a split second if he decided he had to protect something. Nothing could frighten him off then! He was a born Schutzhund or protection dog, but a terrible watchdog.

If one went out with him—especially on the battlefield— he reacted immediately to anything suspicious with a low growl and a frozen stare in the direction of the danger. But he never barked.

My brindle Lux von Ismaning would let anyone into the

house. But when the stranger wanted to leave he would always attack, even bite, if the person didn't freeze. There could be much more written on this topic, because we do not really understand how the dog's mind works in such situations.

But this much we can say for certain: You can probably suppress watchdog instincts, but it can be difficult sometimes to bring them out. And almost any dog can be trained to do Schutzhund work—some better, some worse.

On Beauty And Performance In Dog Breeding [ca. 1960]

Often the outsiders get a false impression when one person talks only of a dog's beautiful appearance, while the other stresses how well the dogs perform their obedience tests. It is false because the goal of breeding is not to stress one above the other. Mainly to get rid of this idea that one must choose either beauty or performance for a breeding goal, I decided to train all my breeding dogs for performance. After all, the same basic drives are anchored in all of our Boxers. If one were going to bred exclusively for beauty and the other only for performance, we would eventually end up with two distinct branches of the same breed.

It is quite understandable if a dog owner, whose animal has not been successful in conformation, turns to performance training successes as a way to harvest something for his awards basket. But much less understandable are those who constantly call out: "Here only conformation! There only performance!"

If the dog comes out of a poor breeding—usually because of convenience or misguided stinginess or maybe just stupidity—and has little promise, then we hear, "Oh, I don't breed for conformation. I breed for performance."

Or the breeder may explain that this dog is a little nervous and should not be bred, but it is a very pretty dog and he does not think it will bite anyone.

It is almost unimaginable how seldom people actually think and plan out a sensible breeding. The real causes for pushing the notion of two kinds of breeding lie in convenience (use the dog down the street), trying to save money on the stud fee, or the breeder just does not know what is the right way. So here is the real question: Are there really two separate elements to breed for, beauty or performance? And the answer is a straightforward, no!

What is beauty anyway? Of course it is not a personal matter, not "in the eyes of the beholder," but must be based on what the standard lays out as the correct features for the breed. One must always say, "Beautiful and correct," when talking about breeding goals. We demand, for example, a straight, firm back (for our athletic Boxers, it should also be short), hindquarters that are powerful and have good bone and correct angulation, and nice tight feet that will hold up under heavy usage. There should also be a deep chest to hold the lungs, etc.

All of these breed characteristics have proven themselves in practical use and must blend together in a harmonic whole. Every breed has its special characteristic—with working breeds they were usually determined by the owners' needs; that's understandable.

For our Boxers, most characteristic is the head and the tight powerful body. If someone believes a Boxer could bite better with a long head, they are simply wrong. Trying to change a breed's primary characteristics does no good. Anyone thinking along those lines should just get a long-headed dog, rather than taking it upon themselves to breed a "modern" Boxer. It only ends in a great fiasco. That is also what happens to the beauty fanatics. The best and most beautiful Boxer is the one that fits the standard best. But it is not enough that the dog is correct. It has to show that to a judge at a dog show, and only a well-raised, confident and outgoing dog can do that in a complete manner!

Today there is a stress on the "nature" of the dog, and we must be careful the stress does not take a toll in the conformation ring. Our Boxers' "nature" has held up well, even if it has not been set as a breeding goal. All we have to do is be careful not to breed those animals that do not have a Boxer's temperament.

Why is training so important then? The owner can get to know his dog's true nature through training. In conformation breeding, we know exactly the faults and strong points of the breeding pair. We know that one might be too long in the back, and the other has bad rear quarters or is missing a good stop. We also know many typey, genetic features, and when we breed those animals we are careful to avoid the wrong match.

We do not know enough about the "nature" of our individual dogs! And it is precisely here that we must proceed in the same manner that we did when breeding only for beauty. The nature of a dog is inherited in exactly the same way that the features of appearance are inherited, at least that is what my extensive experience has shown. Any weaknesses in a dog's nature should be taken into account and balanced out with the other partner's characteristics.

For more than twenty-five years, I have been engaged in training my Boxers and have done fairly well in it. And despite that, when I work with my dogs they still continue to surprise me with how much more I can learn about them during training. It's all a matter of how you approach it. Good intentions and lots of love are certainly a big part of it, because without those nobody will achieve much of any-thing. And you must be patient!

Just why I suddenly decided I would train all my Boxers, I really do not know. Perhaps it was the rumor [in the mid-1930s] that we would be forced by regulation to train all working dogs for military use, which could have been a hardship if we were unprepared. Our Boxer friends all shook their heads when they heard of my plan. They thought it was impossible to find the time, and I really did not know how I would do it either.

But—as is usually the case when something seems almost impossible, I just grabbed the bull by the horns. Luckily, neither my daughter nor I had any idea how much it actually was that I had decided to accomplish in a short time. We had about twenty dogs, counting breeders and adolescents. Every dog lived in the house—I am strongly opposed to pure kenneling of dogs—and had many hours of free running every day. The city dweller is happy to take the dog out for a half-hour stroll. It is necessary and refreshing for both owner and dog. But in contrast, we were overjoyed when we could just sit down for half an hour. We all know farmers (and that's what we were) never have much time. It was only out of a great love for our dogs that we decided to give up all free time and spend it training them.

We found out that we had to plan every minute to make it most useful. And we had to decide which dogs would be most suitable to start with. Eleven dogs were chosen—a big job for two people to do in their "spare" time. Although we excluded the oldest one, at least at first, my daughter did not want to abandon her favorite, Zorn. That was well worth it, because Zorn eventually added a performance degree to his reputation as an excellent sire. Thus, my daughter trained Zorn, Zünftig, Blanka and Blitzmädel, while I took Almuth, Ursel, Wega, and Traun. Each one received the type of training that we felt best fit the dog's personality. Of course, it was understood from the beginning that all would pass the Schutzhund I test. Then some would get courier training, and Zünftig went on to the Schutzhund II degree.

I would not wish to miss mentioning something about the amount of work that involved, but there was also joy in the effort. Anyone who has trained a dog will appreciate that. There were days when we almost felt as though we should give it up, but the dogs were always less tired than we were. That was when we really learned what it is like to train four dogs, one after the other. At first, our method was to take the first dog—probably the best—give him a good work-out, then move to the next, etc. But by the time the fourth dog's turn came, we were tired and usually only worked on one or two items. We became very tired and irritable, and we soon realized the last couple of dogs were not being adequately trained. So we changed our method. We would take one element and train all four in that one, then we would move to another part and go through it all again. Once we started doing it that way, we began to make progress—and rapidly.

By being able to compare the dogs on each exercise, we learned a great deal about the unique features of each dog! Almost every dog required a somewhat different approach to be successfully trained. We quickly learned that courier training required very special characteristics in the dog. Our first messenger dog was the big, elegant, but powerful bitch, Almuth. She loved to jump! No wall or hurdle was too high for her beautiful leaps, and she did her messenger work with almost incredible speed. But we had to remove her from Schutzhund training because she just had no desire to do it. For her partner in training, we picked the smaller but also elegant Wega, and she too ran wonderfully fast, but she was not such an enthusiastic jumper. Wega actually whelped a litter during her training, but only lost about two months' time from training.

As time passed, it became easier for all of us. The animals caught on to what we wanted, and we knew all of their peculiarities. We could see the dogs were becoming more and more enthusiastic about training. Old Zorn took to it with such spirit and eagerness we could hardly believe his age.

We worked together on the messenger training. Actually, that was our favorite training, but it took so much time. The course was about 850 yards, and each dog went back and forth twice, about two miles in all. Since our area is so hilly, much of the time the dogs were running stretches where neither of us was visible. You were often not quite sure if the dog had strayed, especially because we had quite a bit of wild life in the area—or for that matter, it might just decide to take it easy and walk along the way. One time a rabbit jumped up about fifteen feet in front of Zünftig, for a moment he stopped and stared, then he continued on with the message. Another time a strange dog crossed paths with Almuth, who then chased it to a barn, before she ran back and finished the trip. Each dog reacts according to its own nature. Even with people passing by, one dog runs up to be petted, another pays no attention at all, and another might stand and watch them for a few moments and then continue to run the route.

One time we inadvertently sent out two messenger dogs at the same time, one from each end. We immediately realized our error, but we both sat waiting and watching to see what they would do when they met. After a short pause to say hello, both continued on their right paths. It was particularly interesting when the route was winding. The first trip, they always followed the crooked road. After that, each one would invent shortcuts—usually to straighten out the route.

With the so-called "man work" of Schutzhund training (in contrast to tracking and courier), we often had a difficult problem to solve. There were almost no farm boys who wanted to serve as the imitation aggressor. When we did find one willing, then he always had to be trained how to do it. It was impossible to find a really skilled aggressor who knew exactly how to get the best work out of the dog. Despite that, none of my dogs failed the test. Indeed, some were almost too eager.

Attacking the imitation aggressor made the dogs almost deliriously happy. But they did not care much for the restraint that must be shown when they have the aggressor stopped and must stand at bay. If the man stood still and the dogs stood and barked at him—fine. But the more aggressive dogs would circle the man, probably hoping that he would make a move so they could attack again. When we began our training, we only had one good arm protector. That the dogs would circle the aggressor was understandable, but the problem was that no one could stand still under such circumstances. The helpers would quite naturally turn with the dogs to keep facing the danger. But that movement was a signal for the dog to attack the arm again.

Some dogs had an aversion for the protection sleeve. No, it was not the most aggressive, quick biters, because attacking the arm was fine with them. They just loved to grab hold. But it was not the most stupid ones either. No one really knows what goes on in a dog's head. At any rate, there are dogs (especially among Boxers) that prefer to go for the unprotected areas of the helper's body. Boxers even love to greet each other with a friendly bite on the nose. My old Rolf von Vogelsberg used to get occasional nose bleeds from that. Understandably, they often went for the helper's face, just as with a dog. That's not much of a problem for a properly trained helper, but for my farm boys it was impossible to avoid, and they usually changed jobs fast after that happened. We usually did man-training twice a week, but later we found that once a week was enough.

Just when the better animals learned to handle their assignments quite well, something happened that almost caused me to lose the desire for further training. I wished to train my best bitch, Almuth, who already was a faultless courier, to be a record-breaking jumper. Suddenly she came down with a fever, suffered a stroke and died. It was so painful I almost lost my courage.

My daughter struggled greatly with Blitzmädel, mostly in vain. This previously gentle and sweet tempered bitch turned into an aggressive forceful dog when trained. No coaxing or punishment could get her to release the helper's arm after catching him, and she was inclined to jump the helper even when he was not moving and she was supposed to stand at bay. We were now seeing the result of the difficult illness she had when young. It is surely understandable that I did not work with the dogs for a full week then.

Justi, who was a good Schutzhund, would certainly not work out as a messenger for Wega (in place of Almuth). Nor would Ursel be suitable. But I had a dog of my breeding returned to me, Unke, and after a short testing, we decided she was a real winner. She would have to do, especially since we decided to stop training Blitzmädel because of her temperament problems.

Our biggest problem was to find the courier partner for Wega. The bitch Justi was a fantastic runner, as long as she was after something edible. Now we gave her a quick training, which went well with the help of treats.

Many trainers have difficulty with the crawling exercise, but all of my dogs loved it—as soon as they figured out what we wanted. We had them crawling short distances at first, but eventually they were covering quite long stretches. All they needed was praise and encouragement. Almuth had been able to crawl flawlessly for 30-35 yards. The prettiest was Wega. When you saw her crawl, you had to laugh. She moved so rapidly that one could hardly follow her on foot. She held her head up, but her whole body would be flat on the ground, and all the way her tail would be wagging for joy!

For Justi, who was a heavier, more substantive bitch, the jumps were hard. It was different for Almuth and Wega. At first we put up three low hurdles and they handled that. But then we dug a trench and they all failed there. They acted as though they had never made a leap. Surprisingly, the usually reliable Justi went on strike here, a 100% Boxer blockheaded no! She had leaped the trench with ease when it was empty. But when we filled it with water and she fell in because of my clumsiness—as well as hers—that was it! I would have given up on her as a courier then, but I desperately needed a partner for Wega.

Later, my daughter tried giving messenger training to Zünftig. He loved the new obedience exercises, but he performed the run with a thoroughness and calm that just did not match his elegant appearance. Apparently, he believed all that running back and forth made no sense at all. What he loved was tracking, and searching for the aggressor, finding him, holding him at bay and attacking if he moved. Just running with a message was too monotonous.

Justi ran for the treats, which she would even climb a tree for if necessary. Zünftig, who almost seemed to view a treat as an insult, was another story. He only took one to please the giver. Zünftig ran because he was ordered to, and Wega ran because she loved it. If asked, she would run the course ten times—all as fast as possible. Just a word of praise was all she needed. Once you gave her that, she was eager to go again. Her partner would have it hard and we deliberated a long time on who that would be. Either Justi, with her poor jumping, or Zünftig, who did not enjoy the run. In the end, we decided to use all three of them.

One week before the examination, we ran a trial exam, and everything seemed to go all right. Of course, Justi would not jump the trench. You could not even get her near it. The director of the examination had advised me not to let any of them jump during the week before the exam. If the worst came, then I would lose five points. He was right but it irritated me, and I told my daughter what he said. Then she and I had an argument over it. Finally she told me, "You always claim you could get Justi to jump over the moon for a treat. Well, why not the trench then?" That really got to me!

There were still six days before the exam. It was forbidden to practice the last two days before, so there were only three days to get Justi trained to do that jump!

The next day I took ten big sausages with me. We went to the trench. It had been widened to about five feet and my daughter stood on the other side with a sausage. I approached with Justi, who was not leashed. My daughter waved the sausage at her and instead of "jump," I shouted, "Justi, go!"

That was the messenger command, and she associated it with treats. She now saw the sausage, heard the treat-related command, and without any hesitation just sailed over the trench and demanded the sausage. I knew right then that I had finally won.

The next day she cleared 10 feet with no trouble at all, and on the third day she was running ahead and jumped back and forth over the trench—always getting a sausage, of course. Except for her love of Schutzhund work, Justi's only other passion was a treat. When I had her out, I always needed a full bag of treats. Of course, I am well aware of the disadvantages of such training, and I was very careful to keep her away from other dogs. But we had to train those dogs in a very short time, so we took the quickest method possible to get it done.

As a last story, I would like to tell you about a young, eager and capable breeder, whose good efforts still produced nothing. But what happened to him is interesting. Just fifteen years old, the boy had only the best intentions to become a good handler and competitor. He decided to have us train his young brood bitch, Bella vom Dom.

Bella was very lively and had many good features. Unfortunately, taking orders was not one of them, and she had already given her young owner—who lacked experience—some rather hard nuts to crack. On top of that, she became pregnant during her training period. We trained her, making adjustments when necessary, right up to fourteen days before she was due, and everything went fine except for tracking. Then she had her litter.

Bella had an eight-week break, but in contrast to our Almuth, Bella had forgotten almost everything. Now the test was getting close, and her tracking would not have enough time to be polished. Because she was such a good courier, we decided to have her take that exam instead of the Schutzhund. The young owner had also promised to spend extra time working with her at home. Unfortunately, Bella had to stop coming to us a few weeks before the exam, since hoof-and-mouth disease had broken out in her village. But she still took the exam.

We were not too pleased about the bitch's stubborn temperament, but it all went well at first—even the crawl and the water trench were no problem for Bella. But then came the messenger work, and that was her downfall. The first course she ran without any hesitation in excellent time. On the second run she also seemed to be doing well, but then she stopped, started becoming restless—and then took off across the field and out of sight.

Only my husband was able to see her running at full speed to our place, leap the high fence and head down the road toward her home in Toging, about four miles away. The people there were astonished as the bitch arrived out of breath, message tube on her collar, then jumped over the kennel fence and lay down among her puppies. After several minutes of rest, she jumped up and was going to try to get over the kennel fence, probably to continue delivering the message. But they rightfully restrained her, and she lay down again.

What goes on in a dog's brain? And what was the basis for Bella's behavior? In her evaluation, it said she failed the messenger test. My view is that mother-love triumphed over trained duty. I dislike the word "fail" when talking about animals, because it is usually a convenient term to describe something that occurs which our conceited skulls had not expected.

We have so many losers in our training and breeding. Usually, the deeper basis is one of human miscalculation, which sometimes can certainly be very difficult to determine.

For those people who have an understanding and—above all—a heart for animals, such "losers" will still be welcome at home. They force us to rethink our assumptions, because they demonstrate the uniqueness of life and will in our animals.

A dog that goes through protection training with cadaver-like obedience and becomes a machine, is as unattractive to me as a beautiful Sieger that seems to be poured out of a mold. For my part, I always loved doing the training exercises most, because the dog seemed to have the most freedom to show joy, especially in message and tracking work!

On The Question Of Schutzhund Training
[post-WW II]

—Is It A Torture For The Dog?
—Variations Among The Breeds
—Stupidity And Arrogance Of Dog Opponents

For some time now, German dog fanciers have been concerned about cultivating the uniqueness of every breed, through selective breeding and proper training, so they will become as useful to human beings as possible. No doubt there have been sins committed along those lines in earlier days. There were times when people were proud to own a dog from the "Luxury Breeds," dogs that could do nothing. Fortunately, the term "Luxury Dog" has about died out now.

The concept of a "working" dog is known to have spread out from Germany across the globe, even though there have always been dogs and breeds that were truly working dogs. Aside from the hunting dogs, there were also watchdogs, herding dogs, pulling dogs, etc. For many years there were circles that believed the purebred dog was of little use for anything. But today it is different. The purebred dog is recognized everywhere as a useful element, and recent scholarship has helped prove each breed's uniqueness.

The various breeds separate themselves in appearance as well as specific abilities, which humans very early recognized and used. Special requirements of the times often changed the makeup of the breeds, for example with fighting dogs and big game hunting dogs. Most of the time one could hardly call them "purebred" dogs. Only with the Nineteenth Century did a new trend develop toward conformation or beauty breeding, and the working nature of the breeds became unimportant. Despite that, our oldest breeds retained the genetic basis for their working abilities, and eventually the working-dog movement led breeders to seek out the best of those qualities in their breeding programs.

Today, most of the German breeds have been well developed along the lines of usefulness and beauty. Just how firmly the nature of our breeds is anchored can be seen in our service breeds. Even though we have for decades followed the same training and testing programs, the German Shepherd and the Boxer are as different in nature as they are in appearance. And that's all for the best! Only then can one speak of separate work for specific breeds based on their natures and physical structures.

Of course, breeding for utilitarian characteristics (or nature) is severely handicapped because we have no standard to guide us, as we do with structure. This is a broad field, and eventually we will be well informed about how to breed for the desired "purpose" of our particular breed. We already know that purebred dogs have long ago passed mixed breeds in their ability to perform desired tasks, which also helps convince us that the laws of genetics also function in character development. For the mixed-breed dog, in contrast to the purebred, getting a particular nature is a matter of luck. Mixed breeds are in character and appearance just mutts.

Especially breeders of the working dogs know that they must also work with their dogs. It is not only a matter of good performance for a single dog, but is necessary for the advancement, preservation, and definition of the most desired characteristics for that breed. We must seek out those animals with the best nature for the breed and use these animals—along with beauty—in our breeding. The duty of any breeders' organization is to breed for both performance and beauty.

That should not be so difficult for us Boxer breeders, if we just remove the losers from our breeding programs. Luckily, our best and most used sires at vom Dom in the last years were of a very good working nature. It is quite acceptable to me that dogs with performance degrees are judged and evaluated in the conformation ring by a special standard. When it comes to a "working" breed, every dog in every class should be a proven good worker!

The big danger is that particular breeds sometimes venture into areas for which their natures do not fit. For instance the German Great Spitz, which could probably pass a Schutzhund test. But the nature of the great Spitz has very little to do with the demands of Schutzhund training. It would be a shame if such a dog were forced to do something out of his character. As a watchdog, the Spitz has no superiors. Everything necessary for a good watchdog is in the breed. Being a watchdog matches its appearance and nature completely and it would be ridiculous to water down such a finely bred animal. But a Spitz that performs well as a Schutzhund has lost much along the way!

Almost any dog can now pass a test if trained. Still, a false picture of character testing and training can easily be painted, as we see in a long article about animal welfare for dogs. The author asserted, "Every year, thousands of dogs are forced by any means possible to endure police dog training, although they have no use for it at all when they are back home."

Furthermore, the author claimed that acquired characteristics can be inherited! Now, we breeders are not as stupid as he thinks, and the truth is he hasn't a clue as to our present breeds, and he is totally lost when it comes to training.

Race horses are not forced to run faster in the expectation that it will be passed on to the offspring, as the article maintained. Horse races are mainly a test of the animal's heart and lungs. Then the weaker can be sorted out and eliminated from breeding programs. The working-dog tests have the same purpose. Even if only some of these dogs can be used in breeding programs, it still is of great importance to the breed to continue building good working lines.

On the matter of "animal torture" and forced training, which the author of the article was so upset about, we can easily lay that to rest. So many times I have seen a dog, badly spoiled by its owner, turned over to another person for training, and in a very short time the dog is happily working with the trainer. They loved to be with the trainer—the "torturers" in the article—eagerly following their commands.

Just how much dogs love to work can be illustrated by the following examples. My daughter trained the famous Sieger, Lustig vom Dom, for a Schutzhund examination. During Easter there was a break in the training because my daughter left for a few days. Although Lustig had bonded closely with all of us, he seemed to be rather sad during her absence, despite being lord of a large pack. After I turned him loose in the large garden one afternoon, I returned to the house. From a window, I watched as Lustig jumped back and forth over the three-foot hurdle, all alone but still having fun. He repeated the exercise four or five times. Obviously, he was doing by himself what he had learned to love—with her.

Lustig's successor, Ingo von Heger, passed his Schutzhund examination. Every Sunday morning he rode with us some sixty miles to the training field in Munich. One Sunday I had to make a longer trip, but it took me past Munich, so I stopped at the field to excuse my absence that day. Ingo was along and he did not want to get back into the car. He wanted to work. Since his physical resistance did not work, he then began to beg and whine and plead that he be allowed to stay and work with his friends. He really made us feel bad about putting him back into the car and leaving.

These two examples of how dogs love training speak a clear language. Anyone who claims that training is torture only makes himself appear ridiculous in the view of those who know dogs. And if the dog learns things which will never be used later—so what? Isn't it the same way with people? Above all, we train our dogs to be of use to us and to make our lives together easier and more pleasant Even if a much greater number of dogs were trained, it would still not be grounds for the animal rightists to make a justified complaint. Thus, it is amazing what forceful words the author used to describe matters about which he is quite ignorant, in fact quite wrong. No one gains by that, and it causes hard feelings.

We dog lovers and breeders of purebred dogs really do not have it easy. We have dedicated ourselves to an endeavor that not only takes a great amount of sacrifice in time and money, but we also serve the general good. Our dogs were there at the outbreak of war for military use, and nobody could ever claim that what we received for each dog even came close to covering the dog's expenses. All over the world there are trained dogs doing rescue work, being protectors, helping the handicapped—indispensable helpers for humanity. None of us complains of the work that is behind these dogs. But we do have a right to be treated fairly and honestly, and not to have to put up with malicious attacks and lies.

About A Dog's Sense Of Hearing [ca. 1936]

Not too far from us, there lives a little black scrapper, somewhat of a cross between a miniature Dachshund and toy Pinscher. This little mutt bestows unrelenting hate on every owner of another dog. Because I own several Boxers he does not like me at all, and every time I have to go past his place he throws a regular barking tantrum. There is no way around him, since the main street goes right past his house. Just before his place, there is a turn in the road and a steep hill.

The little one's owner assured me that not only can the dog hear the hooves of my horses, he recognizes them out of the hundreds that go by his house. As soon as he hears me coming you cannot hold him back. It does not matter if I am coming with a large wagon of heavy goods or a light, two-wheeled cart, such as used in racing. The traffic in that area is quite heavy—a large feed mill and saw mill are nearby. About six months ago I purchased a motorcycle and was quite proud when I went right past the house without having that little devil come racing out after me. But it never lasted long. I went past undisturbed three times, and then the little mutt caught my scent and flew at me in a rage. After that, it was again impossible for me to travel that neighborhood without being barked at. Apparently it was my Bosch horn—we use horns a lot around here—which he could recognize out of the others.

Well, I changed horns. And when I again came into the area of the mill I blew it several times, and passed unmolested. One day I saw the little guy while driving by. He was taking a nap on a straw pile. When I honked he never even raised his head. Then curiosity began to get to me, and since I was already a ways past his house, I gave a few beeps on the old Bosch horn—which I had just reinstalled. Like a ball, he bounced into the air and raced up to me. After that, there was no hope—no matter which I horn I used, the old Bosch or the new air one, the little terror could hear me from far away, and even when in the house he could hear the horns and went wild to get outside.

It was interesting to test the little fellow. Just to trick him, I went past without honking. But he was now beyond deception. He knew the sound of the motor now. How he did that was a puzzle, because there is a lot of motorized traffic in the area. Every attempt to mislead the mutt misfired. One time I almost succeeded by shifting into a lower gear—I had a heavy load—but it didn't fool him.

I thought about those events quite a bit. It had never really astonished me that our dogs could hear and recognize horses and wagons from a distance that no human possibly could. Our dogs always knew when a team was gone and were always waiting for their return. But it did amaze me that an outside dog could tune in on a mechanical sound. For the sounds of nature, the ancient dog required sharp hearing to survive and does still have a finely honed sense of sound. We know from Menzel's experiments that dogs—despite their good noses—have trouble with chemical smells, but the natural smells around them are no problem at all. And I can understand that. But it does amaze me that they have such sharp hearing that they can distinguish mechanical sounds, such as a horn, a motor, etc. I doubt that even a supremely talented musician would be able to compete with the dog in distinguishing tones.

How Do Dogs Communicate?

Of course dogs—like all animals—can communicate with each other. Their sniffing, greeting, and marking are nothing more than a primitive postal system. Anyone who knows dogs is aware of all that behavior among their four-legged friends. It is the other, less commonly observed, forms of communication that are especially interesting and viewed by only very close observers.

As an example, I bring home some dog food meat from a horse that was ordered to be shot. As usual, my dog Ivein goes with me. When we return, I take the meat to a special building that I use for butchering. The wagon and the meat stay in the building, and Ivein and I go into the house. Immediately all of the dogs surround us. Ivein is inspected from one end to the other, and then suddenly they go wild to get outside and race to the meat shed. I travel often with the horses and my returns are always warmly greeted, but no dog goes running to the meat shed. I should mention that Ivein was not fed at the butcher shop or during the trip.

Here's another case. There are two two-month-old

puppies, and they sometimes do not like to return to the kennel after being outside. Once or twice a day, at various times, I open the kennel doors and let them all take a run. When I feel it is time to return, I just call and they all come back. But these two little ones hesitate. The larger girl seems inclined to obey, but her smaller sister now runs up to her and sniffs in her ear, then she grabs a leaf or stick and away they go! I have a terrible time rounding the two up and getting them back into their kennel. Clearly, they communicated and understood each other.

But the ability of dogs to communicate goes still further. Ivein, who is always out of the kennel, knows that he does not have to worry about anybody all day long. People can pass through our property whenever they wish. But not so with the kenneled dogs. They sound off over anything and everything, and if a stranger passes the kennels they make a hellish racket. Say I am now sitting in my room or in the garden, and Ivein is with me. In the kennel wild barking ensues, but I know that if Ivein makes no motion then it is just a stranger passing through. Everything is fine.

After a while, the yapping outside begins again. Even the most trained human ear could distinguish no difference from the earlier barking, but this time Ivein jumps up, his hair bristles and out he goes. I now know that his speed means trouble. There was a big strange dog sniffing around the kennels. How did Ivein know the situation was different? He could neither see nor smell the other dog. Only the barking could have told him something. I have observed similar events many times. Their barking allows our dogs to know if a stranger, instead of a family member or friend, is passing through. There must be much more that dogs can say to each other by barking than we ever dreamed possible.

About Instinct and Intelligence

These two words have led to many studies, arguments and comments. In most cases, the proponents of a theory exaggerate their examples and often draw completely wrong conclusions from the reactions of the animals. Instead of speculating and theorizing, I would just like to report on some of my dogs' "instinctual" behavior that is far superior to that of rational human beings.

Every year great numbers of fish come up the Isen (a little tributary of the Inn river) to spawn. They are netted and trapped in great amounts and delivered fresh to the markets. With my Boxer, Ivein, I went to the village of Mühle to get some of that fresh fish. The clerks would just reach into a trap, pull out a fish and toss it on the ground. But this time one went flying over the neighboring fence. "Oh, we have to fetch that fish!" They shouted.

But they did not have to move a muscle. Ivein heard the word "Fetch," and he was gone. Over the fence he leaped, stared at the fish for a couple of seconds, grabbed its tail and then quickly switched to a bite right behind the fish's gills. He then jumped back and dropped the fish at my feet. Every fisherman knows that the surest way to grip a fish is behind the gills, but a layman always tries to pick them up by the tail. And that doesn't work. Yet this dog that had never picked up a fish before knew immediately where to grasp the fish to immobilize it. And the fish's skin was not even broken.

Ivein was even "smarter" on another occasion. As my constant companion, he understood everything I said and came to the softest call. He was only lacking in one respect: he loved to fight. In order to avoid unpleasantness, I often had him jump into the wagon and sit behind me when we went past a farm house or a village. Once we were clear, I would just say, "Now, go!" And he would jump down.

But you had to see this dismount! In contrast to his jump into the wagon, I never slowed the horses down when he jumped off. Usually we were at a good trot. From the top of the wagon he would leap forward, often 10 to 15 feet and come down between the traces. It was even more difficult, but just as elegant, with a lower wagon. When he hit the ground right behind the horses, he immediately scooted off to the side. Not once did he fall or even stumble.

Think of the contrast to a person who might wish to jump from a moving wagon. Now, cross your heart—how many of you have never taken a tumble just hopping off a moving wagon? How many warnings have we read in the streetcar to always exit in the direction the car is moving? But we still have the accidents when people fall. My dog, however, did everything right without giving it a second's thought.

Another time I sat at the table writing and Ivein lay beside me. A friend stoked up the stove a bit and a glowing coal fell out. Of course, he picked up the large piece and put it back in the stove, but some glowing pieces still remained. Then Ivein slowly rose and went over to the stove. To my surprise, he began pushing ashes over the glowing pieces. Was that instinct or intelligence? I would say it was surely instinct, and just another example of how the animal's instinctual abilities often are superior to man's intelligence.

About Special Characteristics Of Working Dogs

The only service dog recognized by the German army for many years was the Airedale Terrier. In 1891, Major D. Burkhardt began urging the military to accept dogs for duty on the battlefield and other uses. The only breeds suitable to him were the Airedale and the Boxer. Then the German Shepherd Club began courting the Police Administration to follow the Belgian example and use German Shepherds in police work.

The special nature of the German Shepherd was well grounded. They had a large, powerful body, were well protected against weather, had an aggressive temperament, and were very trainable. Then, too, they had proven themselves for many years in Belgium, and there were quite a few available at low prices. Within one year, the Police Administration had German Shepherds working in some fifty German cities. Other breeds accepted later were Dobermans, Airedales, Rottweilers, Boxers, and lastly, the Giant Schnauzer. Thus the German Shepherd had a good head start, and thanks to good club leadership, they still have it.

Shortly before the outbreak of World War II, the German military declared it no longer was necessary to train dogs for war duty. It was assumed that technological advancements had made the army dog superfluous. But during the war they realized that was not the case. Between the wars, the owners of those breeds considered usable for military work had not sat on their hands. Excellent books came out on obedience and protection training (for example, the basic work by Major Most), as well as improvements in the testing procedure. Although sometimes these procedures seemed to favor one or the other breeds, the start had been made.

Basically, the training emphasized police work. The ideal dog was assumed to be of medium size, intelligent, weather resistant, and have strong drives in fighting, searching, retrieving and nose work. During the war these requirements changed somewhat. A shortage developed for dogs trained in guard post service, patrol duty, assisting in transport work and border duty, and of course also in messenger and first-aid work. The police authorities badly needed good tracking dogs. All of that came when there was actually very little breeding on the home front because of the wartime hardships. Soon the military and other authorities were taking only half-trained dogs, no matter whether purebred or mixed-breed.

After the war, rebuilding the breeds went slowly because there was a lack of good breeding stock. There was a great demand for good dogs, but the times were still difficult. Yet we began a systematic program to rebuild our lines. Meanwhile, the Boxer became the fifth breed recognized as a service dog, and the areas of work for service dogs had been expanded. Especially bothersome were the constant modifications that kept creeping into the testing regulations. Some of those changes went too far.

Our working breeds are all quite good for their work. They have the distinction of different origins, however, and sometimes that leads to an impasse. For that reason, test regulations that are designed with one breed in mind, will often be unsatisfactory for other breeds. It took years of studies and impartial observations to clarify that. An example would be the tracking tests, which are still not satisfactory today.

Let us compare the special abilities of the working breeds for Schutzhund, messenger, first-aid, tracking, guide dog, and companion dog. Today the breeders of working dogs try to breed only dogs that have working degrees. But in doing that, many breeders are actually closing out the possibility of using their dogs in other areas. According to our testing regulations, a dog that passes a messenger test may not take the first-aid test. In the same way, passing the Schutzhund II and III, closes out the Messenger II degree. We now have the possibility among the working breeds, to pick out whichever area we feel suits the dog best. Today's testing regulations for Schutzhund I make it possible for every dog to pursue its talent in protection work or searching or messenger service. That test will probably always be the basic test for a dog's abilities.

In my opinion, the future will require more specialization among the working breeds. Only in that way can the overall level of performance be significantly raised. Anyone who looks at the working dog with impartial eyes, can see that the various breeds have features unique to their breed that allow them to excel in certain types of work. Our job should be to discover those unique features and train our dogs in a manner that would emphasize them.

Many people will certainly disagree with me on that. But we are no longer greatly worried if we have to stop saying that our breed is "suitable for all work." Of course, there would still be some dogs trained in areas no longer considered a particular breed's domain, but that problem could be eased by not being too demanding in the breed requirements. Those dogs of poor breed character and type would not be used in breeding. Thus, a dog with a strong instinct for fighting would certainly go through Schutzhund training. But for the messenger dog, which must have nerves of steel, a strong fighting drive is not desired. And that also goes for first-aid and tracking dogs.

Among the fighting breeds, and the Boxer has to be considered one of those, there are always individual exceptions with weak fighting instincts. Such a dog could possibly pass a messenger test with the highest scores. In that way, the dog would receive its working degree, be admitted for breeding and could even win the Sieger title. But if we use that dog in a breeding program for a breed that is distinguished by its Schutzhund work, then we run the risk of producing more animals with a weak fighting drive and weakening the excellence of the breed in Schutzhund work. Of course, many excellent Schutzhund dogs are completely unfit for courier work, which does not bother most laymen because they think such training is superfluous and only want a protection dog. Everyone knows that I am not an enemy of the messenger dog. In fact, I believe that training dogs for messenger service is probably more fun than any other form of training, and even today it is a very necessary task. It is similar with first-aid and tracking. And tracking involves some of the most difficult and thankless training that there is.

Our testing system today, however, is a significant step forward. Any good dog of sound temperament with proper training can pass the requirements for Schutzhund I. And every dog—even those with little fighting drive—should have to pass them, just as we require every dog to pass the short messenger run in any weather. It should be the same for scent work.

Precisely the Schutzhund I examination allows the trainer to evaluate the abilities and capabilities of the dog in those various areas. But this testing must be correctly carried out, in order to get an impartial evaluation. And that is where much of the trouble lies. It would be very good if the testing were always held in a different place from where the training was done, along with a "villain" who was completely unknown to the dog. The testing ground could be near the training area, and the new helper could be some person who had only been an observer before.

It is very interesting to see what the complete attitude of the dog is under such new conditions. A good judge can get a better picture in just a few minutes of the true character of the dog than during all the other time watching the somewhat boring work. We would be able to avoid the spectacle of a "good" Schutzhund III dog—trained and tested in only one area—being quickly eliminated in tournament competition at a different venue.

I have often observed that the Schutzhund I testing is evaluated differently for different breeds. Of course, it should not be that way, but if it were steered in the right direction that could very well be a welcome step. With Boxers and Rottweilers, both fighting breeds, there could be more stress laid on the man-work side of the test than might be for the Shepherd, whose great talents are for tracking, first-aid and messenger service, although the Boxers—especially the light bitches—usually do quite well in messenger work.

About Linebreeding And Inbreeding
[ca. early 1930s]

In answer to two articles on Terrier breeding—one by a proponent of breeding and the other by an opponent—I would like to state my position as a Boxer breeder. Whether Terriers have a broader genetic base than Boxers—who go back to only five or six animals—is not known to me. Just out of curiosity, I once counted the number of ancestors my Ivein vom Dom had in the fifth generation back. Ivein—who was certainly not a product of inbreeding—ought to have had 32 names in that fifth generation, but there were only 21. But unlike many Boxers, Ivein was completely free of inbreeding in the first three generations.

For those interested in this topic, sit down and work out the pedigree of a dog back to the seventh generation. Many of you will be very surprised. Strictly speaking, all of our Boxers are related. In order to avoid genetic damage through the continued use of this small gene pool, it is best to avoid inbreeding or incest breeding as much as possible. Sometimes beginners and thoughtless breeders trying to save money, or for convenience, or out of ignorance, engage in it, and that is dangerous. It only makes sense when experienced and knowledgeable breeders use it for a sensible reason.

Whether inbreeding of Boxers has accomplished any notable success, only our stud books with the pedigrees of our Siegers can say. Our oldest Siegers came out of matings of dogs that were not closely related. But the closer we get to our present dogs, the stronger is the tendency to use related dogs. We know that inbreeding refines nerves and bones, produces digestive problems and reduces fertility. Those things do not always happen, however, nor do they happen as quickly as often claimed. Our older Siegers were indeed the result of unrelated breedings, but at that time the Boxer was hardly so tightly bred as we demand today.

The first great prepotent sire that came out of inbreeding was Champion Rolf von Walhall. In his second and third generations he went back to Frigga von Vogelsberg. All of our living Boxers have Rolf von Walhall in their pedigrees. As we all know, the repetition of a particular ancestor back in the fourth or fifth generation can hardly be dangerous. Naturally, such an ancestor must not have had a pronounced fault. Rolf von Walhall bred various bitches, some of which had quite different pedigrees from him and from each other.

Especially dominant and significant today are the primarily fawn lines from Egon von Gumbertusbrunnen and the mainly brindle lines from Moritz von Goldrain. Egon came from a mating of Rolf von Walhall and the unrelated Rassel von Birkenhain, who was the result of inbreeding between a son and his mother. Isa, the mother of Rassel, was quite noble and elegant with a not particularly desired head type. The product of the mating, Egon von Gumbertusbrunnen, was flawless in character and in appearance. In just appearance, Egon's descendants were much better balanced than those of Moritz. Egon's most significant offspring show, however, a great variation in character, having all kinds of temperament—from very aggressive to weak.

Moritz, in contrast, came from a mating of two almost

completely unrelated dogs. His descendants were as significant as Egon's, but much less constant in balance. His most important son was Cäsar von Deutenkofen, whose sons Granti, Strutio, Check von Hunnenstein, and also the three Biedersteiners—Buko, Hansel and Hermes—have produced completely different bloodlines, but Moritz's strong character is constant among them all. Has inbreeding, whether present or not, had an impact on those developments?

Of interest is the fact that with Egon and Egon's bloodline there has been strong inbreeding. For example, the Sieger Ajax von der Gralsburg came out of a match between half-siblings, who both were sired by Egon, although the two grandmothers had completely different bloodlines from each other. Neither in appearance nor in nature does Ajax show any of the typical faults of inbreeding. But to add more Egon blood in the next generations would be dangerous. I own a bitch—not of my breeding—who has Egon three times in her second generation. This bitch, a very pretty girl, is absolutely not an inbred type. She is large, big boned, an excellent eater. But her character! She is positively not nervous; she is phlegmatic. Shooting, flashing lights, umbrellas—they do not bother her in the least. All sign of a fight drive or protective spirit are missing. This girl's nature has nothing to do with inbreeding nervousness.

Generally it is believed that inbred animals are prepotent. In the Gumbertusbrunnen line we find quite a few cryptorchids—both uni-and bilateral— in the dogs, and prolapsed vaginas among the bitches—but those are in other lines also, such as from Tasso von der Spree and Bella von Worms. Of course, we must not forget that abnormal offspring can come from other sires also. The increased tendency toward good or bad features however, does seem to increase—sometimes in frightening quantities—when there is an accumulation of one particular blood line. In recent times, some of my best bitches have not conceived after I mated them with unrelated stud dogs. They were total strangers, and that usually makes my bitches over-nervous.

During my twenty-plus years of breeding, I have avoided any incestuous breeding if possible. My first time was when there was a severe shortage of sires during the war, and the second time was when there was a dog quarantine for over three years. Both times, I mated a father with a daughter. In the first, Rolf von Vogelsberg bred his daughter Derby vom Dom. The offspring were excellent! Most noticeable was that it was not Rolf— whose blood was being inbred— that passed on the type, but Derby, who was a red-fawn, small, but noble. If there had been a possibility to exhibit them, the offspring of this match would have played an important role. One of them, Pfiffig vom Dom, is still in many of today's pedigrees. And he was not the best in the litter by far. He was the only fawn Boxer to mate with a fawn bitch and produce brindle puppies. They all had fine temperaments.

In a later experiment, I paired Ivein with his daughter Osra vom Dom. Unfortunately, she lacked enough nutrition, and only two males survived. Both went to farmers and ended up being chained dogs. Both were vicious brawlers and very aggressive, but not really good enough barkers for chain dogs. These animals also took after their mother in type.

I once owned a very beautiful Boxer dog, Lux von Ismaning, who came from a match between mother and son. Although somewhat unusual, Lux never resembled his small, weak-chinned mother and grandmother, nor his very small and large-headed father. He took after his grandfather, Schelm vom Angertor. He had his somewhat long back, narrow upper head and exceeded Schelm in size. In those three instances of my inbreeding, it was not the dog whose blood was concentrated in the offspring that came through most clearly—but the minority bloodline! Lux was one of my most aggressive and reliable Boxers. Because of his aggression, I had to be careful when I played with him. It was very easy to excite him to where he did not always distinguish between play and seriousness. Then you had to force him to calm down, in order to keep from being bitten by him.

What do these observations mean? Over and over it is the same: mating close relatives, such as siblings or parent x offspring is definitely to be avoided. Half-siblings may be paired if two separate bloodlines lie in between. Incestuous breedings do not always bring out the good, desired features of the parents. On the contrary, there is a strong tendency for the obviously weak characteristics to multiply. But there is still one point where I do not agree with the author, and which I would like to discuss. At least in Boxer breeding, the large, dog-like bitches have done nothing for the breed. That does not mean that brood bitches should be small and over-elegant.

So let us sum it all up: Breed only good, healthy, strong animals. You may use a similar bloodline without damage, in fact it is often recommended. Only be very sure that the animal which is emphasized in the pedigree was of the very highest quality. Too close inbreeding (incest) is only to be used after very careful study and consideration because there is always the danger that undesired, recessive features will appear. It is only a very slim chance that a Sieger would come out of such a match, especially as compared to other matings with less closely related animals. A close study of the stud books gives us a clear warning.

Breeding requires a sensitivity on the part of the breeder, a sixth sense, one could say. If that is missing, then the breeder will probably succeed as much by luck as anything. But repeated success will probably never happen.

About Coat And Eye Colors, And Other Special Items
[ca. mid-1930s]

What appears outwardly to be the same is often not at all the case! There are kinds of rabbits that are snow white, but have either blue or red eyes. Most laymen would believe that you could mate a white rabbit with blue eyes with another white rabbit with brown or red eyes and still get white rabbits—that eye color is unimportant to coat color. Wrong! When white animals with different eye colors are mated, you seldom get an all-white offspring. Usually they are checked, or parti-colored. With rabbits, the inner (genetic) type that determines coat color is different for animals with different eye colors, which is noticeable when one mates them and gets offspring that look as though the parents had different colored coats.

To make this clearer, here is another example: I have two dogs with rounded backs. One is caused by poor spinal structure, the other is the result of a badly placed pelvic bone. Probably a mating of the two would produce some puppies with good backs, as the good straight back of one would be matched with the correct pelvis of the other. But in no case should dogs with faults be mated, although the potency of the individual features will play a role here. Why a dog would have a poor back can be determined by its anatomy. It is more difficult with coat color.

For example, Boxers have a definite black mask, some weak and some strong. And those breeds with black masks have a tendency to turn gray at an early age. If we look more closely at the masks, we see that some seem more like a dark brown and only black in the area right around the nose. In such animals, the nose color often lacks an intensive black— the so-called weather-nose. But others have almost bluish black masks with often even the ears being black. Unfortunately, those are the ones that seem to gray the fastest. Thus you can already see by the masks certain genetic conditions and predict how they might turn out in a future match. It is the same with horses. The dapple-grays bleach out fast and become completely white, but the dapple-reds hold their color.

There are two types of eye colors in Boxers. Most puppies have blue eyes, actually running from light blue to a deep navy blue in shades. As the animals grow older, the eyes turn brown, but in the same shading as earlier in blue. That is, the light blues become light brown, etc. Here we find shadings from a light, almost red yellow, to a red brown, to all-black. Those early blue eyes always darken as the puppy ages.

The other color found in puppies' eyes is not blue but gray. Blue is missing, and the eyes appear dark. As the puppy ages, however, the eyes begin to grow lighter. The deep dark eyes usually remain black, but the lighter gray like eyes grow much lighter than those that have the blue eyes.

The gray eyes almost always become too light. I have learned that it is very rare for blue and gray eyes to appear in the same litter.

Another interesting observation: Mating two light-eyed (gray-eyed puppies) produces puppies with colorless, almost white, eyes; but pairing animals that had light blue puppy eyes, even when as adults they had brown or light-brown eyes, can produce a number of dark-eyed dogs. So to sum it up, there is one group of dogs that start with blue eyes, and another group of puppies with gray eyes. The first group will have dark eyes and be dominant for that. Whereas the second group may later have some dogs with darker eyes, but they will not be dominant for offspring. I have seen dogs whose eyes grew lighter as late as the eighth month. Therefore it is worthwhile to make a note of puppy eye color very early because it may come in handy for making later breeding decisions.

Coat color in Boxers is somewhat similar. In the old days—not counting the whites—there were mostly fawns of all shades, brindles of all shades, and the blacks which ranged from almost black to deep black. The light fawns were avoided because breeders feared albinism. But that was the wrong course to take. These lighter fawns always seemed to have black eyes and haws, although sometimes they tended to look rather gray and dirty because of black hairs among the fawn in the coat. Also, we do not pay enough attention to the fact that the light fawns are born as dark colored puppies.

When a fawn is bred to a brindle, the fawn tends to darken. Of course, we soon lost our beautiful golden brindles by repeated fawn-brindle breeding. Twenty years ago, Great Dane breeders were admiring our golden brindles, since they had already lost that coloring. Today we are almost as far in that direction as the Dane breeders. As soon as fawn breeders began trying to get the darker glowing red-fawn color, brindle breeders began to pay less attention to it. In the end, it became just a matter of personal taste whether one preferred silver, or light or gold brindles.

Then suddenly there began appearing very deep red-fawns,

and they were in great demand for their pigmentation. But what a mistake! Those dogs all had white haws and yellow to red-brown eyes, and often very little mask. These characteristics also began to get carried over into the brindles.

A typical example is Check von Hunnenstein, who has a glorious coat color—brilliant red-gold brindle—but his eyes match his coat and are red-brown. The coat and eye colors come through in his offspring! Many of the breeders who have used Check know that. Still, we know much too little about it. Possibly an intensive concentration of those red dogs—although basically weak in pigmentation—led with time to the color of the brown hunting dogs, with their brown noses and eyes. This color has very little to do with the original colors of our Boxers, and it is already gone in the Great Danes. All of these reddish-golden brindles have very little brindling. Therefore it is important that the judges base their eye critiques on the well-marked streaks of brindle. For the judge is by far the best counterbalance to a decrease in pigmentation. The breeder, of course, could do much by making the right selections for breeding.

About Breeding Puzzles [ca. 1935]

During the last 24 years, I have raised 68 litters of Boxer puppies and have always kept exact records. Added to those were the numerous litters of breeder-friends, whose puppies I observed from birth on. Besides that, I have always made experimental breedings of rabbits and other animals, just to get quicker answers to some breeding questions. Any experiments with Boxers were possible only in limited amounts, because sometimes you ended up wasting a whole litter Aside from the expenses, such experiments are not simple, and sometimes the slightest problems will turn out to be the hardest nuts to crack.

Here is a puzzle that all of the old breeders have encountered. From a mating you get a puppy that is a real "cannon." As a rule, the breeding is then repeated with the same parents, but there is no such cannon in the next litter. Some breeders claim that the more often a breeding is repeated, the worse the litter. Of course, that has never been proven. But it is certainly true that a repeat breeding will not always produce the same high-quality animals. Most of the time there is just one outstanding dog in the litter, way above his siblings, who owes thanks to some very unique and special circumstances which just happen to have united in him. You can read in the stud books how one bright star arises out of perhaps thousands of others, even when there have been repeated breedings of his parents.

Why do such repeat breedings appear to produce worse litters? Long ago, breeders talked of Telegony—a theory that suggested previous breedings could have an impact on a later breeding—and used it as the reason why repeat breedings often produced puppies unlike the same earlier match. We do know this much: even with the high quality linebred animals, the repeat matings seldom have the same results as the first. The puppies within that first litter might be very much alike. But if another breeding of the same pair is made, sometimes you can be very surprised.

The second litter is also usually well balanced, but it does not seem to resemble the first at all. An inexperienced breeder might not notice that so much, especially if the puppies are plain and it is difficult to compare markings. But the true fancier sees the differences immediately. Particularly noticeable is when the colors are quite different.

Let us compare my very first and third litter as an example. I purchased Traudel von Steinhausen in 1911, after she had been bred by Rolf von Vogelsberg. She whelped eight puppies, all of which were brindle except one, and all had small white markings—the same as Rolf. Only two brindles were almost fully pigmented. Traudel had been bred many times by her previous owner and ought to have had a long rest, but Rolf had other thoughts. He broke into Traudel's kennel and bred her again.

The result this time was nine puppies, two fawn, three plain brindles, and four whites. This variation in color amazed me, perhaps all the more because I was a beginner.

There was no possibility of an unknown breeding, and all of the puppies were typical children of Rolf.

For many years after that I avoided repeat breedings, until Sigurd reached maturity. He sired all of my litters from Dudel vom Pfarrhaus and Prisma vom Dom. I will describe a few of the results.

Sigurd (fawn) x Dudel (dark gold brindle)

[males listed first]
#1. Litter: 5,4 puppies; 4,2 fawn; 1,2 brindle—all flashy
#2. Litter: 5,6 puppies; 3,1 brindle; puppies plain
#4. Litter: 4,7 puppies; 5 brindle; 6 fawns; lots of flash

An unusual result, given Dudel's dark brindling, plus the three brindle grandparents. In head type they all took after their father. I could probably give many more examples of how different litters from the same pair can vary.

Of course, it is not the individual by which you judge a mating's results but the whole litter.

How would scholarship probably look at these results? We can hardly talk of a "bloodline" or careful genetic selection as the only cause.

I recall the writing of Wrangel in his famous work on horses. He described one case where a stallion first began producing outstanding offspring when in his later years, and all of the foals from him in his earlier years were of no significance. That would suggest that it is not only a matter of genetic heritage, but that age and other factors also play a role.

Another puzzle for many breeders comes when there is a second mating by a different stud dog, or even by several others. Or if it was the same dog, then which mating succeeded. It used to be common practice to have two breedings. We assumed (wrongly) that there would be more puppies because of it. Also, we believed that our chances for a successful breeding would improve if we increased the number of copulations. But others swore a second act was nonsense and an unnecessary burden for the stud dog.

My practice earlier was to breed the bitch on two

succeeding days. Usually the litter appeared in 61 to 63 days. It was not possible to determine which breeding was successful. Actually, Boxers have whelped puppies as late as 67 days after the last breeding. Then I decided that a second act was superfluous when they were so close together, so I moved the second breeding back to three to five days after the first, in order to cover a larger span of fertility. By doing that, I began to have much more success, even with bitches that had missed on every previous breeding.

Now I realized something: I always calculated the day of whelping to be 61-63 days from the first mating, but it always seemed to be the later date. All of which meant that conception was actually occurring during the second breeding. Almost none of the bitches whelped on the first due date. That amazed me. There had to be something wrong! And when I only bred the bitch once, it seemed as though I was about as successful as with a second breeding.

A simple coincidence shed some light on the matter. Sigurd bred a bitch, everything seemed normal, and we sent her back home. But at home, a speedy mixed-breed got to her again and bred her about three days after Sigurd had. And every puppy turned out to be from the mixed-breed! We had to assume that the first breeding had not been successful. Yet Sigurd had bred 49 bitches before her and only a couple did not conceive and two aborted.

To learn more about this matter, I began to experiment with various colored rabbits. Here too the young came almost always from the second mating. How could one explain that? Surely, the first breedings could not all have failed. In the meantime, I had a similar experience with Zorn. A bitch he had bred was bred again four days later by a Schnauzer. The litter had all mixed-breed puppies. Until then I had been convinced that such a long pause after a successful breeding would make it impossible for another mating to take hold. Of course, there are times when there is double ovulation, that is when puppies from two sires are in one litter, but that is very rare.

One interesting case involved a purebred bitch, mated on her eleventh day with a purebred dog. Three days later she escaped and was bred again by a mixed-breed. They were separated and the original dog was again mated to her. The result was an aborted litter of mixed-breeds. How should we understand that? The first two acts were spontaneous. In the first, the dog and bitch romped around in the yard until the deed was done. Why then was the second act the one that succeeded? And why did the third act, hardly half an hour after the second, not conceive?

Once again I turned to the rabbits. I determined that with multiple copulations, the conception almost always occurred with the second, very seldom with the third time. If a person understood the genetic factors, it would be possible to make even more tests. The rabbits' coat colors follow well-known rules of inheritance. But even though I did not know that, I still reached some conclusions of my own.

Breeding two fawn Boxers will never produce a brindle in the litter. Also, in a match between a silver-brindle and a light fawn there is never a red-fawn or a gold-brindle Boxer puppy. Thus when a red bitch is mated with a red-fawn dog, and there is a second act using a brindle dog, we can determine which dog sired the puppies—unless there is that rare double conception. Such experiments have no great risk and do not harm the resulting puppies. It is not too useful to experiment with golden brindle bitches, because even when mated with another brindle they might whelp a fawn puppy. In contrast, the silver-brindle and light-fawn Boxers pass on their colors as well as the red-fawn Boxer.

For years I tried to figure out this puzzle from only my own observations. Then I came across an article in the "Mitteilungen der Fachschaft für Bernhardiner" (Newsletter of the St. Bernard Breed). It was written by professor Koch. He described the litter sizes of several breeds and mentioned that by surgical procedures they were able to establish that many more eggs were produced than were fertilized, around thirty in dogs. A number of fertilized eggs die off and are resorbed by the mother. In a flash, my puzzle had been solved. During the long period of fertility, from seven to fourteen days, the dam repeatedly produces eggs that can be fertilized. If a portion of those fertilized eggs die off, then they would probably be the ones that had first been fertilized.

My original suspicion, that a second and third copulation would destroy the earlier fertilized eggs, had not been entirely satisfactory. There is a limit beyond which repeated acts of breeding will have no impact. But we can draw some practical conclusions from these observations. Only in exceptional situations should a bitch be bred twice, such as when the first act was disturbed by either animal not standing properly. That would benefit the sire and not affect the litter. Above all, breeders should be especially careful not to turn a bred bitch loose among dogs only a few days after the breeding. As shown, the attitude that "now nothing can happen" is an error that could turn out to be quite expensive.

Certainly, the scientists will soon answer all of the questions in that matter. A breeder is surely not going to be making experiments along those lines, and if an "accident" does happen, the breeder will probably keep it quiet. Despite that, it would be nice to know what the outside limit of fertilization really is. And although I have tried to achieve a double conception, it has never happened even when the second act was only a few hours after the first.

On Cryptorchidism And Other Genetic Faults and Peculiarities
[From essays written in 1935-38 and then over 20 years later]

To my sadness, again and again what I hear and read convinces me that people are just not getting the word. It's almost as though you were preaching to deaf ears! So I will now try to bring some clarity into the question of cyptorchidism, at least as far as the available but insufficient material that we have on it will permit.

Unfortunately, the notations in our stud books are still quite limited on this matter. We all know that in a larger litter of say eight or more we let them all survive until about six weeks old or so, and then we sort out those that will eventually be undesirable animals, and the rest we register as normal animals, that means without faults. It also happens often that the breed warden sorts out faulty pups before the registration exam. Of course, the warden does not make a note about cryptorchids at that time. This presorting tends to distort the records on cryptorchidism, since we are not reporting on the full litter.

There are many published studies to explain the causes of missing testicles in dogs. Earlier, it was common to blame it on poor nourishment for the dam, and most common was to blame it on inbreeding. Such claims were in contrast to scholarship, which has established that cryptorchidism follows the Mendelian principles of inheritance. Inbreeding, even when done for several generations, does not bring it on unless the parent animals are carrying the genetic material for it. In order to understand this, we must be acquainted with the principles of Mendel's genetics. Unfortunately, not all breeders have that acquaintance. Thus, a few things can be explained here—but in the simplest of terms.

We know exactly, for example, the rules of coat color inheritance, which are even true for feather colors of birds. Along the same lines, there are laws for inheriting physical and psychological features.

Our Boxers have two colors, namely fawn and brindle. Mix those two and you do not get a third color. If a fawn and a brindle are matched, you will either get fawns or brindles or some of each. Brindle is the dominant color of the two. With large numbers of puppies from such matches, we see a ratio of three brindles to one fawn. Of the three brindles, however, only one will be "pure" brindle. The other brindles are actually mixtures of fawn and brindle. When the pure brindle is mated it always produces only brindles. But if we mate the mixed brindles, we can get brindles and fawns in the litter. Fawn x fawn produces only fawns. But which brindle is pure and which is mixed—that can only be determined by breeding.

If one understand those rules, then one can also comprehend how cryptorchidism is inherited. If I only write of cryptorchidism here (it means hidden testicle), that means either one or both testicles have not descended. I am avoiding the term monorchidism (when only one testicle is present) just for the sake of simplicity. The genetics are the same for both cases.

If we were to mate a normal bitch (compare her to a brindle) with a monorchid dog (compare him to fawn), we would probably get a litter with three out of four males normal and one cryptorchid. Of the three normal-appearing dogs, two will probably be mixed or carriers for the condition, and one might be "pure" normal. The pure normal will always remain so and throw puppies without the problem. Thus, normal is the dominant gene, and cryptorchidism is recessive.

In summary: Brindle coloring and normal testicles are dominant. Fawn coloring and cryptorchidism are recessive.

This recessive or hidden heritage follows definite genetic laws. If the recessive feature is visible, it is pure and will repeat if matched with a similarly pure animal for that feature. In other words, if neither dog nor bitch is a carrier of a cryptorchid gene, their offspring cannot be cryptorchid.

A comparable example would be with our check Boxers [85-100% white]. If this were not a recessive factor it would have been stamped out long ago. But dogs that appear quite normal still carry this coloring as an invisible feature, only known when suddenly a check appears in the litter. It is only possible, however, when both parents carry the feature. If one mates two visible check dogs, you end up with a litter of all checks. Match one check with a plain ["Einfarbige"] Boxer, either fawn or brindle, and you never get a check. And it is similar with cryptorchidism: mate a pure-normal bitch with a monorchid and you get a litter with normal male puppies.

What is often overlooked is that we must also find carrier bitches and sort them out for cryptorchidism. Apparently, we have no visible signs for this condition in bitches, and the only way to determine it is through breeding. At least we can see the condition in males when the male is a double—or pure—carrier.

Monorchid dogs were seldom used for breeding, and today they are never used. The theory seems to be if we do not use the dogs that are pure cryptorchids, the problem will be solved. As easy as this may seem, it is not so easy in practice.

Even if we assume that there are twice as many cryptorchids born than reported in the stud books, and we increased the number of assumed bitch carriers, there still would be only one Boxer out of about twelve that is a carrier. The number of unaffected dogs must still be very high, and removing the carriers should not be too difficult. But the matter has a few very sharp edges.

The biggest difficulty is that carrier-bitches do not show it and are not known, yet they pass it on the same as the males. Those males that are double-carriers will, of course, show it and can be removed from breeding, but the bitches just go on being used in breeding programs. Studying pedigrees tells us very little because we get cryptorchids from both the double and the single carriers, plus the stud books are not too reliable for the cryptorchid statistics.

Only parent animals that have already produced cryptorchids can be identified. Is it proper to exclude them from further breeding? That brings us to the next point and one of the most difficult problems that dog breeders face.

Unfortunately we lack practical information, as this issue is such a hornets' nest! I have always been ready to give information about my dogs because the breeders are the only ones to have the keys to such problems. To hide our dogs' faults for the sake of a monetary victory, a title or a degree, is sometimes successful. But how bitter is the later payment, both for us and others! Yet, the true value of an animal can only be determined in the end by seeing its offspring.

The most important question for us is how we can recognize those double-carrier (homozygous) normal dogs that according to Mendel are present in a 1:3 ratio. You cannot see that in any of them. We have many Boxers that have produced five, six or more litters before a cryptorchid appeared. One example would be Lustig vom Dom, who serviced forty-nine bitches in Germany and never produced a cryptorchid until the very last litter, when two monorchids appeared. So the numbers must sometimes be very high before one can be absolutely sure the dog is not a carrier. It was the same thing with one of Lustig's most famous sons.

Surely, the scientific theories are correct, but such statistics as above make it very difficult for a small kennel to determine very much. We are aware that the greatest problem is with the bitches since it is absolutely impossible to identify the genetic presence of cryptorchidism from appearance alone.

In our kennels, cryptorchidism has become a very serious problem. Although we were often laughed at, my husband and I have always been worried about it—even before the [first] war. We knew the problem from horse breeding, when monorchids were excluded from breeding stock. But at that time there was nothing available on the problem for dogs. We were entirely dependent on our own observations. Many breeders never even knew that a dog was monorchid and used them freely for breeding. We still do not know which of the early sires were monorchids.

Let us take the time to look in my own records. Out of 327 puppies, 167 had the Dom bloodline, and 160 came from other lines. Those with Dom blood had 20 males with undescended testicles, about 12%. Of the 160 from other lines, there were 9 puppies (6%) with the problem. Without doubt the Dom line was seriously affected. Today I realize that this more frequent incidence of cryptorchidism in the Dom line goes back to only a few outstanding animals that were carriers. Of particular interest, however, is the fact that we find cryptorchids coming from outside lines that seem to have never had an affected ancestor; further evidence that the origin of the fault can only be found in the very distant past.

Unfortunately, the laws of inheritance are not as easy to apply as one might think. Eliminating cryptorchidism by excluding affected dogs becomes complicated because other genetic features would often be affected by that. And some of those features we Boxer breeders have worked our tails off to achieve.

Up to about twenty years ago [ca. 1915], Boxer fanciers knew that brindles were superior in elegance but typically had steep shoulders and roached backs. In contrast, the fawns had more substance, short straight backs, and nice front quarters. The faults went with the colors, even when fawn and brindle were mated. Such a match usually produced the same weaknesses in the appropriate color.

Undoubtedly, cryptorchidism is tied up with other—probably highly desired—characteristics. As an example, there was Lustig. Of the many bitches he serviced, the ones that produced the most outstanding puppies were often the same ones that we knew were carriers for cryptorchidism. We have to assume that these bitches passed on their cryptorchid genes to their offspring. And right there we see what makes the elimination of this negative factor almost impossible. We have to breed for many characteristics in our Boxers, i. e. type, temperament and character, also physical appearance. The art of breeding is to recognize that a perfect creation does not exist, that there are always concessions to be made and faults will show up. We will never be able to eliminate cryptorchidism completely, but if we all work together and be honest we can hold it back.

To find one certain bloodline that might be held responsible for the problem will be very difficult, if not impossible—especially today. If one had recognized the fault at the beginning of Boxer breeding, there might have been a chance. But today the blood lines are so interlaced with each other that a pedigree search is of no value. We do still have the chance to evaluate single animals by their offspring, however. Some things must always be kept in mind:

1.   Every animal that produces a dog with undescended testicles (or testicle) is a carrier.

2.   Every animal in a litter containing an affected male puppy must be suspected to be a carrier.

One can never count on getting abnormal puppies from an affected parent. It might be five or six litters before the breeder discovers the unfortunate truth that a parent is a carrier. According to the last stud books, there are an average of 3.5 carrier-animals in each litter. If we figure that a bitch would produce six litters, that would be about 21 female puppies. The other 14 males in the books cannot indicate whether the dam is a carrier. Most of our stud dogs are only used a short time, since many of the best have been sold. By the time we learn something about the inheritance pattern, even by the time the stud book is published, it is usually too late. Even I, for example, have often waited over a year before I learned that Sigurd had sired a cryptorchid.

When I look at the breeding animals of the last years, something occurs to me. Those dogs that are the most beautiful and have the best temperament seem to be the ones most likely affected. Are we now to remove these animals from our breeding programs? If so, then we will be forced to breed inferior dogs. And what about the future? Quite often we will learn after six or more litters that it was all a waste of time. Only too often will we learn that the inferior outsider we have using is also not clear of the fault. By then we have reached the end of our wisdom!

Now, as always, the breed warden should find a way out. I sought out six dogs and four bitches from those I knew were carriers of cryptorchidism. I wished to release their names with the advice not to mate any of their offspring with each other. But I had to admit to myself that was not reasonable. Our brood stock is now so limited, because of foreign sales and increased breeding restrictions, that there is no more room for cutting. We must, therefore, force ourselves at least not to pair two that have already parented a cryptorchid, and certainly not to inbreed them. Eventually we will have to exclude the double carriers, as well as the female puppies in those litters where a cryptorchid has been whelped. I am convinced, of course, that this radical cure will cause great hardships.

It would be wrong, however, to believe that only the Boxer is trapped with this fault. Other breeds do not have it much better, and some have it worse. We do have the distinction of being the first club to publish information on it in our *Boxer Blätter*, even if the warnings over the last ten or more years have been mainly ignored.

We have to ask ourselves, "What good is good temperament and beauty if the strength of life is missing?"

All three of these qualities are vitally important. A weak vitality exhibits itself not only in stillborn and aborted puppies. It is revealed in any weakening of reproductive strength.

Naturally, the experts and non-experts appear from all directions, write and give advice, but they never seem to get to the heart of the problem. They ask, "Why do we have this problem more often now than in the old days?"

There have even been doomsday speeches, talking about the fall of the breed and saying that nothing can be done to stop it. But what we should do—nobody seems to know.

In order to fight the problem we must first be clear about its causes. Recently I examined the records for hundreds of litters and can say for certain: inbreeding has nothing to do with cryptorchidism! It only has an impact when carrier animals are used for the inbreeding, or when a carrier animal is doubled up on. That is the same with any fault or virtue.

No one takes the time to check mixed breeds and street mutts for cryptorchidism, but even they are not spared the problem. There is a Doberman-farm dog cross in our area who is monorchid. Also, such things as malnutrition and illnesses among the parents and puppies do not live up to the important roles they have been given as causes.

Probably all of those claims that the testicles were present but later disappeared are based on errors, just as are those claims that the testicle(s) came down when the dog was from six to nine months old. There are young dogs whose testicles may be difficult to locate, especially for inexperienced breeders. I have had all of those things happen, or at least seem to happen. Up to now, I have examined several hundred male puppies from the earliest age on, and I believe my judgment is now quite certain. Among my own puppies, I am usually able to determine by the fourteenth day whether they are normal or not.

About a year ago, I exchanged a four-month-old male for a bitch. The male had been examined by me and was normal. After two months the owner told me the dog was monorchid!

I replied that it was not possible, but if it were I would replace the dog. Then the owner had a vet examine the animal, and the vet declared the dog normal. I was later told that one testicle was so hard to find a number of witnesses were even fooled. Such incidents, and ones like it, are probably the source of the claims mentioned above.

Nor can we say that cryptorchidism is a sign of physical degeneration. Quite often it is the strongest males that have the problem. Many times I have noticed that such dogs have a restricted gait, which often called my attention to the cryptorchidism. Has this condition really become so prevalent in just the most recent times? In order to determine that, we would have to do the impossible and examine the earlier animals. We can be quite sure that the problem existed then as well, but breeders never paid much attention to it.

More than twenty years ago, I had a sad but also funny case, that can only be forgiven me because of my good intentions and inexperience. I traded a bitch for a four-month-old male, a charming high-stationed fellow, but he remained so refined and delicate that I decided not to use him for breeding. I placed him in a private home. A long time later, after the dog was almost fully grown, I received news that he had indeed turned out to be a well-formed animal, but was lacking in dominance. The owners wondered if they could exchange him for a more aggressive dog.

There were no such animals available in my kennel, so I offered to try to arrange an exchange with somebody else. After a long search, I found an aggressive brindle whose owner also wanted to replace him. Lacking knowledge of the tricks of the dog game, I was really happy that the matter had worked out so well. I even offered to keep the brindle with me for a while and give him some Schutzhund training, so the new owner would get a good reliable protection dog.

The dog turned out to be a wild, unruly rascal who loved to take walks by himself, so I had to work hard with him. Courage and dominance were certainly not missing in the good-looking dog. I was happy when I could finally pack him up. But when I put him in the traveling crate he leaped out. I grabbed him, and he fell over on his back. For the first time, I saw that he was a monorchid! I was horrified. What could I do now? I had done a heap of work, all out of good will, plus I had expenses—and now this mess! I packed him up and shipped him off.

It was not possible to reverse the exchange because the other cryptorchid had already been placed in another home, and the new owners would not give him up. All that was left for me to try was a prayer to the saints that the new owner of the brindle would not check him, assuming that I would never do such a stupid thing. And that is how it went! The new owner of the brindle put him through all his paces, but he never looked in the place where the real flaw lay. It never occurred to him!

That little story illustrates how easily abnormal dogs could have existed unknown in the past, especially if the dog were monorchid. Until that incident, I had not really been too attentive either to be sure the dog had everything in order.

Through such often careless breeding, probably all of today's blood lines are so contaminated that we can hardly speak of a line free of cryptorchidism. But a careful study of the ancestors, at least back to the fifth generation, and detailed records on offspring, can help us find a way out— even though it will be difficult.

Still, it would be wrong to exclude an otherwise excellent sire from breeding just because his litters sometimes contain a cryptorchid. After all, no one would think of excluding a fine animal because he occasionally produced a puppy with light eyes, steep shoulders, poor rear angulation, etc. But we should be certain to use caution in breeding such an animal. We should be more concerned with his litter-sisters, and watch carefully how they produce. The sisters, of course, might or might not also be carriers. The warning should be not to mate animals together that have come out of litters where a cryptorchid has been present. Above all, I warn against using animals that have had the problem present for the last three or four generations.

We often observe that certain features seem to be inherited

together. Earlier we had the carp backs and steep hindquarters in the brindles, faults which did not appear in the fawn puppies in the same litter. And now we seem to see the increase in cryptorchism along with an increase in split noses. Since there were quite a few split-nosed dogs in the past, we can probably assume there were cryptorchids as well. Along with cryptorchidism and split noses, there has also been an increase in the more unpleasant vaginal prolapses. Many bitches—some were top animals—have had to be killed because of that. Aside from the fact that a vaginal prolapses may be a large expense, there is a real danger here for successful breeding in the future. Bitches with the problem might still be bred in some circumstances and produce live puppies. Most of them only have the prolapse during the heat cycle, and if a veterinarian can reposition it, then the bitch can be immediately bred with success. But we know that the mother can pass the condition along, also cryptorchidism.

Some breeders have wondered if the increasing number of problems in our stud dogs might soon make breeding impossible. Such a fear is greatly over-exaggerated, because in practice we can see that while there are always exceptions, even mating two known carriers of cryptorchidism usually produces litters with mostly normal male puppies. Of course, we must clearly identify those litters where abnormal males have been present. Furthermore, we ought to make it possible to identify litter mates of the abnormal dogs in the stud book, which will make it easier for the beginning breeder to select and match breeding pairs.

Also, we must be very careful not to rush to judgment about an otherwise excellent breeding animal because it has produced one or two cryptorchids. Here is an example: Sigurd vom Dom bred a bitch who then whelped a large litter with two cryptorchids, one was unilateral and one bilateral. I warned against a rematch, but the bitch's owner was adamant. The result: four males, all normal! There was a third breeding too, and that produced five normal males. So we can see that in no case should we throw out the baby with the bath water when only an occasional cryptorchid has appeared. But that should also mean that we have no guarantee from a normal litter that the parents are not carriers.

The old master Boppel once said, "Breeding is both an art and a science."

He was right!

A Revived Question

It is already twenty years since the problem of cryptorchidism stirred up the dust and I wrote about it. Unfortunately, the problem is more acute today than ever, and it is also interesting to see how things have gone over this time. If it had not been for the war, which again forced us to use inferior animals and poor pairings, this problem would have been now at least "minor," if not gone. How have the thoughts from so long ago worked out in practice? The total percentage of cryptorchid puppies (both unilateral and bilateral) is still the same as before at 4%. Some years ago I read an article by Professor Hank of Vienna, about research with mixed-breeds. They also had a four percent occurrence of cryptorchids. The fault was recessive, and I do not wish to repeat the whole theory of recessive inheritance here.

We would like to give the example of the white Boxer (the inheritance pattern is the same), however. Checks, when mated to pure fawns or brindles, produce only colored puppies because the full color is dominant. But most of these puppies will not be genetically full-color dogs. They are mixed—part check and part full color, although there might be some that are pure. If a white Boxer is now mated with one of the mixed dogs, there can be many mixed puppies, even a mixture of checks and mixed. The results will not always be the same, but over many breedings they will be quite accurate. Although the genetics of color is much simpler than cryptorchidism—because we can see it in the bitches too—the all-white and check (90% white) Boxers are still with us.

The pattern of inheritance with cryptorchids follows that of the white Boxer. Our only remaining task is to find dogs free of the defect, and that's the rub: there are probably almost no Boxers that are clear of cryptorchidism. Of course, that creates an enormous problem for the breeder.

When my husband was still alive and was the Breed Warden of the German Boxer Club, I wrote some articles about cryptorchidism and its inheritance. Out of that came some noteworthy information. In collecting material, I had only looked at those dogs who had produced many litters, and we learned that it was not correct to believe that the Siegers were the ones most likely to sire cryptorchids. We determined that three groups were visible among the stud dogs.

Group I had a cryptorchid in every four litters.

Group II had one in every 6-8 litters.

Group III had one in every 40 litters.

We could probably call those of Group III non-carriers or pure. If we could base our breeding on those dogs, we would make a great step forward. But is that possible in practice? I will cite some examples from that time out of my own kennels.

The worst producers—in terms of cryptorchidism—were at that time [ca. 1935] the Siegers Edler von Isarstrand, Sigurd vom Dom, and Hansel von Biederstein, three very important dogs. Especially the last two were absolutely essential to our breeding. We recalled some of the monorchid breeders of the past, such as Tasso von der Spree, and tried to avoid those lines. But the lines were all so intermingled that it was not possible to do that. The only possibility left was to find pure animals and bring in a correction through close inbreeding.

I then had some luck. From an inbreeding between two half-siblings (Sigurd was their sire), we obtained Lustig, who—in addition to his other qualities—was about as pure and free from cryptorchidism as a Boxer could be.

Not until the litter #41 did Lustig sire a cryptorchid. Lustig's sire (who was Sigurd's son) was Zorn vom Dom, and he first produced a cryptorchid in the eighth litter.

Lustig's dam, Esta von der Wurm, was apparently pure, despite her carrier-father. When Lustig went to America, he left behind a number of high quality sons, some coming out of carrier-bitches. These offspring, of course, did not all turn out to be as pure as their father. Of the main Lustig sons that did not end up in America, some were indeed non-carriers (Buten von Elbufer, Ernst Lustig vom Zollernhof, Ajax von der Holderburg). Records of their offspring show the same minimal numbers of cryptorchids as their father, Lustig. Inbreeding would have been possible with these animals, but it was only done with Buten, who was also free of the white gene. The other two dogs, as well as Lustig, sired checks, and also the too-light eyes. We did have luck again, when we obtained a large, excellent Boxer that was as clear of the testicle problem as Lustig. That was Karlo von der Wolfsschlucht. His father was Arno von der Holderburg, who was certainly not as clear as his brother Ajax, but nevertheless produced the pure Karlo.

The war ended our efforts to move toward non-carrier breeding; in fact cryptorchidism became unimportant. We could not get to the most desired sires, the condition was no longer noted in the record books, and all attempts to monitor it failed. So today we are still back where we were long ago. If a cryptorchid appears in the litter, the sire is blamed, and over and over we forget that a recessive trait can only develop when the condition is carried by both parents.

As it was twenty years ago, we now use the breed wardens to oversee the condition and record it when it occurs. To do this, it would be best if the testicles were in place at eight weeks. We have learned over the years that a later inspection is also necessary. Two times we have had a puppy that was normal at eight weeks but between four and six months had a testicle pull back and never appear again.

Can testicles disappear, never to return? In the fall of 1944, I had a beautiful litter out of my Anka von Hoffbauer by Hermes von Landl. Anka had never had a puppy before that was cryptorchid, nor did she later. But in this litter there was a beautiful, large boy, whose testicles descended rather late. Yet at three months everything was in place and further inspections seemed unnecessary. When he was five months old, I rather jokingly said to my daughter, "I think I will check our boy, just to be sure everything is OK."

When I laid him on his back I could not believe my eyes; he was monorchid! Many breeders saw this dog and they all understood my concern about this development in such an unusually beautiful dog. After a four-week wait, we decided to place him in a nice home. Three weeks later I had to pick him up, because the owner was unable to get enough food to feed him. I still had hopes that the testicle might have re-descended. But I was even more disappointed: the second testicle had also disappeared.

In the second case, Mr. H. bought a four-month-old normal dog from me. The dog went to an Englishman, who shipped it back in a month because it was monorchid. Because he was interested in the dog's later development, Mr. H. kept it. And in fact at eight months the testicle re-descended and stayed there. The Englishman then took him back, and he is being used as a stud dog in England today. His offspring have not shown a particularly strong tendency toward cryptorchidism.

Sometimes I have noticed that one could feel the testicles in a three or four-week-old puppy, and then they would slowly but surely pull back into the abdomen. Neither massaging nor hormone shots made any difference, although those things have helped in some cases, but not with our dogs.

Scholarship will have to answer this question: Why have testicles disappeared again after they have once descended into the scrotum? According to Dr. Wagner, the two types of cryptorchidism have nothing to do with each other.

Perhaps it is important—at least it is interesting—that in about 99% of the cases of monorchidism it is the right testicle that is missing.

If a puppy's right testicle descends first, then you can almost be certain that the left one will follow, even if it takes awhile.

What is critical is when the left one appears first, because complications often follow. Certainly it is not of much value, and it might even be considered fraud, to attempt to avoid cryptorchidism through surgery. The same goes for hormone treatments, which often drag on, are expensive, and do not always end successfully.

Such treatments should only be of passing interest to breeders because operations should only be done for health reasons—such as cancer—and the affected animal should not be used again for breeding.

As I have already mentioned, Boxer breeders should not only fight cryptorchidism. There are many faults to work against: light eyes, poor shoulders, dewlap, bodies too little or too large, and many others. Let us hope that another powerful sire comes along who is clear of cryptorchidism. If an occasional affected puppy appears in one of his litters, then we should exclude the dam from further breeding. The bitch that produced a cryptorchid from Lustig also had a monorchid father. So it goes.

I know that many things must remain only hoped-for-dreams. In agriculture, people are much more progressive, and faulty animals are quickly removed from any breeding. Dogs that consistently produce cryptorchids ought to be banned from breeding. We know, however, that useful offspring can also come down from those animals. But we must be very careful in using those offspring for breeding. It should only be done by breeders who know what they are doing.

Split Noses and Cleft Palettes

For a long time, problems such as split noses and cleft palettes were unknown among Boxers, and then suddenly they appeared. These abnormalities, which develop from embryonic disturbances, only began showing up in my breeding during 1932/33, after over twenty years of Boxer breeding.

During normal development, the skull and muzzle sections

both grow out of the sides of the upper jaw bones and are finally joined with a small bone structure behind the nose. If that is not the case, there remains between the left and right upper flews a split, the so-called split nose. If the split reaches back into the mouth, leaving an opening between mouth and nose, it becomes a cleft palette. When the bones have indeed grown together properly but the lip does not close together completely, we call that in people a split lip or also harelip. In Boxers, we have found three forms of this fault

1.　Apparently normal developed nose, but a cleft palette.

2.　Split nose, more often lip and nose, with a normal palette.

3.　Split nose with a cleft palette.

The first two types are relatively rare, the usual form being variation three: the complete split of nose and palette. Ordinarily, puppies with that are not capable of surviving because they cannot suck. Often this fault is overlooked, and the breeder wonders why an apparently healthy puppy dies two or three days after being whelped.

It is possible to bottle raise such a puppy, and I have done it myself. But the split did not heal.

Of course, no breeder would think of trying to keep such a puppy alive artificially. But I did read about a doctor who planned to raise such a Chow-Chow in order to use it for breeding to determine if the abnormality were genetic or not. His interest was to use the results in human medicine. Without doubt there are genetic factors involved, and it would have been interesting to learn more about the problem. But as far as I know, the experiments were never carried out.

Of primary interest to us as breeders is the clear fact that split noses and cleft palettes occur much more often in the breeds with short heads (brachycephalic) and shortened muzzles with pronounced stops. It is not surprising that such malformed puppies often appear in the litters of those dogs that have normal brachycephalic heads.

If we page through the pedigrees from now back to 1933, we see that these faults appear primarily among the descendants of two sires, Hermes von der Uhlandshöhe and Sieger Danilo von Königsee. Their pedigrees show no common ancestor to blame for the origin of the problem. Of course, both of these dogs were excellent producers of typey Boxers.

Naturally, it is no wonder that these often-used sires, with their excellent features, have passed on the fault to many animals and lines. As an example, I learned in my America visit that split nosed Boxers were almost unknown until Karlo von der Wolfsschlucht arrived.

This fault is inherited in the same manner as checks and cryptorchidism, which makes it difficult to identify and stamp out. Most of the puppies die quickly, and their presence is either not known or kept secret. But cryptorchidism, on the other hand, is almost always recognized, only that comes when they are older, and almost no one would kill a puppy because of it.

It is almost impossible to control the problems of whites and cleft palettes when the breeders just have them disappear. But with the correct and full information, how much better off our breed would be! There is no evidence, however, that a Boxer with heavy white markings or a split nose is of less value in a breeding program. Every dog passes on something undesirable, but it is important for the breeder to know what the faults are and to plan accordingly.

Every stud dog owner should be fully informed by the owner of the bitch to be bred whether she has whelped a white puppy, a cryptorchid, or a split nose or cleft palette. If any of those are the case, and his stud dog has produced the same fault(s), then they should not be matched together, no matter how tempting the stud fee is. Such a pairing would not be to his advantage—nor to the breed's. When those faults appear in a litter from his stud dog, you can be sure it is the dog that will get the blame. Even worse is that outsiders see such faults and then broadcast that they are typical for Boxers.

Split noses were interpreted in the old days as a sign of a purebred among Bulldogs. Today it is a fault for them. There is reference to split noses in the first Boxer standard, but they are listed as a fault. I have only seen a split nose three times. Once was in 1911, at a large show in Munich, later I also saw one on a mounted puppy head. That puppy had been reared to the fourth month, then killed and its head mounted.

Other than those two, I did have one split nose in a Spitz puppy. Later I heard that a descendent of this little bitch was also throwing split noses. None of those, however, had a cleft palette.

Index